In a Sea of Empires

At the turn of the nineteenth century, the Caribbean was rife with revolutionary fervor and political turmoil. Yet with such upheaval came unparalleled opportunities. In this innovative and richly detailed study, Jeppe Mulich explores the interconnected nature of imperial politics and colonial law in the maritime borderlands of the Leeward Islands, where British, Danish, Dutch, French, Spanish, and Swedish colonies both competed and cooperated with one another. By exploring the transnational networks involved in trade, slavery, smuggling, privateering, and marronage, he offers a new account of the age of revolutions in the Caribbean, emphasizing the border-crossing nature of life in the region. By approaching major shifts in politics, economy, and law from the bottom up, a new story of early nineteenth-century globalization emerges – one that emphasizes regional integration and a multiplicity of intersecting networks.

JEPPE MULICH is Teaching Associate in Global History at the University of Cambridge and St. John's College.

Cambridge Oceanic Histories

Edited by

David Armitage
Alison Bashford
Sujit Sivasundaram

Across the world, historians have taken an oceanic turn. New maritime histories offer fresh approaches to the study of global regions, and to long-distance and long-term connections. Cambridge Oceanic Histories includes studies across whole oceans (the Pacific, the Indian, the Atlantic) and particular seas (among them, the Mediterranean, the Caribbean, the North Sea, the Black Sea). The series is global in geography, ecumenical in historical method, and wide in temporal coverage, intended as a key repository for the most innovative transnational and world histories over the longue durée. It brings maritime history into productive conversation with other strands of historical research, including environmental history, legal history, intellectual history, labour history, cultural history, economic history and the history of science and technology. The editors invite studies that analyse the human and natural history of the world's oceans and seas from anywhere on the globe and from any and all historical periods.

In a Sea of Empires

Networks and Crossings in the
Revolutionary Caribbean

Jeppe Mulich

University of Cambridge

CAMBRIDGE
UNIVERSITY PRESS

CAMBRIDGE
UNIVERSITY PRESS

University Printing House, Cambridge CB2 8BS, United Kingdom

One Liberty Plaza, 20th Floor, New York, NY 10006, USA

477 Williamstown Road, Port Melbourne, VIC 3207, Australia

314-321, 3rd Floor, Plot 3, Splendor Forum, Jasola District Centre, New Delhi - 110025, India

103 Penang Road, #05-06/07, Visioncrest Commercial, Singapore 238467

Cambridge University Press is part of the University of Cambridge.

It furthers the University's mission by disseminating knowledge in the pursuit of education, learning and research at the highest international levels of excellence.

www.cambridge.org
Information on this title: www.cambridge.org/9781108747479
DOI: 10.1017/9781108779289

First published 2020
First paperback edition 2022

A catalogue record for this publication is available from the British Library

ISBN 978-1-108-48972-0 Hardback
ISBN 978-1-108-74747-9 Paperback

For Jacquelyn

Contents

Figures

Tables

Acknowledgments

While the writing of this book was in many respects a process of isolation and solitude, as is probably the case with most historical monographs, it could not have been accomplished without the gracious help of a great number of individuals to whom I owe a deep debt of gratitude. The book began life as a PhD dissertation at New York University's Department of History, and I am particularly indebted to my doctoral advisor Lauren Benton. Not only have our many conversations been invaluable in honing my thinking on law, history, empire, and academic life in general, but she has also been a constant source of advice, criticism, and guidance throughout the long and at times challenging process of crafting this book. There is no doubt that the work would have been worse off and I a much poorer scholar without her support. John Shovlin, my second advisor, has also graced me with more support and encouragement than I could have hoped for. Through our frequent discussions he has challenged me to think critically about the importance of political economy, the development of the state, and the historical craft. Thanks are also due to my other committee members, Ada Ferrer, Daniel Nexon, and Frederick Cooper, who each provided thoughtful feedback, pointed critiques, and inspiring ideas of immense value to the shaping of the dissertation and later the book.

At NYU the Atlantic Workshop was an important source of academic support and illuminating discussions. If there is anything of use to historians in general within the pages of this book, it is in no small part due to the valuable conversations I have had with the members of the workshop – especially Gabriel Rocha, Anelise Shrout, Jerusha Westbury, Daniel Kanhofer, Hayley Negrin, Kate Mulry, Max Mishler, Greg Childs, Timo McGregor, Andrew Lee, Nicole Eustace, and Karen Kupperman. Outside the workshop, other colleagues at NYU gave invaluable feedback on early versions of the work, including Jane Burbank, Thomas Bender, Tony Andersson, and Nadim Bawalsa.

My first academic appointment was at the London School of Economics and Political Science, a place that provided me with vibrant communities at both the International History and the International Relations departments. Several workshop presentations and subsequent conversations at Ye Old White Horse helped sharpen my ideas and analysis, including with George Lawson, Padraic Scanlan, Gagan Sood, Imaobong Umoren, Ronald Po, Martin Bayly, Megan Black, David Motadel, Paul Stock, Joanne Yao, Marc Baer, Tarak Barkawi, and all the participants of the International Theory workshop.

At the University of Cambridge, I have been gifted with an expansive and stimulating academic community. Conversations with my students have been a source of much inspiration and motivation, as have discussions with numerous colleagues, including Johnhenry Gonzalez, Jason Sharman, Saul Dubow, Megan Donaldson, Mark Shirk, Duncan Bell, Andrew Arsan, and Nicholas Guyatt. Thanks are due in particular to Renaud Morieux, who read parts of the manuscript before the final submission and provided vital feedback.

Many other scholars have provided me with constructive criticism, useful prodding, and eye-opening insights. At Yale my academic mentors Steve Pincus, Francesca Trivellato, and Philip Gorski helped sow the early seeds of what would later become this book, and convinced me that good history can also be good social science. Elsewhere, at conference panels, hotel bars, and workshop dinners, a number of fellow-travelers provided fresh perspectives and critical takes on both the substance and the framing of my work. Thanks in particular to Paul Kirby, Linda Rupert, Richard Drayton, Adam Tooze, John Carroll, Julia Costa López, Mauro Caraccioli, Paul Kreitman, Lisa Ford, Halvard Leira, Benjamin de Carvalho, Andrew Phillips, Iver Neumann, Ale Pålsson, Victor Wilson, Bram Hoonhout, Ernesto Bassi, Alex Borucki, Fabrício Prado, Christian Koot, Casey Schmitt, Patrick Jackson, Jordan Branch, Jon Rahbek-Clemmensen, and Edward Keene.

The research for this book has taken place across multiple countries and continents and would not have been possible without the generous help of librarians and archivists at numerous collections and archives. My thanks to staff members at Rigsarkivet and the Royal Library in Copenhagen, the National Archives in Kew, Riksarkivet and the National Library in Stockholm, the Archives nationales d'outre-mer in Aix-en-Province, the Florence Williams Library in Christiansted, the American Antiquarian Society in Worcester, the New-York Historical Society and the Bobst Library in New York City, the Sterling Memorial Library in New Haven, the Cambridge University Library and the Seeley Historical Library in Cambridge, the David Rumsey Map Collection in Stanford, and Gladstone's Library in Hawarden.

I am grateful to David Armitage, Alison Bashford, and Sujit Sivasundaram for the invitation to contribute to the Cambridge Oceanic

xii   Acknowledgments

Histories series, and to Lucy Rhymer, Emily Sharp, and the rest of the team at Cambridge University Press for their patience and assistance. Thanks are also due to the anonymous readers who gave incredibly helpful feedback and provided recommendations for how to improve the manuscript.

Last but not least my heartfelt gratitude to my long-suffering family members, who have both put me up and put up with me every time I have visited Scandinavia for holidays or birthdays, only to disappear into the archives for long stretches of time. My deepest thanks are owed to Jacquelyn Truong for being an unwavering source of motivation and sanity, and for putting up with more academic anxiety and sleepless nights than any person ought to be exposed to. In the time it has taken to write this book, we have followed each other across three continents, calling New York, London, Cambridge, and Hong Kong home. I continue to be humbled by her mental fortitude and deep-seated compassion. This book would likely never have been completed without her support.

1 Introduction

Tiān gāo huángdì yuǎn. [The sky is high and the emperor is far away.]
—Chinese proverb

Besides, interesting things happen along borders – transitions – not in the middle where everything is the same.   —Neal Stephenson, *Snow Crash*

At the turn of the nineteenth century, the Atlantic world was rife with revolutionary fervor and political turmoil. With such upheaval came unparalleled opportunities. Naval officers and privateers, smugglers and seafaring traders, escaped slaves and free people of color all found themselves passing through the busy harbors of the Caribbean in pursuit of profit, freedom, glory, or any number of other ambitions. At the heart of this traffic were the Leeward Islands, an archipelago of small islands in the northeastern Caribbean.[1] These islands represented numerous different European polities, and they exhibited a peculiar type of trans-imperial interconnectedness, characterized by intricate networks of actors and institutions that crossed formal political and legal boundaries. The end of the American Revolutionary War in 1783 refashioned the geopolitical landscape of the Western Atlantic, and many of the Leeward Islands saw new opportunities for trade and prosperity as a consequence. Their role as ports located at the maritime center of transatlantic commerce, transportation, and communication became increasingly prominent, and many of them were to occupy unique positions of regional and oceanic significance during this period.

St. Thomas, a small colony at the heart of the Danish West Indies, and the Swedish island of St. Barthélemy became the preferred ports of call for

---

[1] The geographical demarcation of the Lesser Antilles into Leeward and Windward Islands is a matter of some contention, primarily stemming from different usage in, on the one hand, English and, on the other, French, Spanish, and Dutch. In this book I use the common English definition of the Leeward Islands as stretching from the Virgin Islands in the north to Dominica in the south, while fully acknowledging its origin as a British imperial designation. See Helmut Blume, *The Caribbean Islands* (London: Longman, 1974), 5–6. Further aspects of my definition of the region are discussed later in this chapter.

ships passing through the region with a variety of licit and illicit goods, from privateer loot to smuggled luxury items to illegally traded slaves. British Tortola became the seat of an important prize court in the region's complex web of inter-imperial legal regimes, often luring ships out of their way to bring prizes and legal disputes to that island. White colonial elites on the islands shared a common and increasing fear of the African and Afro-Caribbean slave populations living among them, and on whose backs they had built much of their fortunes. This book turns the lens on these islands in order to illuminate hitherto unexplored characteristics of imperial rule and colonial practice during what C. A. Bayly has aptly termed the first age of global imperialism.[2] No empire existed in a vacuum. By investigating a particular colonial borderland from multiple perspectives at once, we can more clearly see that the entangled and boundary-crossing nature of regional interactions was not an aberrant challenge to imperial rule but an inherent feature of colonial practice.

On a theoretical level, the book presents a framework for analyzing a particular type of interpolity space: the inter-imperial microregion. This phenomenon goes beyond the specific geographical area analyzed in this book, and can be found across the globe during the period of European overseas expansion. The framework encompasses a number of different elements, including political, legal, social, and economic factors, as well as geography, and provides an analytical ideal-type that is pertinent to a variety of historical contexts. This ideal-type draws on recent scholarship in the study of empire, on theoretical innovations stemming from the practice turn in international relations, and on the sociological concept of analytic relationalism.

On a historical level, the book analyzes how cross-imperial practices such as contraband trade, slavery, and opportunistic privateering shaped and defined the Leeward Islands as a politically polyglot zone of thin sovereignty and local integration, characterized more by the interests of intercolonial networks than by those of imperial or national actors. The analysis shows that the Leewards were both geographically and figuratively at the center of early nineteenth-century imperial concerns. Functioning as a microcosm of intra- and inter-imperial relations, the islands serve to illuminate the wider dynamics of overseas empires during this volatile period and to highlight some of the broader historical developments shaping the first half of the highly transformative nineteenth century: the struggle over slavery and the threat of revolution, the tensions between colonial sovereignty and imperial jurisdiction, the

---

[2] C. A. Bayly, "The First Age of Global Imperialism, c. 1760–1830," *The Journal of Imperial and Commonwealth History* 26:2 (1998): 28–47.

expansion of free trade regimes and the challenges of illicit commerce, and the rise of British interpolity hegemony. Crucially, the analysis underscores the unique role played by smaller imperial powers, such as Sweden and Denmark-Norway, within the dynamics of inter-imperial relations in general, and in the process of nineteenth-century British ascendancy in particular. These small empires functioned in ways very different from their larger regional neighbors, with their colonial territories sometimes acting as buffer zones between rival powers and sometimes as political proxies, although they often turned out to be harder to control than their French or British allies hoped.

Spatial and Temporal Scope

Chronologically, the book spans the period from the end of the American Revolutionary War in 1783 to the abolition of slavery in the British West Indies in 1834. These dates signify more than just geopolitical or economic shifts within the Anglophone Atlantic, coinciding with several trajectories in the wider region. The end of the war paralleled and in some ways caused several shifts in the balance between the European colonial powers in the Caribbean: the sacking of Dutch St. Eustatius by British forces began the steady decline of one of the most important centers of trade and transshipment in the Western Caribbean; the emergence of an independent United States and the economic cold war between Britain and her former colonies gave neutral islands in the region new opportunities to profit from the trade restrictions of their larger neighbors; the French and Haitian Revolutions, arguably already on the horizon in the early 1780s, placed the entire region in an increased state of anxiety and, in some cases, led to other armed uprisings; and, as issues of slavery and abolition became gradually more central to political debate in the European metropoles, the West Indian islands came under greater scrutiny of imperial administrators and political reformers.

At the other end of the period covered by the book, the first abolition of slavery in the British West Indies in 1834 had causes and consequences that went well beyond the British Empire. By the 1830s the decline in the plantation economies of the sugar-producing islands was apparent to most economic observers. The forced migration of labor from Africa was gradually being replaced by a new importation of workers from South Asia. British naval hegemony, already emergent half a century earlier, was now a fact of political life in the Atlantic. And the era of widespread privateering, which had been important not just in the Revolutionary and Napoleonic Wars but also in the clashes over Latin American independence, had finally reached its end.

The story told takes place within two larger historical narratives of periodization. The first is that of the long nineteenth century, perhaps one of the most transformative centuries in human history. The second is the period from roughly 1760 to 1830, referred to by Bayly as the first age of global imperialism, as mentioned above. While a multitude of scholars regard the longer nineteenth century as an era of significant and far-reaching transitions, the first age of global imperialism has received comparatively less attention.[3] Although it in some ways overlaps with the older conception of an "age of revolutions," the notion of a first age of global imperial expansion goes well beyond the typically rather narrow Atlantic scope of a focus on political revolution.[4] The concept emphasizes, on the one hand, the worldwide spread of European overseas empires, either through direct colonization or through other commercial and political activities, and, on the other hand, the increasing importance of global flows and connectivity as forces shaping the course of history. One can argue that the early nineteenth century was the first period in which *the global* as a concept had a real role to play on the historical stage.[5]

---

[3] The paradigmatic work on the long nineteenth century is Eric Hobsbawm's famous trilogy, beginning with *The Age of Revolution: Europe 1789–1848* (London: Abacus, 1962). Newer accounts include C. A. Bayly, *The Birth of the Modern World, 1780–1914* (Oxford: Wiley-Blackwell, 2004); Jürgen Osterhammel, *The Transformation of the World: A Global History of the Nineteenth Century* (Princeton: Princeton University Press, 2014); Barry Buzan and George Lawson, *The Global Transformation: History, Modernity and the Making of International Relations* (Cambridge: Cambridge University Press, 2015).

[4] See, for example, R. R. Palmer, *The Age of Democratic Revolution*, vols. 1 and 2 (Princeton: Princeton University Press, 1959 and 1964); Wim Klooster, *Revolutions of the Atlantic World: A Comparative History* (New York: New York University Press, 2009); Bernard Cottret, "La révolution atlantique, une question mal posée?," in *Cosmopolitismes, patriotismes, Europe et Amériques, 1773–1802*, ed. Mark Bélissa and Bernard Cottret (Rennes: Perséides, 2005), 183–98. A notable exception is David Armitage and Sanjay Subrahmanyam, eds., *The Age of Revolutions in Global Context, c. 1760–1840* (New York: Palgrave). See also Armitage, "Foreword," in Palmer, *The Age of Democratic Revolution* (new edition) (Princeton: Princeton University Press, 2014), xv–xxii.

[5] The issue of dating globalization is a hotly contested one. For general overviews, see Michael Lang, "Globalization and Its History," *Journal of Modern History* 78:4 (2006): 899–931; Jürgen Osterhammel and Niels Petersson, *Globalization: A Short History* (Princeton: Princeton University Press, 2009). For arguments for placing its inception in the sixteenth or seventeenth century, rather than in the nineteenth, see Immanuel Wallerstein, *The Modern World-System I: Capitalist Agriculture and the Origins of the European World-Economy in the Sixteenth Century* (New York: Academic Press, 1974); Barry Buzan and Richard Little, *International Systems in World History: Remaking the Study of International Relations* (Oxford: Oxford University Press, 2000); Dennis O. Flynn and Arturo Giraldez, "Path Dependence, Time Lags and the Birth of Globalization: A Critique of O'Rourke and Williamson," *European Review of Economic History* 8(1) (2004): 81–108; Timothy Brook, *Vermeer's Hat: The Seventeenth Century and the Dawn of the Global World* (London: Bloomsbury, 2007). For critiques of the concept of globalization all together, see, in particular, Paul Hirst and Grahame Thompson, *Globalization in Question: The International Economy and the Possibilities of Governance*

I argue that this early globalization did not take the same shape as what we might now think of as global connectivity. Rather, it emanated from increasingly integrated regional spaces, composed of layered networks of trans-polity connections and activity – from tightly knit maritime microregions at the local level to transoceanic migratory and commercial flows on the global level. A study of early globalization is a study of networks within networks – of both the interdependence and integration of locally anchored regional actors and the influence of larger global forces on them.

The book presents an analysis of one such microregion – that of the Leeward Islands in the Caribbean – by exploring a specific set of processes. Rather than paying equal attention to the entirety of the archipelago, the analysis focuses on three islands, or groups of islands, in particular: the British Virgin Islands, the Danish Virgin Islands, and Swedish St. Barthélemy. There are important analytical reasons for focusing on these colonies. They were all key nodes in the commercial and legal inter-imperial networks of the Caribbean in general and of the Leeward Islands in particular, and none of them has received much attention in the scholarly literature. What is more, they represent two smaller imperial players in the global arena – the Swedish and Danish-Norwegian empires – that have been all but overlooked by anyone outside the national histories of those countries but that played critical roles during the period of British ascendancy. Although the historical narrative is focused on the Leeward Islands in particular, it is not limited to them, and when historical events or connections call for it, the analysis expands to a number of other regional players, including Caribbean colonies of the Dutch, French, and Spanish empires as well as Haiti and the newly independent republics of the continental Americas.

Scholars engaged in transnational historical research, especially in the study of borderlands, find themselves faced with a dual challenge of comparison. On the one hand, if the topic is truly transnational – that is to say, if it spans the formal borders of multiple polities – then it will almost unavoidably call into question the traditionally accepted boundaries of state-level units, making it hard to justify a comparative analysis focused on those units.[6] On the other hand, the people inhabiting the

---

(Cambridge: Polity Press, 1996); Frederick Cooper, "What Is the Concept of Globalization Good For? An African Historian's Perspective," *African Affairs* 100:399 (2001): 189–213.

[6] See, for example, Michael Werner and Bénédicte Zimmerman, "Beyond Comparison: *Histoire Croisée* and the Challenge of Reflexivity," *History and Theory* 45:1 (2006): 30–50. For an argument for the compatibility between comparison and entanglement, see Jürgen Kocka, "Comparison and Beyond," *History and Theory* 42:1 (2003): 39–44.

historical spaces very likely made similar comparisons themselves –
weighing the desirability of declaring allegiance to this or that crown or
making choices of migration from one territory to another in the face of
changing local conditions. Allowing space for native comparisons, while
still avoiding the trap of reifying the categorical units being critiqued, is a
serious balancing act.

This book, then, is not a work of comparative history per se. In order to
compare different empires, these units have to be discretely defined, but
one of the core arguments made in the pages that follow is that the
different colonies present in the Caribbean in this period were not discrete
entities at all. Rather, their very entanglement was one of the defining
characteristics of the region and of the practices that composed it. At the
same time, some comparison is inevitable in an analysis such as this, not
least because of the constant comparative observations made by the
historical actors living in the region.[7] Often these observations led to
practical action, such as relocating from one island to another in search
of better opportunities or claiming subjecthood under a different empire
or republic in times of turmoil. Ignoring such contemporary comparisons
would lead to misrepresentations of historical constraints and possibilities.

Geographically innovative regional approaches to history have become
increasingly important over the last few decades. As national histories
have at long last lost some of their hold on the discipline, other frameworks have come to the fore amid widespread debate over how to think of
history in a way that does not privilege the national and political boundaries of the present day. This debate is useful insofar as it forces historians to reflect on the important role played by the spatial framing of their
work and to consider the importance of actors and structures that might
have been left entirely out of view in more traditional perspectives.
New definitions, however, can also become unnecessarily restrictive, in
essence replacing one set of unhelpful and arbitrary boundaries with
another or, in other cases, merely renaming without doing much analytical reframing. This has been especially true in the case of Atlantic
history – one of the more widely debated, disputed, and ultimately
embraced new fields to emerge in the discipline over the past two
decades.[8] While an Atlantic perspective can serve to increase awareness

---

[7] For an illuminating discussion of comparisons made by historical actors, see Renaud
Morieux, "Indigenous Comparisons," in *History after Hobsbawm: Writing the Past for the
Twenty-First Century*, ed. John Arnold, Matthew Hilton, and Jan Rüger (Oxford: Oxford
University Press, 2017), 50–75.

[8] For a modest sample of the historiographical debate, see Bernard Bailyn, *Atlantic History:
Concept and Contours* (Cambridge, MA: Harvard University Press, 2005); Peter
A. Coclanis, "Atlantic World or Atlantic/World?," *The William and Mary Quarterly* 63:4

and understanding of transnational, inter-imperial, and cross-cultural exchanges and links within this particular geographical space, it can also blind us to those connections that go beyond the Atlantic basin and to those parallels that we might find elsewhere on the globe. These blind spots are not an inherent limitation of the field, but rather a potential danger – one exacerbated by the recent tendency toward narrowness.

The book is Atlantic in scope insofar as it deals with a geographical area that is located within the Atlantic basin, and is embedded in multiple different trans-Atlantic networks.[9] The scope is also global, however, as the same networks inevitably span wider than a single body of water, and the processes of global imperialism and commercial activity across continents influence the developments in the Caribbean to a significant extent, particularly in the nineteenth century. To a certain degree, the analysis can thus be characterized as Atlantic in scope but global in approach. Rather than operate under such programmatic disciplinary labels, however, the book takes specific theoretical insights from Atlantic history and other approaches, using these to sharpen the focus and shape the conceptual framing of the historical analysis. Three related trends have been particularly influential for the present book. First is the new focus on spatiality and maritime or liminal geography in Atlantic history, as exemplified by the work of Linda Rupert, Michael J. Jarvis, Paul Pressly, Karwan Fatah-Black, and Ernesto Bassi.[10] Second is the particular focus on social networks, championed in many accounts including those by Kerry Ward, Alison Games, David Hancock,

(2006): 725–42; Alison Games, "Atlantic History: Definitions, Challenges, Opportunities," *The American Historical Review* 111:3 (2006): 741–57; Jack P. Greene and Philip D. Morgan, eds., *Atlantic History: A Critical Appraisal* (Oxford: Oxford University Press, 2009); David Armitage, "Three Concepts of Atlantic History," in *The British Atlantic World, 1500–1800* (2nd edition), ed. Armitage and Michael J. Braddick (New York: Palgrave Macmillan, 2009), 1–12; Lauren Benton, "The British Atlantic in Global Context," in ibid., 271–89; Armitage, "The Atlantic Ocean," in *Oceanic Histories*, ed. Armitage, Alison Bashford, and Sujit Sivasundaram (Cambridge: Cambridge University Press, 2018), 98–102.

[9] According to David Armitage's most recent typology of Atlantic historiography, the present study would likely qualify more specifically as an "infra-Atlantic history." See Armitage, "The Atlantic Ocean."

[10] Linda Rupert, *Creolization and Contraband: Curaçao in the Early Modern Atlantic World* (Athens: University of Georgia Press, 2012); Michael J. Jarvis, *In the Eye of All Trade: Bermuda, Bermudians, and Maritime Atlantic World 1680–1783* (Chapel Hill: University of North Carolina Press, 2012); Paul M. Pressly, *On the Rim of the Atlantic: Colonial Georgia and the British Atlantic World* (Athens: University of Georgia Press, 2013); Karwan Fatah-Black, "A Swiss Village in the Dutch Tropics: The Limitations of Empire-Centred Approaches to the Early Modern Atlantic World," *BMGN – Low Countries Historical Review* 128:1 (2013): 31–52; Ernesto Bassi, *An Aqueous Territory: Sailor Geographies and New Grenada's Transimperial Greater Caribbean World* (Durham, NC: Duke University Press, 2017).

Christian J. Koot, and Fabricio Prado.[11] Third and last is the view of empire as being composed of various sets of practices. This type of practice analysis has been particularly pronounced in historical scholarship on colonial law, in studies of slave societies, and in the study of imperial knowledge production.[12]

The Islands at a Glance

The Leeward Islands were given their name by European explorers due to their downwind location relative to ships arriving in the Caribbean from the eastern coasts of the Atlantic basin, making it easy for these ships to reach Leeward ports by simply sailing with the wind. They are made up of the northern half of the Lesser Antilles, spanning from the Virgin Islands in the northwest to Dominica in the southeast (see Figure 1.1). Found among them are some of the smallest populated islands in the Caribbean Sea. At the turn of the nineteenth century, the colonies of the Leeward Islands belonged to a multitude of European empires, including those of Britain, Denmark, France, the Netherlands,

---

[11] Kerry Ward, *Networks of Empire: Forced Migration in the Dutch East India Company* (New York: Cambridge University Press, 2009); Alison Games, *Webs of Empire: English Cosmopolitans in an Age of Expansion, 1560–1660* (Oxford: Oxford University Press, 2009); David Hancock, *Oceans of Wine: Madeira and the Emergence of American Trade and Taste* (New Haven: Yale University Press, 2009); Christian J. Koot, *Empire at the Periphery: British Colonists, Anglo-Dutch Trade, and the Development of the British Atlantic, 1621–1713* (New York: New York University Press, 2011); Fabricio Prado, *Edge of Empire: Atlantic Networks and Revolution in Bourbon Río de la Plata* (Berkeley: University of California Press, 2015). See also David Prior, "After the Revolution: An Alternative Future for Atlantic History," *History Compass* 12:3 (2014): 300–309.

[12] For uses of practice in legal history, see Lauren Benton, *Law and Colonial Cultures: Legal Regimes in World History* (New York: Cambridge University Press, 2002); Mary Sarah Bilder, *The Transatlantic Constitution: Colonial Legal Culture and the Empire* (Cambridge, MA: Harvard University Press, 2004); Daniel J. Hulsebosch, *Constituting Empire: New York and the Transformation of Constitutionalism in the Atlantic World, 1664–1830* (Chapel Hill: University of North Carolina Press, 2005); Ken MacMillan, *Sovereignty and Possession in the English New World* (Cambridge: Cambridge University Press, 2009); MacMillan, *The Atlantic Imperial Constitution: Center and Periphery in the English Atlantic World* (New York: Palgrave Macmillan, 2011). For practice analyses in histories of slavery, see, for example, Stephanie Camp, *Closer to Freedom: Enslaved Women and Everyday Resistance in the Plantation South* (Chapel Hill: University of North Carolina Press, 2004); Kristen Block, *Ordinary Lives in the Early Caribbean: Religion, Colonial Competition, and Politics of Profit* (Athens: University of Georgia Press, 2012); Vincent Brown, *The Reaper's Garden: Death and Power in the World of Atlantic Slavery* (Cambridge, MA: Harvard University Press, 2008). For the practice perspective in histories of imperial knowledge production, see, in particular, Richard Drayton, *Nature's Government: Science, Imperial Britain, and the "Improvement" of the World* (New Haven: Yale University Press, 2000).

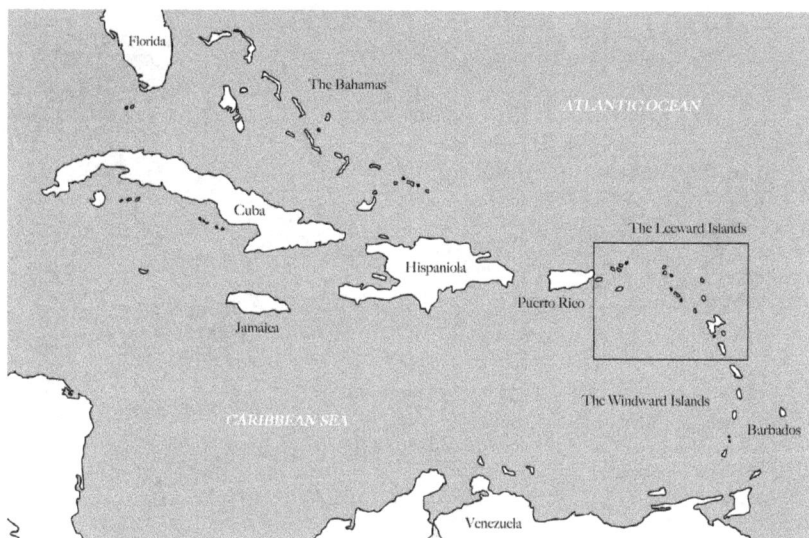

Figure 1.1 The Leeward Islands in the greater Caribbean.

Spain, and Sweden (see Figure 1.2). Besides European settlers and their descendants, the populations included a great number of Africans and Afro-Caribbeans, a variety of creole peoples, and, on the larger islands, remnants of the indigenous Taíno and Carib peoples. Leeward Islanders were highly polyglot and diverse, most of them speaking several languages and able to communicate across colonial and imperial boundaries. The main languages of the region were Dutch, English, French, and Spanish, alongside a number of local creoles.[13]

The Virgin Islands are a distinct group of islands within the Leewards, consisting at the turn of the century of island colonies belonging to the Spanish, Danish, and British empires.[14] The colonial government in

---

[13] Indeed, at the turn of the century the most common language spoken across the Leeward Islands, including in Danish, Dutch, and Swedish colonies, was Creole English.

[14] The Virgin Islands are a distinct island chain in a geographical sense as they are separated from Puerto Rico to the west by the Virgin Passage and from the rest of the Lesser Antilles to the east by the Anegada Passage. The Anegada Passage is typically seen as the dividing line between the Greater and the Lesser Antilles, but the period of colonization saw significant maritime traffic connecting the Virgin Islands to their neighboring colonies in both directions. In this sense they came to form a bridge of sorts between the Greater and Lesser Antilles, and in the period studied here they were seen by both Danish and British empires as a key component of the Leeward Islands, both geographically and administratively. The Virgin Islands' proximity to each other is even greater than that of the other islands in the Lesser Antilles, although island density is not at the same level as within the Bahamas to the northwest.

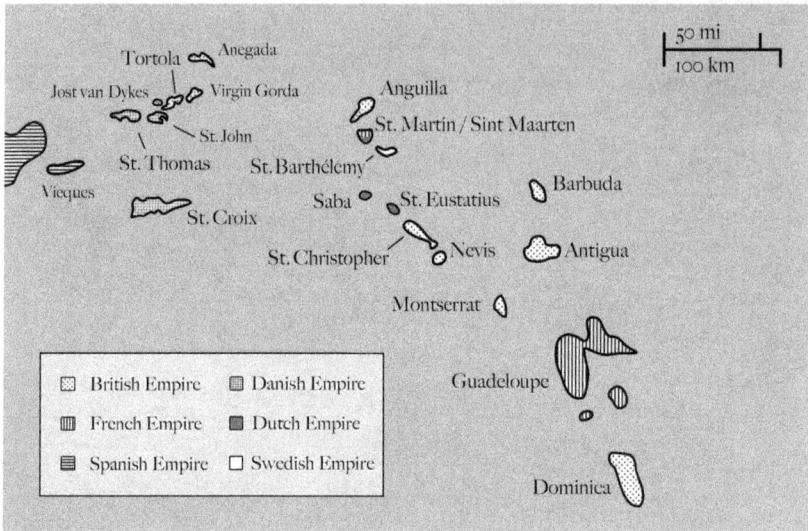

Figure 1.2 Empires in the Leeward Islands, 1815.

Puerto Rico administered the Spanish Virgin Islands of Vieques and Culebra, while the British and Danish islands made up their own colonial units. The British Virgin Islands consist of four main islands – Tortola, Anegada, Virgin Gorda, and Jost Van Dyke – alongside a number of smaller islands and keys, most of which were uninhabited. The Danish West Indies, today the US Virgin Islands, likewise consist of three larger islands – St. Thomas, St. John, and St. Croix – as well as a great number of lesser surrounding islands. The Danish or US islands are volcanic, geographically a continuation of the central mountain range of Puerto Rico, whereas the British are low limestone islands.[15] Most of the Danish and British Virgin Islands are exceedingly small, ranging in size from Jost Van Dyke's 3.1 square miles to St. Thomas's 32 square miles, with the exception of St. Croix, which not only is located further away from any of the other islands but also is by far the biggest, measuring a total of 82 square miles (see Figures 1.3 and 1.4 for their relative location).[16]

---

[15] William F. Keegan and Corinne L. Hofman, *The Caribbean before Columbus* (Oxford: Oxford University Press, 2017), 5–6.

[16] The islands in order of size are as follows: Jost Van Dyke (3.1 square miles), Virgin Gorda (8.1 square miles), Anegada (14.7 square miles), St. John (19.7 square miles), Tortola (21.6 square miles), St. Thomas (32 square miles), and St. Croix (82 square miles).

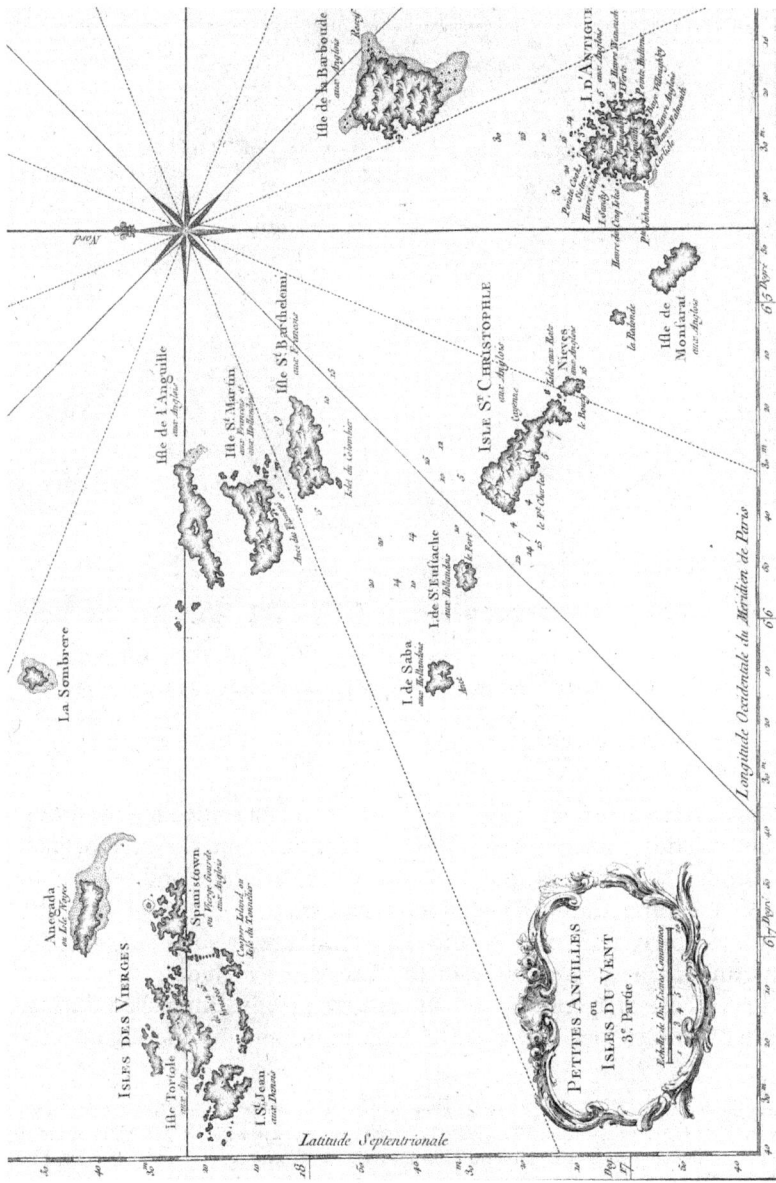

Figure 1.3 Chart of the northern Leeward Islands, 1764. From Jacques Nicolas Bellin, *Le petit atlas maritime recueil de cartes et plans des quatre parties du monde.*
Source: The David Rumsey Map Collection

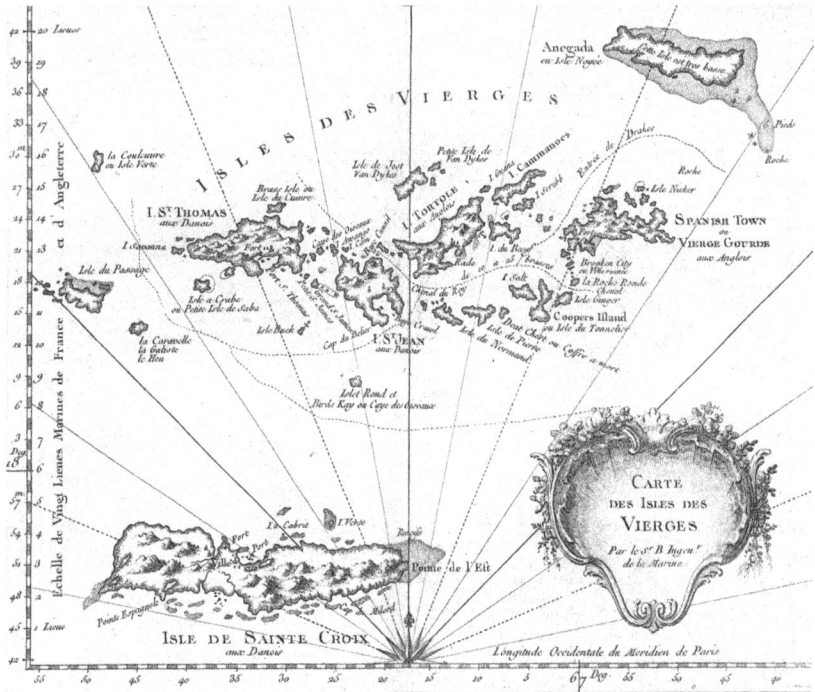

Figure 1.4 Chart of the Virgin Islands, 1764. From Jacques Nicolas Bellin, *Le petit atlas maritime recueil de cartes et plans des quatre parties du monde.*
Source: The David Rumsey Map Collection

Ortoiroid people arriving from South America first settled the northern Leeward Islands some three thousand years ago, but the archipelago went through several subsequent phases of displacement and repopulation. By the time European explorers first made contact in the late fifteenth century, members of the Taíno culture, also originating in South America, inhabited most of the Leewards, including the Virgin Islands.[17] These indigenous populations were greatly diminished during the initial centuries of European colonization, and by the eighteenth

[17] Irving Rouse, *The Tainos: Rise and Decline of the People Who Greeted Columbus* (New Haven: Yale University Press, 1992), 6–21, 66–67. For more on the history of the region prior to colonization, see Keegan and Hofman, *The Caribbean before Columbus*, 134–42, 197–237. There is some confusion in the historical literature over the terminology used to describe indigenous Caribbean peoples. Some of this confusion stems from the fact that European colonizers often referred to most inhabitants of the Lesser Antilles as "Caribs," while twentieth- and twenty-first-century archaeologists make clear distinctions

century their numbers on the Virgin Islands were so reduced as to have vanished almost entirely from colonial records.[18]

Both European empires and individual sailors and privateers made use of the islands throughout the sixteenth century, but the process of formal colonization was not undertaken until the seventeenth century. Many of the islands then passed through multiple empires, including the Dutch, French, Spanish, English, and even the Knights of Malta, who briefly controlled St. Croix in the 1650s. Danish colonial efforts in the Caribbean began with the settlement of St. Thomas in 1671, followed by the settlement of St. John in 1718 and the purchase of St. Croix from the French in 1733. The British for their part conquered the remaining Dutch Virgin Islands in 1672 with the outbreak of the Third Anglo-Dutch War, focusing their initial development efforts on Tortola and gradually spreading to the other three islands over the next decades.

St. Barthélemy, a volcanic island, is geographically similar to the smaller of the Virgin Islands, measuring a total of 9.7 square miles and having a mostly arid and rocky interior. It lies in close proximity to St. Martin, Anguilla, Saba, and St. Eustatius, and has a large natural harbor. The island was first colonized by French settlers from St. Christopher in the 1650s, but saw little use in the subsequent century, despite a brief military occupation by the British in 1758. The island's population numbered less than a thousand in this period, and there was very little agricultural production taking place in the interior. Sweden acquired the colony in 1784, as part of a deal granting French merchants trading privileges in the Swedish port of Gothenburg, which proved the culmination of a decade-long search on the part of the Swedish crown for a colonial possession in the Americas.[19]

The Danish, Swedish, and British islands all saw significant population growth across the eighteenth century. Much of this growth stemmed from the importation of large numbers of enslaved Africans, who were used both as plantation labor and as workers in the islands' port towns. When looking at the greater Caribbean region, the Leeward Islands stood out in their demographic composition at the turn of the nineteenth

---

between the "Island-Caribs" inhabiting the Windward Islands and the Taíno peoples inhabiting the Greater Antilles and most of the Leeward Islands. Even this dichotomy is misleading, as it betrays the cultural and linguistic diversity of precolonial Caribbean peoples. See Samuel M. Wilson, "The Cultural Mosaic of the Indigenous Caribbean," *Proceedings of the British Academy* 81 (1992): 37–66.

[18] "Vanished" is perhaps a misleading word, as much of their displacement took place through organized violence and the spread of deadly contagious diseases.

[19] Ingegerd Hildebrand, *Den Svenska Kolonin S:t Barthélemy och Västindiska Kompaniet fram till 1796* (Lund: P. Lindstedt, 1951), 1–33.

Table 1.1 *Free and enslaved populations in the Danish West Indies, the British Virgin Islands, and St. Barthélemy, 1812–1815*[a]

	Whites	Free people of color	Slaves	Total population
St. Thomas	2,122	2,284	4,393	9,525
St. John	157	271	2,306	2,734
St. Croix	1,840	2,480	24,330	28,650
The British Virgin Islands	486	1,472[b]	7,285	8,709
St. Barthélemy	1,958	1,128	2,406	5,492

[a] Exact population numbers are not generally available year to year. The numbers presented here for the Danish and British islands are from 1815, while the ones for St. Barthélemy are from 1812. A more detailed breakdown of the population over time is provided in Chapter 5 of this book. The numbers are taken from Neville A. T. Hall, *Slave Society in the Danish West Indies: St. Thomas, St. John and St. Croix* (Mona: University of the West Indies Press, 1992), 5 and 180; Yolande Lavoie, Carolyn Fick, and Francine-M. Mayer, "A Particular Study of Slavery in the Caribbean Island of Saint Barthélemy: 1648–1846," *Caribbean Studies* 28:2 (1995): 382–84; "Statistical tables of the British Virgin Islands at two periods," in TNA, CO 239/9.
[b] This number includes 534 so-called liberated Africans – people who had been transported to the region to be sold into slavery, only to be seized by imperial authorities and placed in apprenticeships as part of the abolition of the slave trade. See Chapter 6 for more on the apprenticeship system.

century (see Table 1.1). While a majority of the population was still enslaved, the share of free people – both white and of color – was generally higher than in the larger plantation islands surrounding them. Within the Leewards there was still a relatively clear divide between plantation islands and entrepôts. The smaller, more urban islands of St. Thomas and St. Barthélemy were thus comparable to other entrepôts in the microregion, such as Dutch St. Eustatius, which had a total population of 2,591 in 1817, of which 67 percent were enslaved, 13 percent were free people of color, and 20 percent were white.[20] The contrast to the plantation island of St. Croix is striking, with its total population of 28,650, of which 85 percent were enslaved. In this way St. Croix was more similar to the other sugar-producing islands of the region, although not quite of the same size or scale as French Guadeloupe – the largest of the Leeward Islands – which had a population of almost 100,000 in 1817, of which four in five people were enslaved.[21]

[20] Herman Benjamins and Johannes Snelleman, eds., *Encyclopedie van Nederlandsch West-Indië* (Leiden: Martinus Nijhoff, 1917), 627.
[21] Alexandre Moreau de Jonnès, *Recherches statistiques sur l'esclavage colonial sur les moyens de le supprimer* (Paris: Imprimerie de Bourgogne et Martinet, 1842), 19.

Despite the demographic differences between plantation colonies and entrepôts, all of the Leeward Islands qualified as slave societies in the sense typically deployed by Caribbean historians, meaning a society in which social and political institutions were fundamentally organized around slavery.[22] Indeed, the islands were all deeply embroiled in the system of slavery, but this system was not experienced in uniform ways across colonies. While some islands produced high-value commodities for export through the toil of slave labor, others acted as nodes in maritime networks that facilitated these production chains by hosting intraregional slave markets or offering convenient ports of transshipment.

The Inter-imperial Microregion

In the history of European empires, and overseas empires in particular, political interactions at the so-called periphery rarely took the form of well-defined interpolity relations but were more often examples of cross-polity exchanges embedded within networks that crossed, blurred, and sometimes subverted the formal boundaries, and thereby the sovereignty, of states and empires. Such networks could result from a number of different historically and regionally specific circumstances, with varying degrees of official sanction from any or all of the involved polities. The political space created by these networks extended beyond the sphere of inter-imperial or foreign policy, and came to include certain sets of practices and institutions that constituted some functions of governance most often thought of as being the sole domain of the state. European overseas colonialism of the eighteenth and nineteenth centuries was especially prone to this trend, given its particular imperial repertoire, which included economies reliant on some type of unfree labor, be it in the form of slavery or indentured servitude; commercial activities tied to long-distance maritime networks; political frameworks focused, at least in part, on inter-imperial rivalry; legal regimes that were both adaptable and intelligible across imperial borders; and a tendency to rely on relatively small but well-equipped military forces at the local level.

---

[22] See, in particular, the groundbreaking work of Elsa V. Goveia, *Slave Society in the British Leeward Islands at the End of the Eighteenth Century* (New Haven: Yale University Press, 1965). It is worth noting that Goveia's work on the topic, originating with her doctoral dissertation in 1952, predates the oft-used binary of "slave society" and "society with slaves" formulated by classicist Moses Finley. See Theresa Singleton, "Islands of Slavery: Archeology and Caribbean Landscapes of Intensification," in *What Is a Slave Society? The Practice of Slavery in Global Perspective*, ed. Noel Lenski and Catherine Cameron (Cambridge: Cambridge University Press, 2018), 290–309.

In its ideal-typical form, an inter-imperial microregion is defined as a geographical area inhabited by multiple polities, with a particularly high density of relations and interactions between and across the formal boundaries of these polities. Such connections can include the movement of goods, information, and people; the transference, dissemination, and adoption of legal, commercial, and political practices; the formation of informal communities of groups and individual actors, tied together by language, ethnicity, economic interests, or political identity; and the shared internal and external threats to security and social order posed by slave uprisings, revolutions, and inter-imperial war, alongside local interpolity rivalries. The polities in question need not all be imperial, but at least some of them must have connections of authority that stretch outside the microregion, placing their subjects in a situation of potential conflict between regional and metropolitan interests. The last point also implies the existence of some type of imperial intermediaries – actors operating locally as representatives of a metropolitan authority that is geographically removed from the region. These agents operate alongside more inherently local actors, such as settlers, merchants, sailors, slaves, and indigenous groups, whose interests are primarily, although not always exclusively, tied to the regional context. For some of the latter actors, their ties to the region are due to a chosen relocation to the area, while others have had their ties to outside contexts forcefully severed through involuntary displacement.[23]

In the last few years a number of volumes have come out by historians and social scientists shaped in part by what is now a thriving academic debate over the nature of empire.[24] A key component in this literature has been Daniel Nexon's work on early modern imperial systems and

---

[23] For an insightful treatment of how distinctly regional identities and relations can develop following forced migration, see Jane G. Landers, *Atlantic Creoles in the Age of Revolutions* (Cambridge, MA: Harvard University Press, 2010).

[24] Notable examples include Charles S. Maier, *Among Empires: American Ascendancy and Its Predecessors* (Cambridge, MA: Harvard University Press, 2006); John Darwin, *After Tamerlane: The Rise and Fall of Global Empires, 1400–2000* (London: Penguin, 2007); Karen Barkey, *Empire of Difference: The Ottomans in Comparative Perspective* (Cambridge: Cambridge University Press, 2008); Jane Burbank and Frederick Cooper, *Empires in World History: Power and the Politics of Difference* (Princeton: Princeton University Press, 2010); Julian Go, *Patterns of Empire* (Cambridge: Cambridge University Press, 2011); Andrew Phillips, *War, Religion and Empire* (Cambridge: Cambridge University Press, 2011); Paul K. McDonald, *Networks of Domination: The Social Foundation of Peripheral Conquest in International Politics* (Oxford: Oxford University Press, 2014); Anthony Pagden, *The Burdens of Empire, 1539 to the Present* (Cambridge: Cambridge University Press, 2015).

their dynamics of rule.[25] This approach casts empires as specific types of structural arrangements, which

differ from hegemonic and unipolar orders because they combine two features: rule through intermediaries and heterogeneous contracting between imperial cores and constituent political communities. These characteristics constitute ideal-typical empires as a form of political organization with particular network properties. Ideal-typical empires comprise a "rimless" hub-and-spoke system of authority, in which cores are connected to peripheries but peripheries themselves are disconnected – or segmented – from one another.[26]

When considering the view of empires as social and political configurations presented by Nexon, the inter-imperial microregion can be seen as a distinct variation of the ideal-type. As shown in Figure 1.5, actors and groups of actors of different polities are tied together in overlapping and layered networks within the region, leading to a system that differs from regular imperial compositions in important ways. The direct ties of authority between imperial cores, local intermediaries, and local groups exist alongside a myriad of non-authority ties between local groups of different imperial peripheries, creating grounds for relationships, institutions, and practices that can potentially undermine and subvert a given core's control of its periphery. While organized cross-colonial resistance to imperial authority is not an automatic consequence of such composition, the possibility of mobilization across imperial boundaries exists as a constant threat.[27] Furthermore, imperial and colonial institutions on the ground necessarily function differently in a setting with such a degree of inter-peripheral integration than they do in locations with stronger intra-imperial ties of authority and less exposure to external polities.

The inter-imperial microregion consists of numerous networks, and these operate at what are at once different and overlapping levels of interaction and authority. There are at least three distinct levels of cross-polity interactions in most inter-imperial microregions. The first is that of *inter-imperial politics*, meaning those interactions between formal imperial actors that influence the region in some way, including

[25] Daniel H. Nexon, *The Struggle for Power in Early Modern Europe: Religious Conflict, Dynastic Empires and International Change* (Princeton: Princeton University Press, 2009); Daniel H. Nexon and Thomas Wright, "What's at Stake in the American Empire Debate," *American Political Science Review* 101:2 (2007): 253–71. See also Daniel H. Nexon and Paul Musgrave, "States of Empire: Liberal Ordering and Imperial Relations," in *Liberal World Orders*, ed. Tim Dunne and Trine Flockhart (Oxford: Oxford University Press, 2013), 211–30; Morten Andersen, "Semi-cores in Imperial Relations: The Cases of Scotland and Norway," *Review of International Studies* 42:1 (2016): 178–203.
[26] Nexon and Wright, "American Empire Debate," 253.
[27] See Nexon, *The Struggle for Power*, 108–10, 125–26.

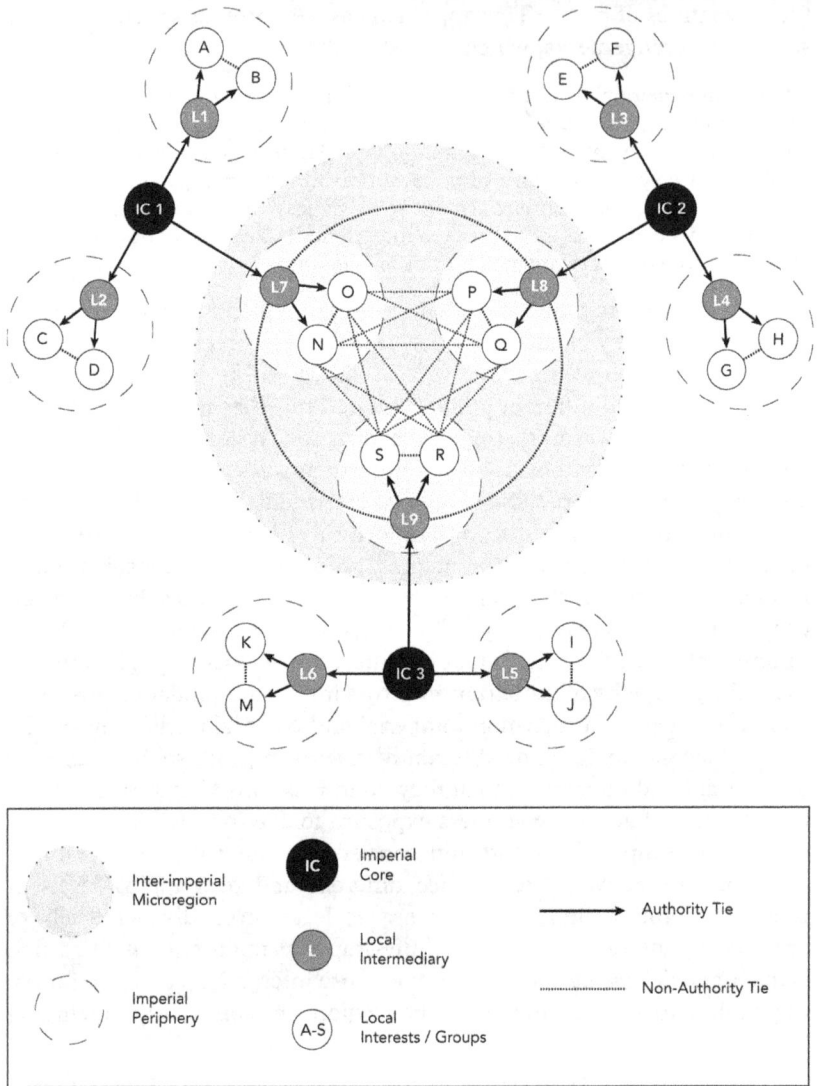

Figure 1.5 An ideal-typical inter-imperial microregion.

declarations of war and peace, formations of alliances, and negotiations of trade agreements. The second is that of *intercolonial relations*, a category that encompasses interactions and exchanges taking place at the level of local political and legal authority, such as claims to and contestations of sovereignty, dissemination of perceived best practices in governance and policy implementation, and local colonial competition and cooperation. The third is that of *trans-imperial networks* – social, commercial, or political. Such networks can be composed of numerous different types of actors and spring from an even greater myriad of activities, but common to all of them is that they cross the nominal boundaries of different polities without the same degree of institutionalized formality as the previous two types. This observation does not imply that they are necessarily without inherent relations of authority or power, but rather that they operate outside the norms of regular diplomatic or jurisdictional channels. The first two levels of interaction thus take place as a consequence of state structures and initiatives, while the third set of interactions often circumvents or outright subverts those structures.

The categories outlined here represent useful analytical distinctions, but they are not isolated from one another, nor do they imply that actors are limited to participation at a single level. Rather, they exist in a complex system of mutual interaction, and many of the specific networks or transactions within any given microregion will likely be at once transimperial and intercolonial, involving both actors that are moving within the political institutions of the colonies and others who are defying or subverting these. While inter-imperial politics can usually be thought of as more of an exogenous force for the region in question, the actions at any one level will often have important ramifications for the other two, moving either from the global to the local or vice versa. Trans-imperial networks were of course not limited to specific microregions, but are found everywhere in the world of competing imperial polities. What makes the inter-imperial microregion a distinctive political space is the comparatively high density of networks and clear porousness of sovereignty, qualities that together create the necessary conditions for a number of mutually constitutive practices and institutions not usually found in more imperially homogenous areas.[28] Such practices and institutions could span the spectrum from commercial activities and political exchanges in the public sphere to tasks that are usually thought of as being held solely in the hands of the state, including internal security and institutionalized legal norms. In the specific case of the Leeward Islands, the internal threats of slave uprisings and colonial rebellions thus led to a certain level of mutual reliance on military aid between the colonies of different empires in times of crisis and, related to this, a low level of preparedness for significant external threats and invasions. Illicit commercial practices created, and were in turn shaped by, informal

---

[28] Few if any colonial spaces were truly imperially homogenous prior to the late nineteenth century, so this is more a distinction of degree than of kind.

cross-colonial regional markets, often at the detriment to more formal imperially sanctioned markets.[29] The dissemination and circulation of news and other information created and was taking place in locally anchored trans-imperial public spheres, which were in some cases further integrated by the use of local pidgin or creole dialects.[30] Finally, the jurisdictional practices by many colonial magistrates and their adoption of perceived best practice among neighboring colonies led to the formation of more or less institutionalized intercolonial legal norms at the regional level, officially sanctioned or otherwise.

In these and other ways microregional spaces were a well-known fact of life for historical contemporaries. They shaped the lives of groups and individuals living or operating within them, and provided both challenges and opportunities for imperial administrators. The merchant mariner who happily crossed imperial borders in order to get the best price for his goods, the plantation owner who bought imported slaves on a neutral island only to smuggle them into British territory, the captive who fled the colony of one empire for the fleeting possibility of freedom in another, the privateer who sailed with three different flags and four different letters of marque, in case he should get caught by the wrong imperial cruiser – all these actors existed within political and legal spaces that were more than just those of neighboring colonies. Politically polyglot space fostered politically adaptive people and vice versa, leading to practices and perspectives that were decidedly different from the neat

---

[29] For detailed treatments of such interactions, see Eric Tagliacozzo, *Secret Trades, Porous Borders: Smuggling and States along a Southeast Asian Frontier, 1865–1915* (New Haven: Yale University Press, 2005); Alan L. Karras, *Smuggling: Contraband and Corruption in World History* (Lanham: Rowman & Littlefield, 2010). For specifics on smuggling in the Caribbean, see Bram Hoonhout, "Smuggling for Survival: Self-Organized, Cross-Imperial Colony Building in Essequibo and Demerara, 1746–1793," in *Beyond Empires: Global Self-Organizing, Cross-Imperial Networks, 1500–1800*, ed. Cátia Antunes and Amélia Polónia (Leiden: Brill, 2016), 212–35; Wim Klooster, "Inter-imperial Smuggling in the Americas, 1600–1800," in *Soundings in Atlantic History: Latent Structures and Intellectual Currents, 1500–1830*, ed. Bernard Bailyn and Patricia Denault (Cambridge, MA: Harvard University Press, 2009), 141–80; Rupert, *Creolization and Contraband*, 67–101.

[30] See, for example, Julius C. Scott, *The Common Wind: Afro-American Currents in the Age of the Haitian Revolution* (London: Verso, 2018); Scott, "Crisscrossing Empires: Ships, Sailors, and Resistance in the Lesser Antilles in the Eighteenth Century," in *The Lesser Antilles in the Age of European Expansion*, ed. Robert L. Paquette and Stanley L. Engerman (Gainesville: University Press of Florida, 1996), 128–43; Gregory L. Childs, "Scenes of Sedition: Politics, Publics, and Freedom in Late Eighteenth Century Bahia, Brazil," PhD dissertation (New York University, 2012). For more on the formation of regional creole dialects, see Philip Baker and Peter Mühlhäuser, "Creole Linguistics from Its Beginnings, through Schuchardt to the Present Day," in *Creolization: History, Ethnography, Theory*, ed. Charles Stewart (Walnut Creek, CA: Left Coast Press, 2007), 84–107.

and unambiguous territorial ordering we might be tempted to project back in time from the vantage point of the present.

In analytical terms, the inter-imperial framework stresses a relational approach, one that looks at the interactions between groups or individuals as they take place within a given historical context, thereby highlighting the importance of the autonomy of agents, the influence of institutions, and the role played by physical and material reality, without having to resort to either character-driven narratives or structural determinism.[31] Indeed, this is one of the aspects that distinguishes the microregional study from a traditional microhistory, with the latter's emphasis on actor-centric analyses and the close examination of the "exceptional normal," to use Edoardo Grendi's oft-quoted phrase.[32] The microregional lens, in contrast, is focused on uncovering new connections and practices that are simply not visible through the examination of any single archive or bounded locality. A similar point can be made in relation to the regional version of the world-systems approach employed by some global historians, most prominently the distinguished Africanist Donald R. Wright.[33] While the model presented here has some features in common with the work of scholars such as Wright, it does not rely on the same structural underpinnings, nor does it necessitate a view of historical change based primarily on macroeconomic patterns. Somewhere between world-systems analysis and microhistory in scope, the microregional perspective seeks neither abstracted simplicity nor complexity for its

[31] See, in particular, Mustafa Emirbayer and Jeffrey Goodwin, "Network Analysis, Culture, and the Problem of Agency," *American Journal of Sociology* 99:6 (1994): 1141–54; Emirbayer, "Manifesto for a Relational Sociology," 281–317; Margaret R. Sommers, "'We're No Angels': Realism, Rational Choice, and Relationality in Social Science," *American Journal of Sociology* 104:3 (1998): 79–98; Jackson and Nexon, "Relations before States," 291–332.

[32] Edoardo Grendi, "Micro-analisi e storia sociale," *Quaderni storici* 35(1977): 512; Giovanni Levi, "On Microhistory," in *New Perspectives on Historical Writing*, ed. Peter Burke (Philadelphia: Pennsylvania State University Press, 1992), 93–113; Carlo Ginzburg, "Microhistory: Two or Three Things That I Know about It," *Critical Inquiry* 20:1 (1993): 10–35; Matti Peltonen, "Clues, Margins, and Monads: The Micro-Macro Link in Historical Research," *History and Theory* 40:3 (2001): 347–59. It is worth noting that the original Italian microhistorical approach is somewhat different from the version more commonly found in the Anglophone literature, as the latter tends to place more emphasis on narrative history than on theoretical innovation. See the useful discussion of the field in Francesca Trivellato, "Is There a Future for Italian Microhistory in the Age of Global History?," *California Italian Studies* 2(1) (2011): 1–21.

[33] Donald R. Wright, *The World and a Very Small Place in Africa: A History of Globalization in Niumi, the Gambia* (3rd edition) (New York: M. E. Sharpe, 2010). For world-systems analysis more broadly, see Wallerstein, *The Modern World-System I*; Janet Abu-Lughod, *Before European Hegemony: The World System A.D. 1250–1350* (Oxford: Oxford University Press, 1989).

own sake, but rather attempts to map out and make sense of the messiness and entanglement of networked institutions and practices.[34]

The inter-imperial microregion is both a social and a physical space. Interdependence and cross-group connections rather than formal geographical criteria, such as ecological generalizability or uniformity, define its composition and limits.[35] This distinction is especially important for the spatial boundaries of the microregion, which are not strictly conterminous with a particular physical area but instead depend on the shifting lines of interaction of the groups operating within it. Indeed, a clear demarcation of the microregion is inherently impossible, as malleable networks of people, rather than political borders or geographical markers, make up its primary constituents. Microregional spaces can therefore be mapped out only in a tentative and provisional way, by indicating the reach of their networks rather than charting fixed geographical boundaries.[36] That is not to say that there is no physical dimension to the microregion and that it is only a social space, as the density of interactions that ultimately constitute the region are anchored in particular spaces and enabled by the nature of those spaces. In this sense the Leeward Islands, characterized as they were by their close proximity to one another, their coastlines dotted with natural harbors and hidden coves, and the deep but narrow waters between them, made the frequency of boundary-crossing practices possible and facilitated the formation of trans-colonial networks. Meanwhile the density of connections within the microregion should not be interpreted as leading to isolation. Larger regions are often made up of multiple microregions, intersecting with one another at specific points. The microregion of the Leeward

---

[34] For the role of complexity in microhistory, see, in particular, Jacques Revel, "L'histoire au ras du sol," in *Le pouvoir au village: Histoire d'un exorciste dans le Piémont du XVIIe Siècle*, trans. Monique Aymard (Paris: Gallimard, 1989), i–xxxiii.

[35] In geographical terms, the microregion is defined as a functional rather than a formal region. See Roger Minshull, *Regional Geography* (London: Hutchinson University Library, 1967), 38–59.

[36] The literature on the shifting boundaries of regional and subregional spaces has seen a recent revival in history, building on previous insights from critical geography and political economy. See in particular Martin Lewis and Kären Wigen, *The Myth of Continents: A Critique of Metageography* (Berkeley: University of California Press, 1997); John Allen, Doreen Massey, and Allan Cochrane, *Rethinking the Region* (London: Routledge, 1998); Celia Applegate, "A Europe of Regions: Reflections on the Historiography of Sub-National Places in Modern Times," *The American Historical Review* 104:4 (1999): 1157–82; Elliott Young, "Regions," in *The Palgrave Dictionary of Transnational History*, ed. Akira Iriye and Pierre-Yves Saunier (New York: Palgrave Macmillan, 2009), 882–87; Sebastian Conrad and Prasenjit Duara, *Viewing Regionalisms from East Asia* (Washington, DC: American Historical Association, 2013); Michael Goebel, *Overlapping Geographies of Belonging: Migrations, Regions, and Nations in the Western South Atlantic* (Washington, DC: American Historical Association, 2013).

Islands was in no way isolated from other, broader circulations and connections, but rather embedded into larger spaces and bodies of water including the Caribbean, the Atlantic, and indeed a gradually emerging global space of trans-oceanic connectivity.

The discussion of the microregion's geographical nature leads to the question of environmental characteristics, namely, the distinction between maritime and landlocked spaces. While insular or coastal regions have the benefit of less costly and more reliable seaborne lines of travel, communication, and transportation than those reliant on inland routes, examples such as the eighteenth-century Ohio Valley and the upper Mississippi Valley illustrate that the formation of interpolity networks and considerable cross-colonial integration can also be found in landlocked regions.[37] Thus, even though maritime areas, and especially those with a multitude of islands or extensive coastlines, seem more likely to produce the conditions of porousness and interconnectedness that enable the formation of inter-imperial microregions, proximity to the sea is not an inherent necessity in a definitional sense.[38]

It is important to note that the networks in which interactions were imbedded were rarely based on positional equality between actors, but more often built upon relations of power and hierarchical ordering. The idea of a hierarchical network might sound paradoxical given some of the typical analytical uses of networks in the social sciences, but unequal distributions of power and specific logics of hierarchy are often at the very core of networked interactions, even when these take place through processes that go beyond the traditional practices of power politics or military exchanges.[39] The positions of individuals or groups within relational networks mediated commercial, social, legal, and political

---

[37] For a closer examination of the benefits of maritime lines of communication, see Kenneth J. Banks, *Chasing Empire across the Sea: Communication and the State in the French Atlantic, 1713–1763* (Montreal: McGill University Press, 2006), 65–100. For more on the North American examples, see Michael N. McConnell, *A Country Between: The Upper Ohio Valley and Its Peoples, 1724–1774* (Lincoln: University of Nebraska Press, 1992); Jane T. Merritt, *At the Crossroads: Indians and Empires on a Mid-Atlantic Frontier, 1700–1763* (Chapel Hill: University of North Carolina Press, 2003).

[38] For recent studies of other maritime regions with complicated legal and social entanglements, see W. Jeffrey Bolster, *The Mortal Sea: Fishing in the Atlantic in the Age of Sail* (Cambridge, MA: Harvard University Press, 2012); Renaud Morieux, *The Channel: England, France and the Construction of a Maritime Border in the Eighteenth Century* (Cambridge: Cambridge University Press, 2016); Bassi, *An Aqueous Territory*; Guillaume Calafat, *Une mer jalousée: Contribution à l'histoire de la souveraineté* (Paris: Éditions du Seuil, 2019).

[39] For a more traditional take on international networks, see Margaret E. Keck and Kathryn Sikkink, *Activists beyond Borders: Advocacy Networks in International Politics* (Ithaca, NY: Cornell University Press, 1998). For the role of hierarchies in interpolity

exchanges in the nineteenth century – positions that could be both a source and effect of the power held by these actors. What is more, these networks were not static and strictly spatially bounded phenomena, but rather dynamic structures that mobile actors external to them could enter and manipulate, provided they were familiar with the locally specific practices by which they operated.

A key aspect of the microregional framework is its focus on diplomacy and foreign relations at the margins of imperial systems – similar to what Renaud Morieux has termed "diplomacy from below."[40] By placing the interaction of individual colonies, or in some cases clusters of colonies or quasi-colonies, at the center of a study of inter-imperial relations, the crucial role of imperial magistrates, agents, intermediaries, or middlemen becomes clear. Whatever term we use to characterize these actors, their contributions to the shaping of inter- as well as intra-imperial policy and practice are fundamental to a fuller understanding of the dynamics of alliances, rivalries, and legal contestations. Placed as they were between metropolitan decision makers, local elites, colonial citizens, and marginalized groups of slaves or indigenous peoples, they clearly had a central role in determining the daily governance of imperial states.[41] But they were likewise positioned as the first arbitrators of intercolonial disputes and as the physical and political representatives of their respective empires. Often lacking any policy dictates beyond the most superficial, and faced with numerous and unforeseeable challenges, these individuals had to walk the tightrope between rapid and responsible decision-making, attentive to their local conditions and policies that would not fly in the face of the monarchs and governments to whom they were ultimately responsible. When they succeeded at this balancing act they could continue their work with the support of both local and imperial interests, but if they veered too much to either side they would end up falling out of favor with local, regional, or national actors. At times the challenge of independence

---

relations, see David A. Lake, *Hierarchy in International Relations* (Ithaca, NY: Cornell University Press, 2009); Alexander Cooley, *Logics of Hierarchy: The Organization of Empires, States, and Military Occupations* (Ithaca, NY: Cornell University Press, 2012); Ayşe Zarakol (ed.), *Hierarchies in World Politics* (Cambridge: Cambridge University Press, 2017).

[40] Renaud Morieux, "Diplomacy from below and Belonging: Fishermen and Cross-Channel Relations in the Eighteenth Century," *Past and Present* 202:1 (2009): 83–125.

[41] This aspect of imperial intermediaries is the focus of a number of excellent studies, including Jerry Bannister, *The Rule of Admirals: Law, Custom, and Naval Government in Newfoundland, 1699–1832* (Toronto: University of Toronto Press, 2003); Lisa Ford, *Settler Sovereignty: Jurisdiction and Indigenous Peoples in America and Australia, 1788–1836* (Cambridge, MA: Harvard University Press, 2010).

might outright paralyze them, reducing them instead to passive observers of the developments and opportunities of the colonial world.

If officials and magistrates are fundamental elements of the inter-imperial microregional framework, local actors with few direct imperial affiliations are another. The mobility of individual merchants, sailors, adventurers, and speculators in the maritime world of the colonial Caribbean was high indeed, and navigating the networks of smuggling, trade, and privateering was as profitable, dangerous, and natural to these actors as was navigating the high waters of the oceans themselves. The movement of people across imperial borders, whether temporary or more permanent, was an integral aspect of the microregional system, and it serves as much to question the notion of imperial sovereignty over discrete political and geographic units as do the autonomous political actions taken by the nominal agents of imperial authority. In fact, this movement often acted to expose just how tenuous these agents' hold on power was, demonstrating as it did the strength of the informal networks that crisscrossed and often subverted official authority.

None of this is to say that studies of inter-imperial interactions at the metropolitan level should be dismissed. A host of decisions were made at the highest level of political authority, and employing a framework that highlights relations and agency at the local level does not necessitate simultaneously ignoring these other processes. What it shows is how imperial aims and decrees translated into action on the ground, and how actors outside the formal hierarchy of political decision-making could influence and steer the course of events toward their own interests, whatever they might be. In this way, the inter-imperial microregional framework fits well with the emerging paradigm of new transnational political history, employing a ground-level perspective on events that were previously seen exclusively through the eyes of diplomatic elites.[42]

The microregional framework is a methodological approach that fits particularly well with historical studies of world politics, as the relatively narrow lens of regional history is combined with a perspective that emphasizes transnational and inter-imperial interactions and connections, enabling historians to conduct studies that are at once local and global. The framework is equally useful for works of comparative history, as distinct areas can be compared and contrasted across time and space

---

[42] For examples of this approach to diplomatic history, see Matthew Connelly, *A Diplomatic Revolution: Algeria's Fight for Independence and the Origins of the Post–Cold War Era* (Oxford: Oxford University Press, 2002); Rafe Blaufarb, "The Western Question: The Geopolitics of Latin American Independence," *The American Historical Review* 112 (2007): 742–63.

through the use of the inter-imperial microregion as an ideal-typical model in the Weberian sense.[43] Using the model in this way – as a "conceptual instrument for *comparison* with and *measurement* of reality" – one can identify the parallels between various inter-imperial configurations while also highlighting the way in which individual historical cases diverge from the ideal-type, thereby illuminating the distinctive character of specific regions while placing them in the context of a global history of connectivity and patterns.[44]

---

[43] See Max Weber, "Objectivity in the Social Sciences," in *The Methodology of the Social Sciences*, ed. Edward Shils and Henry Finch (New York: Free Press, 1949), 50–112. Among the best discussions of analysis through ideal-typification in the social sciences is Patrick Thaddeus Jackson, *The Conduct of Inquiry in International Relations: Philosophy of Science and Its Implications for the Study of World Politics* (New York: Routledge, 2011), 142–52. For some sophisticated critiques of Weber's approach to ideal-typification, see Seyla Benhabib, "Rationality and Social Action: Critical Reflections on Max Weber's Methodological Writings," *The Philosophical Forum* 12:4 (1981): 356–75; Stefan Eich and Adam Tooze, "The Allure of Dark Times: Max Weber, Politics and the Crisis of Historicism," *History and Theory* 56:2 (2017): 197–215.

[44] Weber, "Objectivity," 97. For more on the concept of connected histories, see Sanjay Subrahmanyam, "Connected Histories: Notes towards a Reconfiguration of Early Modern Eurasia," *Modern Asian Studies* 31:3 (1997): 735–62; Victor Lieberman, *Strange Parallels, Southeast Asia in Global Context, c. 800–1830, vol. 2: Mainland Mirrors: Europe, Japan, China, South Asia, and the Islands* (Cambridge: Cambridge University Press, 2009), 1–84.

2   Free Ports and Black Markets

In the colonial Caribbean, mammon was king. As wars and revolutions swept through the region, trade remained the highest priority and profit the ultimate concern for most colonial elites, perhaps nowhere more so than in the Leeward Islands. Here networks of commerce trumped imperial allegiances time and again, and whether practiced de facto through illegal means or de jure under the sanction of imperial free port policy, free trade was the dominant trend at the turn of the century.

While most of the larger Caribbean islands, including Jamaica and Hispaniola, were ideal for large-scale agricultural production, many of the smaller islands in the Lesser Antilles had natural environments more suited for trade than for farming. The rocky interiors of Tortola, St. Thomas, and St. Barthélemy made it difficult to maintain large plantations, but the islands' expansive coasts and plentiful coves created optimal conditions for smuggling and clandestine maritime activities.[1] All three islands were also gifted with excellent natural harbors, around which most social and economic activity came to gravitate. In this way urban life became central to these island societies, despite the fact that towns such as Charlotte Amalie and Gustavia remained small in size relative to those on larger Caribbean islands that were predominantly rural spaces.[2]

---

[1] This geography did not keep plantations from being built on many of the smaller islands, but they were generally less profitable and expansive than was the norm in the region. As an example, the French had all but abandoned St. Barthélemy as a failed plantation island before the Swedish acquisition of the colony. In the Danish West Indies, the sugar production on St. Croix and St. John far outgrew that on St. Thomas. See Jens Vibæk, *Vore Gamle Tropekolonier, bind 2: Dansk Vestindien, 1755–1848* (Copenhagen: Fremad, 1966), 126–31.

[2] Despite the tendency in Caribbean historical studies to focus on plantation societies, a few works have emphasized the role of urban spaces in the history of the region. See Franklin W. Knight and Peggy K. Liss, eds., *Atlantic Port Cities: Economy, Culture, and Society in the Atlantic World, 1650–1850* (Knoxville: University of Tennessee Press, 1991); Anne Pérotin-Dumon, *La ville aux îsles, la ville dans l'île: Basse-Terre et Pointe-à-Pitre, Guadeloupe, 1650–1820* (Paris: Editions Karthala, 2000); Alejandro de la Fuente, *Havana and the*

27

If plantation agriculture was the overwhelming concern for most Caribbean imperial administrators in the eighteenth century, the smaller islands gained increasing attention at the turn of the nineteenth century.[3] The growth of long-distance overseas trade and the expanding circuits of maritime commerce, combined with growing global competition and production chains, meant that strategically placed entrepôts, such as those of the smaller Leeward Islands, were propelled to prominence while some of their larger sugar-producing neighbors gradually became less central to imperial economies than they had been in previous decades. This shift proved especially important for neutral powers in the region, as the inter-imperial wars that dominated the last decade of the eighteenth century and the first two decades of the nineteenth century provided independent merchants with a host of opportunities for trade and profit.

The trans-imperial trading networks of the Caribbean were expansive and well developed, holding considerable economic and political clout in both colonial and metropolitan spheres. British and Dutch merchants were particularly prevalent across the Leewards, and neutral islands were popular ports of call for many of these traders, leading to considerable quantities of goods and capital tied to islands such as St. Barthélemy and the Danish West Indies. It was likewise common for proprietors in the region to own land and estates across different islands and empires. Thus many landowners on the Danish islands also held property in nearby Dutch and British colonies, and not a few resided on Tortola or St. Christopher.[4] Prior to the outbreak of war with Denmark in 1807, British subjects operating in the region petitioned the Privy Council, expressing their apprehension at the potential conflict since British property on St. Thomas, "which is to a very great amount, may be confiscated by the Danish government, or become liable to be plundered by the French from Martinique or Guadeloupe."[5] While such pleas did not prevent war between the two empires, much care was taken to

---

Atlantic in the Sixteenth Century (Chapel Hill: University of North Carolina Press, 2011); Jorge Cañizares-Esguerre, Matt Childs, and James Sidbury, eds., *The Black Urban Atlantic in the Age of the Slave Trade* (Philadelphia: University of Pennsylvania Press, 2013); Marisa J. Fuentes, *Dispossessed Lives: Enslaved Women, Violence, and the Archive* (Philadelphia: University of Pennsylvania Press, 2016), chapter 1.

[3] Besides sugar, which accounted for just over half of Caribbean exports in 1820, the colonial economies also produced large quantities of molasses, rum, coffee, and cotton. See Victor Bulmer-Thomas, *The Economic History of the Caribbean since the Napoleonic Wars* (Cambridge: Cambridge University Press, 2012), 105–11.

[4] Land registers of St. Thomas and St. John, 1755–1778, RA, AA 63.83.1–3.

[5] Petition dated August 1807, in TNA, PC 1/3786.

protect local property rights during the prolonged period of British occupation of the Danish colonies.

The present chapter considers the microregion of the Leeward Islands in terms of political economy and commercial practices. Since cross-imperial trade played such a crucial component in the formation and development of the region's intercolonial networks, an understanding of the extent and texture of this trade, as well as the related dynamics of smuggling and investment, is key to fully grasping the other aspects of the microregion. Not only did commercial practices drive contact and com-petition between colonies and groups, but the flow of trade was also a crucial concern for the various regulatory attempts of individual empires in the region, in terms of both inter-imperial interaction and intra-imperial legislation. In this sense the analysis of the present chapter forms part of the foundation for the following chapters, by examining the networks and structures of the inter-imperial microregion and some of the ways in which European metropoles responded to local conditions. The chapter also illuminates some of the shifts taking place within the region as a consequence of the emerging globalization of the early nine-teenth century, a process that the Leeward Islands were initially at the center of in the Atlantic context but that ultimately led to their near-disappearance from the global economic stage.

Colonial Companies

At their inception, in the 1670s and the 1780s, respectively, both the Danish and Swedish Caribbean colonies were controlled not by the imperial states themselves but rather by imperially sanctioned trading companies: the Danish West India and Guinea Company (Vestindisk-Guineisk Kompagni) and the Swedish West India Company (Svenska Västindiska Kompaniet). While not full-fledged company-states, like the British East India Company or the Dutch Vereenigde Oostindische Compagnie in Asia, the Scandinavian trading companies enjoyed con-siderable autonomy in the governing of their colonial territories.[6] They operated under royal charters that were renewed on a regular basis, and they drafted the rules governing the Caribbean territories in cooperation with government administrators in Copenhagen and Stockholm.[7] As a

---

[6] Philip J. Stern, "'Bundles of Hyphens': Corporations as Legal Communities in the Early Modern British Empire," in *Legal Pluralism and Empires, 1500–1850*, ed. Lauren Benton and Richard J. Ross (New York: New York University Press, 2013), 21–48; Stern, *The Company-State: Corporate Sovereignty and the Early Modern Foundations of the British Empire in India* (Oxford: Oxford University Press, 2011), 3–17.
[7] "Rules for the trade and government of St. Barthélemy," RKA, TSC, 757/B/12/1/190.

general rule, chartered companies' attitude toward smuggling and free trade was different from that of other merchant communities. They enjoyed a near-monopoly on the most lucrative commodities in the overseas colonies, primarily sugar and slaves, but kept a relatively hands-off approach when it came to other goods.

Unlike their British or Dutch counterparts, the Scandinavian ventures never proved especially profitable. By the 1780s the Danish West India and Guinea Company had already disappeared from the political stage, losing both its Caribbean and African colonial holdings. Three decades earlier, in 1755, the Danish Chamber of Revenues had taken control of the West Indian islands after deeming the company to be mediocre merchants and even poorer governors, and a few years later, in 1776, the company was finally liquidated after a period of prolonged financial difficulties, culminating in the selling of their remaining forts on the Gold Coast to the Danish crown.[8]

The Swedish West India Company followed a somewhat different trajectory. Having been chartered around the founding of New Sweden in the Delaware region in 1637, the company was relatively inactive from the Dutch conquest of that North American colony in 1655 to the acquisition of St. Barthélemy in 1784.[9] It then proceeded to run the Caribbean island for two decades, operating a monopoly on the sugar export to Sweden and a near-monopoly on the regional Swedish slave trade.[10] Three-quarters of the profits derived from taxation and tariffs on the island went to the company and one quarter to the Swedish state. Despite these lucrative privileges, the company ran into financial difficulties on multiple occasions and clashed with the imperial state on several issues, including a short-lived ban on the importation of coffee in 1794.[11] Unlike the Danish company, the Swedish company operated a free port alongside its monopoly on the sugar trade, and the company's administrators proved to be both uninterested in, and rather poor at, governing the colony, preferring a laissez-faire approach to

---

[8] For the history of the Danish West Indies during the company era, see Waldemar Westergaard, *The Danish West Indies under Company Rule, 1671–1754* (New York: Macmillan, 1917); J. O. Bro-Jørgensen, *Vore Gamle Tropekolonier, bind 1: Dansk Vestindien indtil 1755* (Copenhagen: Fremad, 1966).

[9] For Sweden's colonial projects in the wider Atlantic world, see Eric Schnakenbourg, "Sweden and the Atlantic: The Dynamism of Sweden's Colonial Projects in the Eighteenth Century," in *Scandinavian Colonialism and the Rise of Modernity: Small Time Agents in a Global Arena*, ed. Magdalena Naum and Jonas Nordin (New York: Springer, 2013), 229–42.

[10] The preeminent work on the Swedish West India Company in St. Barthélemy is Hildebrand, *Den Svenska Kolonin S:t Barthélemy*.

[11] Ibid., 291–94.

those areas of trade that did not directly relate to their own activities. This haphazard approach to governance ultimately led to the suspension of the company's political and commercial privileges in 1805, as the Swedish imperial state took over the full administration of the distant island.[12]

Even though both the Danish and Swedish companies were thus active only in the early days of their respective colonies, they nonetheless point us to two important aspects of the Scandinavian empires' approach to their Caribbean possessions. First, neither empire was particularly interested in the actual governance of their overseas colonies. The day-to-day administration was parceled out to semi-autonomous third parties, both because of a lack of capacity on behalf of the metropolitan governments and due to a general disinterest in colonial affairs on their part. Second, the formation of these companies was an example of the widespread mimesis found in European imperial practice. They were shaped in the image of rival European companies, drawing on the perceived best practices of the Dutch and the English colonial company-states in particular. In a perhaps-foreseeable twist of fate, the Scandinavian ventures also followed the same path as their foreign counterparts, eventually being dissolved by metropolitan governments that would take over the ultimate responsibility of local governance, however reluctantly.[13]

The Contraband Trade

Commercial activities in the Caribbean had included illicit components ever since colonial empires began vying for control in the region. The wide-ranging trade restrictions imposed by imperial administrators coupled with the general lack of enforcement capabilities fostered an environment ripe for nominally illegal commercial practices. Whether one labels imperial policies of this era as mercantilist or uses a different and less historically fraught term, it is clear that a major aim for most imperial polities, obsessed as sovereigns were with obtaining a positive

---

[12] "Slut-sedler," 1807, RKA, TSC, 757/B/12/1/191. For an in-depth discussion of Swedish maritime and trade policy after the dissolution of the Company, see Per G. Andreen, *Politik och Finansväsen från 1815 års riksdag till 1830 års realisationsbeslut* (Stockholm: Almquist & Wiksell, 1858).

[13] The Dutch West India Company (*Geoctroyeerde Westindische Compagnie*) was likewise dissolved and its Caribbean and West African territories taken over by the Dutch Republic in 1791, after a prolonged period of decline. At that point the English Somers Isles Company and the French West India Company (Compagnie française des Indes occidentales) had already been defunct for close to a century.

balance of trade, was to restrict the flow of foreign trade into their colonial territories, particularly in the rich West Indies.[14] This type of restrictive trade regime inevitably created a certain disconnect between metropolitan lawmakers and local merchants, not only in terms of their differing aims but also with regard to the only partially overlapping networks that formed around legal and illegal trade practices.

Smuggling was not always a local reaction against imperial policy. In some cases, support for smuggling was the goal of centrally administered policy, perhaps most well documented in the case of the Dutch Empire.[15] Draconian trade restrictions on the part of one empire often encouraged neighboring powers to circumvent these restrictions, either to obtain specific goods, as with Spanish silver in the Americas, or to access particular markets for export, as with the Sino-European trade in the Pearl River Delta. This was also common practice for neutral powers during wartime in the long eighteenth century, as uninvolved parties traded with both sides of a conflict and neutral ports became hubs for the transshipment of goods between belligerent powers.

It is worth distinguishing analytically between this type of imperially sanctioned smuggling and more locally driven activities without any sort of metropolitan oversight, even though such boundaries were often quite blurry. While the former set of practices took place within a larger framework of inter-imperial relations and sometimes contributed to specific aims connected to the destabilization or undermining of rival imperial enterprises, the latter trans-imperial and intercolonial practices were more clearly motivated by the sole goal of maximizing profits.[16] What is more, locally driven smuggling often undermined not only the sovereignty of the colony with which the trade took place but also that of the empire from whence the smugglers themselves hailed. Thus a St. Thomas trader selling slaves brought from the Danish Gold Coast

---

[14] The historiographical touchstone in the scholarly debate over mercantilism remains D. C. Coleman, ed., *Revisions in Mercantilism* (London: Methuen, 1969). For newer contributions, see Lars Magnusson, *Mercantilism: The Shaping of an Economic Language* (London: Routledge, 1994); Istvan Hont, *Jealousy of Trade: International Competition and the Nation-State in Historical Perspective* (Cambridge, MA: Belknap Press, 2005); Paul Cheney, *Revolutionary Commerce: Globalization and the French Monarchy* (Cambridge, MA: Harvard University Press, 2010); Steven Pincus, "Rethinking Mercantilism: Political Economy, the British Empire, and the Atlantic World in the Seventeenth and Eighteenth Centuries," *The William and Mary Quarterly* 69:1 (2012): 3–34; Philip J. Stern and Carl Wennerlind, eds., *Mercantilism Reimagined: Political Economy in Early Modern Britain and Its Empire* (Oxford: Oxford University Press, 2014).
[15] See, for example, Wim Klooster, *Illicit Riches: Dutch Trade in the Caribbean* (Leiden: KTLV Press, 1998); Rupert, *Creolization and Contraband*, 67–101.
[16] For a comprehensive analysis of different smuggling practices, see Karras, *Smuggling*, 73–108.

to a Spanish buyer in Puerto Rico transgressed not only against Spanish import restrictions but also against Danish imperial policy regarding the trade in slaves from Danish ports and under the King's flag, which generally confined the sale of such slaves to Danish colonial territories.[17]

Despite recurring imperial proclamations to the contrary, locally anchored intercolonial trade was widespread in the Caribbean throughout the eighteenth century and even into the first half of the nineteenth century. Informal markets were often at least as big as more formalized markets, and in many colonies the normalization of smuggling practices meant that some degree of free trade was an economic reality – de facto if not de jure.[18] Historian Wim Klooster has argued that smuggling in the Caribbean and Americas was an all-encompassing phenomenon, "often overshadowing legal trade between 1600 and 1800."[19] This statement is hard to verify empirically since by its very nature illegal commercial activity is near impossible to measure accurately, particularly given the fragmented and incomplete archival holdings. Yet the archival record indicates that this type of de facto free trade was indeed the common state of affairs on many of the Leeward Islands throughout most of the early colonial period, and well into the eighteenth century.[20]

The informal trade in the Leeward Islands took place within transimperial networks that ranged from tightly knit communities to loose and flexible webs of familiarity. The microregion of the Leewards was a deeply multicultural and multilingual space, characterized by a certain kind of thin sovereignty.[21] Not only were the colonies of various empires porous in regard to territorial control, but they also exhibited a pronounced sense of imperial transience. Many islands shifted from one European empire to another over the course of the long eighteenth century, and their populations often comprised diverse peoples with a number of different cultural, linguistic, and political affiliations. As an example, the population of the three islands in the Danish West Indies varied significantly. The majority of the white populations of St. Thomas and St. John were of Dutch descent, while immigrants from Britain and British colonies in the Americas quickly came to be the

[17] Despite such restrictions, Danish slave traders were important suppliers to the slave markets in the Spanish Caribbean. For more on this topic, see Chapter 6.
[18] It is worth noting that a significant part of the plantation trade never went directly through any colonial ports, free or otherwise. Large plantations often had their own wharves where goods would be picked up and shipped directly to Europe. Some of this traffic is caught by the official archival record left behind by colonial authorities, but certainly not all of it.
[19] Wim Klooster, "Inter-imperial Smuggling in the Americas," 141.
[20] See, for example, Koot, *Empire at the Periphery*, 181–214.
[21] For a discussion of concept of thin sovereignty, see Chapter 3.

dominant European group on the former French island of St. Croix.[22] Intercolonial migration was at least as common as immigration from Europe, and it contributed significantly to the multinational and multi-cultural nature of the islands, while often infuriating local administra-tors, who saw some of their wealthiest or most skilled inhabitants move away from their territories in search of greater opportunities for profit and prosperity elsewhere.[23]

The mobility and diversity of Leeward Islanders had clear implications for commercial practices in the region.[24] British, Dutch, and French trading diasporas were prevalent across the Caribbean. These networks were based on linguistic, cultural, and, at times, familial commonalities, with strong connections to both European cities and other colonies in the Americas and elsewhere.[25] The trading networks of the Leewards were far from limited to those of national or linguistic groupings, however. Many microregional networks were trans-imperial, and thus trans-national, in composition, based on connections forged across political and linguistic borders. Because imperial or national allegiances had relatively little purchase in the mercantile Caribbean, profit was often a much stronger motivator than shared cultural heritage for shaping endur-ing commercial ties. Since island ports such as Gustavia on St. Barthél-emy, Charlotte Amalie on St. Thomas, and Oranjestad on St. Eustatius were already linguistically polyglot, with natives of multiple European empires and other Atlantic polities calling them home, it was only natural that the networks within which these merchants and sailors operated were equally polyglot.[26] Given that much of the informal and illegal trade of the Leeward Islands transgressed against existing imperial law in various ways, patriotism was hardly the first concern for members of these networks.

A plurality of trading partners was not just convenient for many Leeward merchants but often a necessity, especially for the smaller

[22] Notes taken by Councillor of State Martfeldt concerning the Danish West Indies, 1765, RA, CPC, Private Collections, 410, Miscellaneous. See also Hall, *Slave Society in the Danish West Indies*, 9–19.

[23] This view is clearly expressed in reports from the British Leeward Islands, as more and more British colonists traveled to St. Croix in the mid-eighteenth century despite inter-imperial political rivalries at the regional level. Governor Matthew to the Council of Trade and Plantations, Montserrat, March 19, 1734, in *Calendar of State Papers Colonial, America and West Indies*, vol. 41 (London: HMSO, 1953).

[24] These demographic factors are discussed further in the following chapters.

[25] For a detailed and enlightening examination of how cultural diasporic trading networks function, albeit in a different oceanic setting, see Trivellato, *The Familiarity of Strangers*.

[26] See, for example, Norman F. Barka, "Citizens of St. Eustatius, 1781: A Historical and Archeological Study," in *The Lesser Antilles in the Age of European Expansion*, ed. Paquette and Engerman, 223–38.

national groups such as Swedes and Danes. In order to prosper in the diverse region, one could not be limited to trading with countrymen, who were often in the minority even within their own colonies, and a certain level of flexibility was paramount to prospering. Furthermore, the lines of nationality and subjecthood were tenuous at best. The inhabitants of the Danish West Indies or of St. Barthélemy could claim nominal Danish or Swedish citizenship since they resided within the colonial territory of those empires, but they were also often able to claim subjecthood to the British or French crowns due to lineage, landownership, or personal connections. Issues of subjecthood and political-jurisdictional placement were even more fraught for the growing populations of free people of color on the various islands, who in the nineteenth century in particular were deeply engaged in trans-imperial commercial practices. They did not have quite the same flexibility of subjecthood as their European neighbors did, but many of them had access to different sets of intra-regional connections based on networks that did not involve the white colonials.[27] In this sense free people of color were *of* the region to a much greater extent than were their neighbors of direct European descent.

While smuggling was prevalent across the eighteenth and nineteenth centuries, the patterns of the illegal trade were far from static. Whereas the eighteenth century was characterized by aggressive, state-sponsored practices, primarily targeting the Iberian empires in the Americas, the introduction of free port legislation in many colonies in the second half of the eighteenth century changed this pattern, as described in further detail later in this chapter. At the same time, the widespread inter-imperial warfare of the 1790s and the early 1800s created new opportunities for neutral ports to serve as spaces for what would otherwise be considered illegal trade between warring parties. The boundary between smuggling and the so-called neutral trade was often blurry, and the definition of both terms relied on the political and national outlook of the observer. This tension led to a number of clashes between administrators, at both the intercolonial and the inter-imperial levels, especially as the British Empire attempted to assert its emerging hegemonic dominance in the region and dictate the trade policy of other imperial powers. Numerous Swedish and Danish vessels were thus seized by British forces for trading with the French Empire during the 1790s, leading to a steady stream of diplomatic complaints over London's infringement on the neutrality of

---

[27] See W. Jeffrey Bolster, *Black Jacks: African American Seamen in the Age of Sails* (Cambridge, MA: Harvard University Press, 1997), 158–89; Scott, "The Common Wind"; Scott, "Crisscrossing Empires," 128–43; Landers, *Atlantic Creoles*, 15–53.

those polities.[28] The Swedish governor of St. Barthélemy, Carl Fredrik Bagge, was particularly vocal in his criticism, writing repeatedly to his British counterparts "to insist of the rights of the armed Neutrality."[29]

In a seemingly paradoxical historical twist, the increased degrees of freedom granted to colonial ports in terms of foreign trade at the turn of the century did not lead to an immediate or significant decrease in unsanctioned trans-imperial smuggling. Rather, the trade highlighted the ongoing struggle between imperial authorities and their representatives, on the one hand, and microregional networks and communities, on the other, as empires attempted to assert control over their colonial territories. Colonial magistrates were placed in sometimes profitable but always difficult positions, as their allegiances to both imperial rule and regional autonomy were put to the test. Since these magistrates would often be officeholders immediately below the governor within the colonial hierarchy, they were responsible for carrying out many imperial policies that at times would go against local, and even their own, interests. Thus, while these local elites were key to implementing metropolitan policy on the ground in their respective colonies, they were also frequently the weakest link in the chain of imperial command and even a potential source of resistance, defending local autonomy in the face of perceived unwarranted encroachments from metropolitan administrators.[30]

Such dynamics should not be thought of as indicative of a clear-cut dichotomy between imperial centers and local peripheries but rather as a display of a complicated set of partially overlapping networks and interests. As I describe in further detail below, the networks in which colonial magistrates participated often spanned across imperial boundaries just as much as they spanned the divide between colonial and metropolitan spheres. Even within the more strictly controlled hierarchy of imperial agents, there were many different factional divides, especially in the British Empire. Many debates taking place in European metropoles mirrored similar discussions in overseas colonial territories, and while local interests might seem united against exercises of imperial power, the interests of plantation owners and regional merchants were at other times

---

[28] Several cases from the St. Christopher Vice Admiralty court against Swedish vessels are found attached to a letter from Governor John Stanley to Henry Dundas, July 31, 1793, TNA, CO 152/74, f. 4.

[29] Ibid.

[30] See Lauren Benton and Lisa Ford, "Magistrates in Empire: Convicts, Slaves, and the Remaking of the Plural Legal Order in the British Empire," in *Legal Pluralism and Empires, 1500–1850*, ed. Lauren Benton and Richard J. Ross (New York: New York University Press, 2013), 173–98.

strongly opposed. As other demographic groups grew in size over the course of the nineteenth century, most importantly creoles and free people of color, new alliances formed and old networks changed, altering the dynamics among local, regional, and imperial levels and interests.[31]

Imperial bans or restrictions on intercolonial trade were often challenging to implement in practice, and when colonial authorities did enforce them, news spread fast in the regional public sphere. In 1804 the North American merchant James Dryburgh placed a full-page report in a local Charleston newspaper, *The City Gazette*, describing his recent tribulations "as a caution to all supercargoes and ship masters, bound for the island of St. Thomas."[32] The report consisted of transcriptions and translations of a number of consular and legal documents from the island. The case concerned the import of trade goods by Dryburgh on his schooner *Mercury*, ostensibly en route from Charleston to Trinidad. A few days after the American merchant had arrived in the port and passed through the customs house, the commandant of St. Thomas, Casimir von Scholten, ordered Dryburgh arrested and his property seized, accusing him of "having committed smuggling." This accusation was based on an invoice held by a local merchant and brought forth by the accuser, listing a good deal more cargo than what was declared to the customs house upon the *Mercury*'s arrival.[33]

After a brief investigation, the lower court concluded that Dryburgh might well have neglected to "enter that part of the flour he might have had on his arrival here," but that the consequences of this action should not amount to more than a symbolic fine. Not satisfied with this outcome, von Scholten and the king's attorney, Mr. Lind, decided to appeal the case at the colony's higher court, which took a less benign approach to the case. The key rationale for the eventual sentence of this court is worth quoting at length since it deals with not only the specific case in question but also the larger issue of combating perceived smuggling in the free port of Charlotte Amalie:

The goods that are liable to pay duties which are imported in vessels whose principal cargo consists in toll free produce, is also free from toll imposition, but it results there from, that such goods ... be entered, so that the concerned can judge what part thereof is toll free, or if the whole can be entered free. This Dryburgh has not done, and he ought therefore to be reprimanded and considered as liable to punishment; the judge has sentenced him to pay a fine

---

[31] Some of the consequences of these shifts are discussed in further detail in Chapter 5.

[32] *The City Gazette*, 23, 5270, August 5, 1804, Charleston, South Carolina.

[33] Ibid. Compared with the Danish court documents concerning the case held in RA, COC, 555, Miscellanea, 1769–1844.

of 25 pieces of eight and the expenses of the suit. The court considers this fine to be too trifling and disproportional with the value of money in this island, and which will occasion that more will be mislead and do the same.[34]

The court thus overturned the ruling of the lower court and instead sentenced Dryburgh to pay the expenses for the two court cases as well as a fine and the neglected tariff, the total sum of which was many times larger than the twenty-five pieces of eight decreed in the lower court.

An interesting aspect of this case is the fact that Dryburgh reacted to his sentence by sharing his experience in *The City Gazette*, a Charleston-based newspaper that circulated relatively widely in the greater Caribbean. It is clear from the article that he did not deny the illegal trade but rather expressed outrage over the fact that he had been prosecuted and punished so harshly for it and barely managed to leave the island with his schooner and cargo intact. This outcome does seem to have been a rare exception in the Danish port at the time, which had been known as a haven for illicit trade throughout the eighteenth century. Given that Dryburgh was an active trader in the Leeward Islands and the greater Caribbean region, it seems plausible that he also spread the word about St. Thomas and its over-vigilant commandant through more interpersonal methods while traveling the region.

Despite the attempts by some colonial administrators such as von Scholten to enforce imperial trade policies, most magistrates were themselves deeply entangled in the networks of illicit trade. It is thus worth noting that both Mr. Lind and Commandant von Scholten were relatively new in office, replacing a series of seemingly less vigilant predecessors. As mentioned above, the trans-imperial networks of the gray markets were thoroughly entrenched in the microregion, and since most magistrates were drawn from the local population, they almost inevitably had some ties to these networks. This was especially true for low-level magistrates, and certain offices made it very easy for the persons holding them to profit personally while at the same time contributing to the flow of contraband economies.

One such office was that of collector of customs. It proved notoriously difficult for imperial authorities in the smaller island colonies to fill customs offices with individuals who were trustworthy and effective in carrying out their duties. In May of 1821 the collector of customs of Dominica arrived at Tortola "on a special enquiry into the conduct of Mr. Francis Ingram," the then-presiding customs officer on Tortola. Ingram was suspected by British colonial administrators to be deeply

---

[34] Court transcripts, RA, COC, 555, Miscellanea, 1769–1844.

involved in various smuggling activities in the Virgin Islands. His colleague from Dominica acted quickly on arriving in Road Town – suspending Ingram; appointing an interim replacement, Mr. Bridgewater; and calling an assembly of the local magistrates to evaluate and resolve the situation.[35] Interestingly, the smuggling of regular goods in itself was not what had brought the ire of imperial agents upon Ingram. Rather, it was his alleged trade in and mistreatment of illegally imported African slaves, or "apprentices," that caught the eye of his superior. While open breaches of the slave trade abolition were enough to catch the attention of higher authorities in the empire, Ingram's extremely liberal interpretation of Tortola's free port status, going so far as to ignore most if not all trade restrictions and to neglect to charge the required tariffs, seemed to have sparked little notice prior to the thorough investigation by the Dominica magistrate, despite the fact that Ingram had held the office for several years.

No doubt part of the explanation for this seeming disinterest is to be found in the attitude of the island's other magistrates, who for the most part had little interest in reporting breaches of trade laws in which they were themselves more than likely to be involved, either directly or indirectly. Imperial officials had long regarded Tortola as a particularly problematic colony, with locals doing little to uphold the letter or the spirit of the law. In 1778 George Suckling, a Halifax lawyer and career magistrate in the British Atlantic, spent fourteen weeks in Tortola, having been stationed in the Virgin Islands as Chief Justice. However, he found himself unable to obtain his commission, and came away from the region with a rather poor impression, describing Tortola as "a shocking scene of anarchy, miserable indeed, and disgraceful to Government" – a characterization that would resonate for decades.[36] Indeed, investigations into the trading practices on the island in 1831, a decade after the suspension of Ingram, show that contraband trade was still a widespread and indeed endemic problem in the colony.[37] The breach of the slave codes was a different matter, however, and allegations of mistreatment were particularly likely to be noticed on Tortola, just a decade after the trial of Arthur William Hodge for the murder and mistreatment of slaves.[38]

---

[35] Letter from Mr. Clement to Earl Bathurst, August 4, 1821, TNA, CO 239/7, Misc.

[36] George Suckling, *An Historical Account of the Virgin Islands in the West Indies* (London: Benjamin White, 1780), 66–67.

[37] The 1831 report from Governor Maxwell is contained in TNA, CO 239/25/66.

[38] Lauren Benton, "This Melancholy Labyrinth: The Trial of Arthur Hodge and the Boundaries of Imperial Law," *Alabama Law Review* 64:1 (2012): 91–122. See Chapter 6 for a discussion of the illegal slave trade after the 1807 abolition and Chapter 5 for more on the case of Arthur Hodge.

Accusations of smuggling were also made in the same period against officials on St. Barthélemy, but here the target was a man with considerably more authority: the island's governor, Johan Norderling. In the case of the Swedish colony, accusations came not from within the empire but rather from other powers in the region. In the early 1820s Gustavia had developed a reputation as a smugglers' cove, a place that went well beyond what was expected of a free port by opening its harbor to all manners of contraband traders and privateers. A large part of the merchandise under scrutiny came from questionable seizures conducted by privateers from the newly independent Latin American republics. Others were old-fashioned contraband goods smuggled in from French or British islands. This traffic led to complaints from a number of imperial officials in the region, Spanish as well as French and British.[39]

For his part Norderling acknowledged the need to engage with smugglers, arguing that he had little choice in the matter and that it was an unfortunate result of circumstances in the colony prior to his arrival and the competitive trade environment of the Leeward Islands more generally. Much as British magistrates would later do on Tortola, Norderling compared his island's financial challenges with the prosperity of the neighboring Danish free port: "St. Thomas has all the advantage of a steady supply of Baltic, Mediterranean, English, and Dutch goods to attract both buyers and sellers; we plod along in our old routine fighting for English and French smuggled cargoes of sugar and rum to pay for American shipments, that is all.... What a mess I've come to!"[40] The transgressions were not just against the laws of other empires, however. If inhabitants of St. Barthélemy had to circumvent the trade restrictions of its own empire at times, it was only because Swedish merchants and manufacturers were too "inactive and inert, although they have hundreds of articles which could be disposed of here to advantage," thus forcing locals to look elsewhere in order to cover their most basic needs.[41]

Unlike Ingram on Tortola, Norderling was secure in his position as governor of St. Barthélemy despite the host of accusations officials and merchants of foreign empires made against him. The explanation for this security should not be sought in the comparative importance of his office alone, but also in the way in which the Swedish Empire functioned more broadly. Tortola was part of a larger British imperial system in the

---

[39] Letters from Johan Norderling, February 12 and December 4, 1820, RKA, SBS, 2411/2/VII A.

[40] Quoted in Ernst Ekman, "A Swedish Career in the Tropics: Johan Norderling (1760–1828)," *The Swedish Pioneer Historical Quarterly* 15:1 (1964): 21.

[41] Ibid., 21–22.

Caribbean with multiple colonies in both the greater region and the microregion of the Leeward Islands competing over political power and influence within their own intra-imperial hierarchy. There were limited political and jurisdictional resources available within the empire, including region-wide offices and institutions such as prize courts, free ports, and governorships.[42] Competition over these resources was at times fierce, and while smaller islands such as Tortola had little chance of reaching the top of the regional intra-imperial hierarchy, they did manage to gain access to some influential institutions, such as the important prize court located in the British Virgin Islands during the Revolutionary and Napoleonic Wars.[43]

This type of legal-political competition and positioning within the British regional system meant that the autonomy of individual islands functioned in different ways from that of islands belonging to smaller empires with only one or a few Atlantic colonies. Thus while Tortola stayed out of the majority of factional infighting over high-ranking political offices in the British Leewards in order to be left alone when it came to more locally important issues of commercial practices, news of a potential scandal was much more likely to attract attention from other imperial agents in the region. The governor of St. Barthélemy, in contrast, was given a high degree of autonomy by the government in Stockholm in regional political affairs as long as he followed the spirit of his overall mandate. Political grievances from foreign regional powers at the intercolonial level were thus easy to ignore, as long as they did not reach the higher levels of inter-imperial diplomatic crises or high-level official complaints aimed at Stockholm rather than Gustavia.

A revealing window into the specific practices of nineteenth-century smugglers can be found in an unlikely place – the legal records of a case brought before the prize court on Isla Margarita in Gran Colombia. In early 1820 a ship originating in St. Thomas owned and operated by one captain Lang was captured by republican privateers in the waters between the Lesser Antilles and the coast of Venezuela. The ship was taken into the port of Isla Margarita, where Lang contested the legality of the capture and demanded the return of his ship and its cargo. The prize proceedings were carried out in February 1820 at the local court, its

---

[42] The British Leeward Islands functioned as one colonial territory with a single governor from 1671 until 1816, when the islands were divided into two separate colonial entities. The seat of the governorship and the de facto government of the islands shifted a number of times between St. Christopher, Nevis, and Antigua, and the 1816 split was in part due to a political power struggle between those islands.

[43] See Chapter 4 for more on the imperial infighting over this court.

magistrates operating "by appointment of the Congress of Colombia."[44] While the court documents show all the formal signs of a proper legal proceeding, it is uncertain what chances the captain had for getting his lost goods back, not just because of ulterior motives on the part of the presiding judge of the prize court but also because Lang was by all indications a seasoned smuggler, caught in the act of carrying illegal goods to the Spanish Americas.

Ultimately the judge ruled against Lang's claim, arguing that neither his cargo manifest, which did not correspond to the actual cargo aboard the ship, nor his Danish shipping records, indicating his status as a neutral party to the ongoing conflict and thus not a legitimate target for Colombian privateers, held up to closer scrutiny.[45] Lang's problem was not that he was a Spanish or Portuguese merchant in disguise but rather that he was a Caribbean smuggler, carrying out illegal trade between the Danish and British West Indies and the Spanish colonies in the region. This trade required him to carry a variety of flags and papers, and evidently led to certain irregularities in his cargo manifest, in order to escape the notice of Spanish colonial authorities and allow him to dock in the ports of multiple empires. While such practices were widespread among Lang's colleagues in the Leeward Islands, the questionable nature of his paperwork threw his claims of being a legal resident of St. Thomas into doubt and provided the Colombian prize judge with more than enough justification to dismiss any requests for compensation on the grounds of political neutrality. When sailing the treacherous waters of the conflict-ridden region, even the most cunning smuggler had to navigate both formal and informal currents, or face the consequences when finding himself caught in a storm.

The Free Port Acts

At the level of inter-imperial commercial policy, few if any acts were as important for commercial development of individual colonies in the Leeward Islands as the granting of free port status. Concurrent with the growth of informal markets, a different type of imperially sanctioned free trade emerged in the region in the latter part of the eighteenth century. The system of free ports became a de jure institution not just in the British colonies, which pioneered their jurisdictional formalization, but across empires, and a growing number of Dutch, Danish, and Swedish

---

[44] Court papers from Isla Margarita, February 1820, RA, Government-General, 2.41, Files concerning piracy, 1818–1825.
[45] Ibid.

colonies were declared ports of free trade at various points in the second half of the century.[46] In some cases these declarations represented a continuation and formalization of existing imperial policy, as with the Dutch islands, while in other instances it meant a more obvious shift in commercial policy, as with most of the British and Danish colonies. The free port system did not lead to an end of smuggling across the board, since free ports were not places without trade regulations or even places free of fees and duties. Rather, they were ports where access for foreign ships and goods was far more open than under earlier, more restrictive, commercial regimes.[47] In this sense the de facto free trade carried out by smugglers and contraband traders was partially replaced by an institutionalized and officially sanctioned de jure system of free trade, but illegal commercial practices were far from eradicated.

While much of the state-sponsored smuggling of the eighteenth century was replaced by legalized free trade, other smuggling practices more subversive to imperial authority continued more or less uninterrupted. The clearest case of this continued smuggling was the trade in plantation staples such as sugar, molasses, and coffee, which the free port acts either prohibited foreign vessels from exporting entirely or placed rather severe restrictions on. Another example was the refusal by merchants to pay the necessary duties when importing or exporting goods from free ports, either by misreporting their cargoes on arrival and departure or by circumventing official ports all together. The many coves and inlets of the Leeward Islands made this latter option exceedingly feasible, especially for small vessels like the single-masted sloops so common in the region. It is interesting to note that the introduction of relatively standardized free port legislation in the second half of the eighteenth century in this way marked a key shift in the definition of contraband trade, from essentially any type of trade that crossed imperial borders to trade in specific and carefully delineated commodities.

Prior to the sacking of St. Eustatius in 1781, the Dutch West Indies were seen as the pinnacle of Caribbean trading colonies, and their free trade policy formed a blueprint of sorts for British legislators to expand

---

[46] While never going so far as its Northern European neighbors, the French Empire also experimented with introducing partial free ports within the framework of the commercial *exclusif* system in their West Indian colonies during the last decades of the ancien régime. See John Shovlin, "Rethinking Enlightened Reform in a French Context," in *Enlightened Reform in Southern Europe and Its Atlantic Colonies, c. 1750–1830*, ed. Gabriel Paquette (Baltimore: Johns Hopkins University Press, 2009), 47–62; Jean Tarrade, *Le commerce colonial de la France à la fin de l'Ancien Régime: L'evolution du régime de "l'Exclusif" de 1763 à 1789*, vols. 1 and 2 (Paris: Presses Universitaires de France, 1972).

[47] Frances Armytage, *The Free Port System in the British West Indies: A Study in Commercial Policy, 1766–1822* (London: Longmans, Green and Co., 1953), 1–3, 28–44.

on. As Adam Smith noted in his famous inquiry, "Curaçao and Eustatia ... are free ports open to ships of all nations; and this freedom, in the midst of better colonies whose ports are open to those of one nation only, has been the great cause of the prosperity of those two barren islands."[48] Free port status was in this sense a form of sanctioned smuggling, at least when seen from the Spanish, Portuguese, and French perspectives, but unlike the state-sponsored smuggling of previous decades the free port system attempted to place such trading practices within a more clearly defined legal framework. On the one hand, this enabled Northern European empires to refute allegations of smuggling and in turn accuse their French and Iberian rivals of being mercantilist and backward in their views of political economy, much as they would later do against their European and indigenous commercial rivals in Asia.[49] On the other hand, the free port system granted imperial administrators more direct control over the trading activities of their Caribbean territories, thus serving the intra-imperial purpose of reining in rampant smuggling and commercial practices that were otherwise beyond the reach of imperial authorities.

While the implementation of the British free port acts was rather limited on their initial introduction in the 1760s, encompassing trade only on the islands of Dominica and Jamaica, the system gained renewed momentum following the end of the American Revolutionary War in the 1780s. Thus, a number of new British free ports were declared in the last decades of the century, and more resources were being devoted to the implementation of the acts. This shift was due in part to the changed geopolitical landscape of the greater Caribbean, including the arrival of new imperial powers and the emergence of an independent United States, and in part to the reignited debates over free trade in the British public sphere. While a number of free ports were established across the region, as shown in Figure 2.1, the exact privileges extended to these ports varied, and although foreign vessels were welcomed, the specific goods they could buy and sell were often very limited.

Tortola applied multiple times to become a free port, and local merchants intensified their lobbying efforts in the first decade of the nineteenth century, particularly following the granting of free port status to the city of Nassau in the Bahamas at the turn of the century.[50] While limited free port status was granted to Tortola in 1802, this act did not include

---

[48] Adam Smith, *An Inquiry into the Nature and Causes of the Wealth of Nations*, ed. Edwin Cannan (London: Methuen & Co., 1904), 194.
[49] See, for example, Bayly, *Imperial Meridian*, 101–5.
[50] Armytage, *The Free Port System*, 100–103.

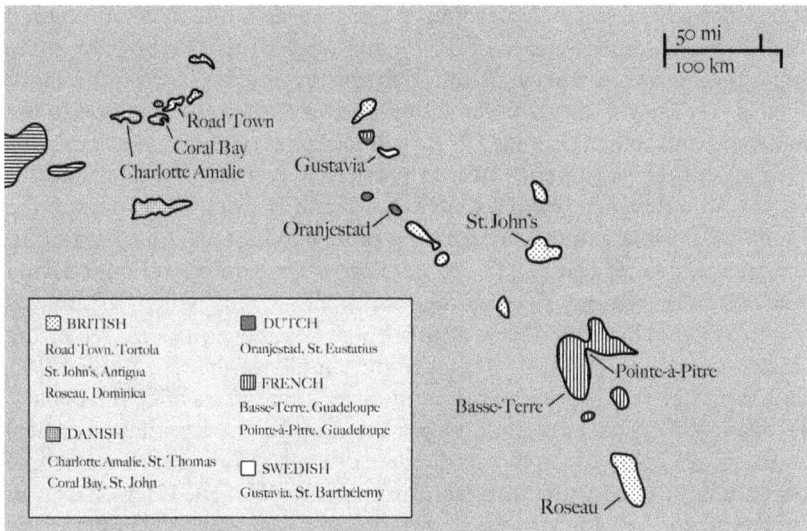

Figure 2.1 Free ports in the Leeward Islands.

the island's major sources of income, sugar chief among them.[51] In 1804 the Tortola Assembly, as well as several individual merchants, lodged requests to London urging the government to consider expanding the colony's free port status and referencing the fierce competition from neutral ports in the region.[52] While the government of William Pitt the Younger was initially reluctant to extent the free port system further in the Caribbean, a consolidated free port act was eventually passed in 1805, making a number of previously temporary acts perpetual.[53]

It is important to note that free port legislation was not necessarily an expression of liberal free trade ideology. Rather, it was an integral part of the inter-imperial competition for trade and profit in the Caribbean and elsewhere. A major political rationale for the granting of free port status was thus to divert commerce and capital away from the neighboring ports of rival empires, including the trade of British merchants. In the case of the Leeward Islands, explicit targets of such policy included the neutral islands of Denmark, Sweden, and the Netherlands, and especially the port of St. Thomas. In 1806 a bill was proposed in parliament to make Road Town in Tortola a full free port, focusing in particular on the

[51] "Tortola Trade Act," 42 Geo. III, c. 102.
[52] Letters to the Privy Council, June 1804, TNA, PC 1/3605.
[53] "Importation and Exportation Act," 45 Geo. III, c. 57.

transshipment of sugar. According to Lord Temple, the newly appointed Vice-President of the Board of Trade and a prominent landowner in the West Indies, the primary motivation for proposing the bill was "to make British merchants vest their capital in Tortola, which they now do in the neutral island of St. Thomas."[54] British parliamentarians did not universally accept this argument since, as Spencer Perceval put it in a continuation of the debate a few days later: "It would be impossible ... that the island of Tortola could ever be in the same situation as the island of St. Thomas; the latter being in the possession of a neutral power, and having a privilege of trading all over the world; neither of which advantages Tortola could have by virtue of this bill."[55] Perceval, the leader of the Pittite opposition in 1806, was a prominent ally of the late William Pitt and would go on to become prime minister three years after the debate. He was a strong proponent of the abolition of the slave trade and critical of the West Indian lobby in parliament, so his reluctance to grant free port status was no great surprise. For his part, William Eden, Baron of Auckland and President of the Board of Trade, defended the bill, arguing that it was "a measure of sound policy" since its object was to

render Tortola a carrying island, and to take from St. Thomas's some part of the carrying trade in the possession of that island, in which a number of British shipping were employed. This was a measure which ... would therefore be beneficial to our commerce and our navigation, whilst, with respect to our West India trade, it would not be injured, nor did any of those persons concerned in that trade, or connected with West India interests, ... make the least complaint, that any such injury was likely to result from it. As to the dangers Which the noble duke apprehended, there was an express provision in this bill for the purpose of preventing the importation into this country of foreign sugar, as there was a clause by which no more sugar was to be imported into this country from Tortola than the amount of the average annual produce of that island.[56]

Despite the reluctance of the opposition, a majority in parliament ultimately approved the Tortola Free Port Bill and on July 3, 1806, George III gave his royal assent to passing the bill.[57]

These parliamentary debates illustrate some of the key arguments for and against free trade in the British colonies and show how central comparisons to other imperial entrepôts were to discussions of British

---

[54] HC Deb May 19, 1806, vol. 7 cc253–54.   [55] HC Deb May 23, 1806, vol. 7 c364.
[56] HL Deb June 20, 1806 vol. 7 cc779–80. Sugar was, of course, not the only thing being transshipped through Road Harbour. While sugar was the largest export of the Leeward Islands, there were a number of other materials being grown in the colonies, and many different products passed through the free ports, including cotton, indigo, molasses, timber, rum, and mules. See Armytage, *The Free Port System*, 146–60.
[57] HL Deb July 3, 1806 vol. 7 c900; "Tortola Trade Act," 46 Geo. III, c. 72.

commercial policy. They also highlight the complex nature of British colonial policy, as the West Indian lobby operated across traditional partisan lines, relying more on the trade and property interests of individual politicians than on their ideological leanings. In this sense the commercial networks of the West Indies extended far into the capitals of European empires. Two decades later, in the pages of an 1826 pamphlet, the prominent abolitionist and parliamentarian James Stephen urged the British public to beware the power of the West Indian lobby, whose influence, he argued, extended well beyond the obvious advocates of its cause:

[F]or what with the personal influence that so many members must naturally have with other gentlemen sitting in the same assembly, and the widespread connexions of Colonial proprietors with the land-holders and merchants of this country, by means of which many members may of course be influenced, it may be reasonably computed that at least twice the number of those who are known to be bound by the West Indian cause, are directly or indirectly, by particular interests, or personal feelings, attached to it.[58]

The obsession with the trading power of rival colonies was not limited to British imperialists. Free trade advocates from St. Barthélemy also frequently referred to Dutch and Danish islands as the primary commercial hubs to overcome in the regional context – St. Eustatius in the 1780s and early 1790s and St. Thomas in the following decades. The internal Swedish debates over free trade were further influenced by foreign advocates, including from the newly independent United States, who welcomed the addition of a new neutral trading power in the Caribbean theater. In a letter to Erik Magnus Staël, the Swedish ambassador to France, Thomas Jefferson explicitly referenced the possibility that St. Barthélemy might divert US trade from St. Thomas and St. Eustatius, and made the American preference for free port status clear: "The interest of the United States then is that St. Bartholomew be made a port of unlimited freedom; and such too is evidently the interest of Sweden."[59]

Swedish ambitions of creating a powerful entrepôt in the region were set, and Gustavia was declared a free port by the king in September of 1785, following the handover from the French Empire the previous year.[60] While the first decade of Swedish rule saw relatively little growth of any

---

[58] James Stephen, *England Enslaved by Her Own Slave Colonies: An Address to the Electors and People of the United Kingdom* (London: R. Taylor, 1826), 63–64.

[59] Letter from Thomas Jefferson to Erik Magnus Staël, 1785, quoted in Ernst Ekman, "St. Barthélemy and the French Revolution," *Caribbean Studies* 3:4 (1964): 19.

[60] *Kongl. Maj:ts Nådige Kungörelse, Som förklarar Ön St. Barthelemy i Westindien för en Fri Hamn eller Porto Franco.* Drottningholm, September 7, 1785. For an insightful analysis of Gustavia's commercial development in the first decades of Swedish rule, see Victor Wilson, *Commerce in Disguise: War and Trade in the Caribbean Free Port of Gustavia, 1793–1815* (Turku: Åbo Akademi University Press, 2016).

kind, the Revolutionary Wars and the regional upheaval in the French
Caribbean at the end of the century influenced the development of Gustavia significantly. The town rapidly expanded, with the urban population
outgrowing the rural by the mid-1790s, in large part due to the growth of
the port as a place of transshipment as well as the influx of French and
Dutch émigrés.[61] Merchants and settlers in neighboring islands, including
St. Eustatius and St. Martin, were drawn by the emergence of a new
neutral port in the microregion, especially one that seemed to be governed
in such a laissez-faire manner. Furthermore, from the perspective of white
French settlers in the region, St. Barthélemy was a colony with francophone origins but without the political turmoil of nearby Guadeloupe or
St. Martin caused by the French Revolution.[62]

Part of the appeal of the Swedish free port was as a place where one
could gain Swedish subjecthood and sail under neutral Swedish colors.
This option proved particularly convenient for French and American
merchant mariners, who were otherwise frequently barred from trading
with British colonies during the prolonged inter-imperial conflicts at the
turn of the century. While this practice projected the Swedish colonial
presence across the region despite the fact that the Swedish West India
Company itself was remarkably inactive, it did relatively little to fill the
coffers of the colonial administration. Thus, even as Gustavia merchants
grew wealthy during the Revolutionary and Napoleonic Wars as a result of
the neutral trade, the empire itself saw relatively little of this prosperity.[63]

As imperial administrators attempted to adopt the best practices of
foreign colonies in terms of commercial policies, the biggest challenge
often turned out to be the actual on-the-ground implementation of
adopted legislative language. Thus the Danish free port acts, which
closely resembled those of the British colonies in their wording and
seeming implications, proved challenging for local officials to turn into
practice given the limited resources and manpower available to them.[64]

[61] Yolande Lavoie, "Histoire sociale et démographique d'une communauté isolée: Saint-
Barthélemy (Antilles françaises)," Revue d'histoire de l'Amérique française 42:3 (1989):
411–27. See Chapter 5 for more on the divergence of urban and rural demographics in
the Swedish colony.
[62] See Ekman, "St. Barthélemy and the French Revolution."
[63] It is hard to get at the exact growth rates due to the nature of the archival records, but
partial overviews are contained in St. Barthélemy Accounts, 1793–1816, RKA, SBS
2411/4/XXV A-D, XXX A-B, and XXXI A-B. These indicate that the most significant
growth took place during the second half of the Napoleonic Wars, from 1808 to 1815 –
coinciding with the British occupation of St. Thomas.
[64] Lack of enforcement due to weak state capacities in smaller Caribbean free ports was a
widespread phenomenon at the turn of the nineteenth century. See Alan L. Karras,
"Transgressive Exchange: Circumventing Eighteenth-Century Atlantic Commercial
Restrictions, or The Discount of Monte Christi," in Seascapes: Maritime Histories,

Such policies therefore tended to turn into general guidelines rather than hard and fast rules, and they often served as a veil of legitimacy for what was in reality a continuation of earlier years' informal trading practices and laissez-faire approach to upholding official restrictions.

Despite the efforts of a few colonial administrators, including von Scholten on St. Thomas, it was arguably only during the British invasion and occupation of the Danish West Indies that the colonies' existing free port status was fully implemented. Several of the British administrators who controlled the colonial governance of the Danish islands from 1807 to 1815 came to St. Thomas with prior experience of the practical implications of the British free port system, and they had access to more resources directed at implementation than did their Danish predecessors. Their experience proved applicable to the Danish colonies, and following the end of occupation the reforms implemented by the foreign empire were largely kept intact. These reforms included a more formalized tariff system in the port and a greater emphasis on monitoring and controlling maritime traffic, including the keeping of detailed logbooks and statistics of the nationality and cargo of all incoming and outgoing ships.[65] The newly appointed Danish magistrates implemented further reforms throughout the 1820s, as local administrators faced with a lack of metropolitan backing from Copenhagen found other ways to provide the needed increase in resources for the customs house and harbormaster's office. As an example, a new decree in 1825 required all vessels originating from the Danish islands to carry new papers certifying registration in the colonies, obtained and paid for at the customs house in Charlotte Amalie.[66] This rule served very little judicial purpose, but was an effective way of increasing the income of the local administration.

When considered as an attempt to harness and direct the widespread informal trade of the microregion, the introduction of free port legislation in the Leewards only partially succeeded. Unsanctioned smuggling continued to be prevalent throughout the free port era, but the introduction of mechanisms that were at once less restrictive and more narrowly targeted in their aims seems to have been effective, at least in some ports. As a way to get access to the otherwise closed markets of foreign empires in the wider region, the free port system was also a mixed bag. While the British colonies had some limited success with this project, the neutral

---

Littoral Cultures, and Transoceanic Exchanges, ed. Jerry H. Bentley, Renate Bridenthal, and Kären Wigen (Honolulu: University of Hawai'i Press, 2007), 121–34.

[65] "Extracts and calculations concerning the West India trade, customs, and shipping, 1764–1856," RA, COC, 490; "Naval officer's returns, St. Thomas, 1811–14," TNA, CO 259/3.

[66] Examples of certificates are kept in RA, Government-General, 2.41.

ports of the smaller empires benefited greatly from trade with a variety of foreign ships. For the majority of free ports, the result was less profitable for their respective empires than it was for the individual merchants operating within and between them, leaving the port administrations underfunded and with a lack of resources to enforce tariffs and regulations. The turn of the century was a golden age for intercolonial trade in the Leeward Islands, one that would carry on into the first decades of the nineteenth century before entering a fateful decline, as global economic changes swept through the microregion.

Regional Networks and Global Shifts

What took place within the inter-imperial microregion of the Leeward Islands was in many ways an early example of the dynamics of nineteenth-century globalization. Regional integration spurred on by trans-imperial commercial networks served to tighten relations among colonial territories of multiple empires, fostering a growing degree of economic interdependence in the process. Local economies saw tremendous growth due to their placement within wider, and more loosely integrated, transatlantic networks of trade and production. The tightly knit microregional network of the Leeward Islands functioned as a central component of the wider networks of the Caribbean region as a whole, which were in turn key parts of the Atlantic networks that for their part existed within a number of gradually emerging global networks. Due in part to spatial and technological limitations, commercial and political economic globalization of the nineteenth century did not emerge at the level of worldwide connectivity from the outset. Rather, it expanded outward from increased regional interaction in a process with multiple levels of networked structures anchored in specific geographical spaces – from the microregional to the regional to the oceanic to the global.

In this respect the inter-imperial microregion of the Leeward Islands was not a unique phenomenon, but rather indicative of a wider pattern of configurations across the world of European overseas expansion and competition. Similar spaces could be found throughout the nineteenth century, including in the Pearl River Delta, in the Río de la Plata, on the West African Coast, and in Mauritius and Seychelles. These different microregions were all composed of trans-polity networks based on economic interests and polyglot commercial practices, with varying degrees of official national, imperial, or colonial involvement. Global connectivity expanded from such regional configurations, as flows of commodities and people bound together these and other spatial nodes in increasingly integrated global networks, in effect creating a pattern of regional globalization: gradual global integration alongside continued trans-national regionalization. While some aspects of nineteenth-century glob-alization were very much the result of top-down processes, often closely linked to European imperialism and imperial political economy, it behooves us to pay attention to the ways in which individual agents on the ground formed and shaped their own trans-polity networks.[67] Since these bottom-up processes were much more closely tied to spatial and geographical realities, it seems natural that they would be shaped primar-ily by local and regional factors, rather than by global forces.

On the islands of St. Barthélemy and St. Thomas the locally anchored globalizing trends of the early nineteenth century are perhaps most clearly visible in the official shipping logs, documenting the incoming and out-going maritime traffic, however sparse and poorly preserved they are. The information contained in these registries illustrates just how inter-imperial the island ports were, with vessels of many different flags and from various parts of the region passing through and conducting trade there. The type of vessel is rarely noted in these logs, but tonnage sometimes is, which can give us an idea of the type of traffic appearing in the ports. While these numbers vary significantly from year to year and nationality to nationality, they average between forty-five and ninety tons per vessel in the early nineteenth century. These numbers indicate a preponderance of mid-sized vessels, particularly brigs and schooners, both of which were common in the Caribbean, rather than a significant number of larger, full-rigged ships.[68] This pattern would also fit with the more detailed accounts available from the British Virgin Islands, documenting known wreckages off the nearby island of Anegada during the same period.[69]

By the first decade of the nineteenth century, St. Barthélemy had become thoroughly integrated into the region and was among the

[67] For the relationship between imperialism and nineteenth-century globalization in the British context, see Gary B. Magee and Andrew Thompson, *Empire and Globalisation: Networks of People, Goods and Capital in the British World, 1850–1914* (Cambridge: Cambridge University Press, 2010).
[68] "The St. Barthélemy Customs Journal, 1811–1813," RKA, SBS 2411/4/XXVI A; St Thomas Harbour Master 1819–1867, "Statistics concerning incoming vessels," RA, WILA 25.6.1. This conclusion is further supported by the fact that some months show significantly higher average tonnage, which corresponds with the documented arrival of larger ships. This is the case for the German ships arriving every few months in Charlotte Amalie during the 1820s, with an average tonnage closer to 250.
[69] This information is contained in a number of reports and charts located in TNA, CO 239/10, and TNA, CO 318/82. More than sixty vessels were wrecked on the Anegada Reef in the first three decades of the nineteenth century, providing an interesting sample of the maritime traffic in the region. For a discussion of some of these wrecks, see Chapter 6. While there were a few larger ships and smaller sloops among the wrecks, the majority were either schooners or brigs.

Table 2.1 *Vessels arriving in Gustavia, 1811–1813*[a]

Nationality of vessels	1811, percentage	1812, percentage	1813, percentage
Britain	54	51	35
Sweden	9	18	46
United States	29	18	2
Spain	8	12	16
Portugal	<1	1	1

[a] The numbers of incoming ships used in the table are found in "The St. Barthélemy Customs Journal, 1811–1813," RKA, SBS 2411/4/XXVI A. The majority of ships sailing under the Swedish flag were registered in St. Barthélemy rather than in Europe. It is also worth noting that while the number of US vessels was smaller than that of British in all three years, the total tonnage carried by American vessels was larger than that of British vessels in both 1811 and 1812.

primary nodes in the commercial networks connecting North America and the Caribbean. As indicated by the shipping statistics in Table 2.1, a variety of British, Spanish, American, and Portuguese vessels passed through the harbor. While no vessels officially sailing under French flags entered Gustavia during this period of the Napoleonic Wars, a not-inconsiderable number of local St. Barthélemy vessels sailing under Swedish colors can be presumed to belong to French owners. As described above, it was relatively easy to obtain local papers in the Swedish colony, and this was a common practice of regional traders during the war years. That US merchants also exploited this possibility is evidenced by the shift in numbers following the outbreak of the War of 1812, as vessels sailing under the US flag fell from 18 to 2 percent, while Swedish vessels, primarily registered in St. Barthélemy, rose from 18 to a staggering 46 percent. As British officials applied pressure on the Swedish administration to block access to Gustavia for US vessels, American captains found ways to circumvent such restrictions.[70] Not only were Swedish ships in the port thus rarely in the majority, but they were also likely to be Swedish in flag only.

The total number of vessels passing through the free port of Charlotte Amalie fell slightly from a yearly average of 2,831 in the 1820s to 2,571 in the 1830s. The nationalities of the ships changed, as illustrated in Table 2.2, becoming increasingly international as the percentage of vessels sailing under the Danish flag fell from an average of 36 percent

[70] This diplomatic pressure is documented in several exchanges between Secretary of Colonial Affairs Gustaf Wetterstedt and Governor Stackelberg of St. Barthélemy, February 1812, RKA, LC 2414/12.

Table 2.2 *Vessels arriving in Charlotte Amalie, 1820–1839*[a]

Nationality of vessels	1820–1829, percentage	1830–1839, percentage
Denmark	36	18
Britain	25	28
United States	17	16
France	9	7
The Netherlands	6	4
Sweden	4	3
Spain	1	17
Gran Colombia	2	4
Haiti[b]	<1	1

[a] The numbers of incoming ships used in the table are found in St. Thomas Harbour Master 1819–1867, "Statistics concerning incoming vessels," RA, WILA 25.6.1. Besides the nationalities shown here, a number of other flags are presented in the data, which collectively amount to less than 2 percent of the total. Gran Colombia was composed of several former Spanish American colonies that would go on to become its successor states after the dissolution of 1831, namely, Colombia, Venezuela, and Ecuador.
[b] These percentages hide the importance of trade between St. Thomas and Haiti. Despite the relatively low number of official Haitian vessels arriving in the port in the 1820s, the free port of Charlotte Amalie was one of the few places where Haiti could continue to trade, despite trade barriers put up by the larger Atlantic empires. See Julia Gaffield, *Haitian Connections in the Atlantic World: Recognition after Revolution* (Chapel Hill: University of North Carolina Press, 2015), 23–60.

in the 1820s to an average of 18 percent in the 1830s, partly as a consequence of the falling prices of sugar – by far the largest export to Denmark. What the numbers in the table do not show is the degree to which regional rather than European trade dominated the maritime traffic. While vessels from European ports such as Liverpool, London, Copenhagen, and Amsterdam arrived in Charlotte Amalie on a monthly basis, transatlantic shipping was not the dominant trend. Judging from the logbooks of the harbormaster of St. Thomas, the most common places of origin of the incoming vessels were either neighboring Caribbean islands, such as Tortola, Puerto Rico, St. Eustatius, St. Barthélemy, Guadeloupe, and Trinidad, or North American port cities, particularly Baltimore, Philadelphia, New Orleans, and Charleston.[71]

This is not to say that the beginning or end points of those vessels were necessarily regional, but rather that Charlotte Amalie became a hotspot for transshipping and a favored stopover point for merchants and sailors

[71] St. Thomas Harbour Master, "Pilot journals of incoming ships," 1821–1835, RA, WILA 25.4.1–2.

passing through the region in search of trade, supplies, and gossip. While the flow of those most prized exports of the previous century – sugar and coffee – fell considerably in the nineteenth century, a myriad of new goods was transshipped through St. Thomas. These included provisions, dried foodstuffs, manufactured goods, mules and cattle, and loot obtained through privateering and piracy.[72] The main reasons for such transshipping were to be found in the advantageous customs policy of the free port, the high concentration of potential sellers and buyers located there, and the possibilities of passing on goods of questionable legality with less risk of confiscation than in neighboring ports. Even as the widespread smuggling and contraband trade of the eighteenth century had become less common, or at least less visible, in the 1820s and 1830s, the island's free port status and the active neutrality of its Danish colonial administration continued to make it one of the most popular ports in the Leeward Islands for international and intercolonial travelers.

As profitable as the Revolutionary and Napoleonic Wars proved to be for the commercial networks of the Leeward Islands, the wars were in many ways the beginning of the end for the region's long period of economic growth. Political and economic shifts in both global and regional contexts spelled the end of prosperity for colonial landowners and merchant elites, particularly in the colonies of Northern European empires. The late 1830s saw sugar, the primary crop produced by most plantations in the Leewards, being grown on an even greater scale in Brazil, on the large Spanish islands of Cuba and Puerto Rico, and in the Dutch East Indies, especially Java.[73] This trade contributed to a fall in global sugar prices that had significant consequences for the economies of smaller Caribbean islands.[74] At the same time, cotton, which had been among the main secondary exports from the Leeward Islands, was being grown more cheaply and more efficiently in the southern United States and in South Asia.[75] Primary reasons for this general shift away from the

---

[72] Vibæk, *Vore gamle tropekolonier*, bind 2, 301–10; Ulla Katic, "The Transportation of Mules from South America to the West Indies in the 1860s," *Historia Medicinae Veterinariae* 23 (1998): 3–25.

[73] J. H. Galloway, *The Sugar Cane Industry: An Historical Geography from Its Origins to 1914* (New York: Cambridge University Press, 1989), 120–42.

[74] The growth in sugar beet production in continental Europe, following the loss of the French Empire's Caribbean colonies, no doubt also contributed to the changing prices beginning in the 1820s. See George M. Rolph, *Something about Sugar: Its History, Growth, Manufacture and Distribution* (San Francisco: John J. Newbegin, 1917), 100–115; E. Muriel Poggi, "The German Sugar Beet Industry," *Economic Geography* 6:1 (1930): 81–93.

[75] See, for example, Sven Beckert, *Empire of Cotton: A Global History* (New York: Alfred A. Knopf, 2014), 199–241.

West Indies included the abolition of slavery in the non-Spanish Caribbean, the rapid expansion of global production cycles, and the consequent emergence of new and highly competitive suppliers.[76]

The geographic shift in the production of raw materials was not the only reason for the diminishing role of Caribbean port cities in the wider Atlantic and global economy; the transformation of trade was exacerbated by other factors, prime among them technological innovations. The increased use of steamships for transatlantic cargo transport in the second half of the nineteenth century meant that a growing number of merchant mariners no longer had reason to set anchor in West Indian ports on their way to or from the continental Americas.[77] The Caribbean became an unnecessary stopover, and the lack of competitively priced products for sale further decreased the incentive for opportunistic traders to plan their journeys around local ports, despite the opportunities provided by free trade and lowered tariffs. Thus, the era of the Leeward entrepôts came to an end, the island colonies falling victims to the globalizing commercial processes they had themselves been at the center of a few decades earlier.

Conclusion

The search for profit in one way or another drove the majority of colonial enterprises in the Leeward Islands. Planters, merchants, sailors, and magistrates all played their part in networks of trade and commerce that spanned the entirety of the Leewards, crossing colonial and imperial borders in the process and extending their reach far outside the Caribbean microregion. The basis of many such trans-imperial networks was free trade of a sort, with goods and capital moving more or less freely between the colonial territories of any number of European empires.

---

[76] Despite the importation of South Asian indentured labor following the abolition of slavery in the British Caribbean, the sugar-producing colonies fell far behind Brazil and Cuba in terms of output. See Madhavi Kale, *Fragments of Empire: Capital, Slavery, and Indian Indentured Labor in the British Empire* (Philadelphia: University of Pennsylvania Press, 2011), 1–11; Sidney Mintz, *Sweetness and Power: The Place of Sugar in Modern History* (New York: Penguin Books, 1985), 50–73; Galloway, *The Sugar Cane Industry*, 143–50.

[77] Gordon Boyce, *Information, Mediation, and Institutional Development: The Rise of Large-Scale Enterprise in British Shipping, 1870–1919* (Manchester: Manchester University Press, 1995), 26–43; Edward W. Sloan, "The First (and Very Secret) International Steamship Cartel, 1850–1856," in *Global Markets: The Internationalization of the Sea Transport Industries since 1850*, ed. Clara Eugenia Núñez (Seville: Universidad de Sevilla, 1998), 41–48; Frank W. Geels, "Technological Transitions as Evolutionary Reconfiguration Processes: A Multi-level Perspective and Case-Study," *Research Policy* 31:8 (2002): 1257–74.

Given the restrictive trade policies of the eighteenth century, such freedom was often to be found outside the boundaries of imperial law, and even when official policies of free and unrestricted trade were introduced at the turn of the century, smuggling was still a widespread practice among many of the region's entrepreneurial actors.

If smuggling was a common phenomenon in the Leeward Islands, it was at least in part because the geography of the microregion was so conducive to these activities. With a multitude of keys and inlets all across the region, it was almost impossible for the understaffed and poorly equipped colonial authorities to patrol their own waters and safeguard their coastlines from smugglers and their ilk. This task was made all the more Sisyphean by the active participation of many local communities in the illegal trade, including a large number of magistrates and other officials who realized that if this activity was going to take place in any case, one might as well make a profit from it. The strength of these smuggling networks and the knowledge of routes and passages that they held go some way toward explaining why the illegal slave trade was so widespread in the Leewards after 1807, as men who had previously smuggled sugar and molasses now began to carry African bodies in their holds as well.[78]

The trade networks that formed the basis of the inter-imperial microregion were important well beyond the context of political economy, and the connections forged between different colonies served to foster a decidedly trans-imperial space. This was especially true when it came to conflicts between imperial authorities and colonial interests, since many of the issues over which they initially clashed were related to the freedom of trade and the protection of perceived national interests. Indeed, the free ports themselves became sites of political and jurisdictional contestation and one of the key resources over which political struggles were fought, both within and between empires. The free port legislation was created to harness the preexisting practices of intercolonial trade taking place in the region, but it was only ever partially successful in controlling the networks fostered by these activities.

On a different level, the regional integration brought about by the trading practices analyzed in this chapter was in many respects a manifestation of a particular form of early globalization. As the borders between different political entities were crossed, whether in the name of free trade policies or by more subtle and pragmatic contraband traders, relationships of economic interdependence were created and a

---

[78] For more on the illegal slave trade, see Chapter 6.

distinct regional interest formed – an interest that valued stability and the security of private property well above more patriotic concerns such as which empire held which island. The Leeward Islands formed a space where regional and global trade met, located at the center of transatlantic commerce and with strong maritime connections to almost all the major trading hubs on the rim of the Atlantic. This centrality of place did not last long. As other microregions became integrated into expanding global imperial economies, and as a host of political and economic factors conspired to make the Leewards less competitive in a widening market, the region quietly slipped into economic decline in the middle decades of the nineteenth century.

3   Imperial Warfare, Colonial Violence

The Caribbean of the eighteenth and early nineteenth centuries was a world at war. European empires clashed with one another in a series of conflicts, many of which spilled over into their Atlantic colonies. Yet these naval and military engagements were not the only type of organized violence in the region. White elites relied on the collective use of force to preserve the hierarchical and repressive social order on which their colonial system was built. Living in a state of constant fear of slave uprisings, the white settler populations of the islands depended on neighboring colonies to provide unspoken security guarantees against the perceived common threat to the prevailing social order. This mutual reliance on security was among the strongest forces of intercolonial integration in the region.

Despite the informal collective security arrangement fostered by these conditions, the Leeward Islands were not immune to the impact of broader inter-imperial conflict, and warfare between European powers often turned into colonial skirmishes and occupations. In the wake of the Revolutionary and Napoleonic Wars, the largely uncontested position of British naval and military superiority became increasingly apparent, and the colonies of smaller empires came to occupy ever more precarious spaces between the larger Atlantic powers of the region.

The perpetually meager state of island defenses left colonies poorly prepared for internal and external threats alike. Most of the military infrastructure was woefully underfunded, with weather-beaten fortifications left to rot on hills and beaches. There were never enough soldiers garrisoned on the islands, and those who were in residence frequently spent more time bedridden than on active duty because of the disease environment. Local militias, of which many members were recruited from the growing population of free people of color, were as much a source of concern as of reassurance for white colonial commanders. Together, these factors made the individual colonies of the Leeward Islands essentially defenseless against foreign invaders and more often than not reliant on outside support when faced with organized slave uprisings.

Mutual reliance on security among its constitutive colonies helped to establish the inter-imperial microregion. From the early decades of the Caribbean slave regime, insurrections posed a constant threat to the colonial order. Since the black populations on the sugar-producing islands quickly outnumbered whites, sometimes by as much as fifteen to one, an organized uprising represented an existential threat to both the lives and livelihoods of white planters.[1] This was true across the Caribbean, especially at the turn of the nineteenth century when the specter of large-scale slave revolts such as the one in Saint-Domingue pushed the white elites of rival colonies closer together.[2] But in the Leeward Islands, cooperation across imperial borders was both stronger and more deeply rooted than among the larger islands, as poor defenses and geographical proximity came together to foster intercolonial security practices – even when these clashed with metropolitan directives.

While later chapters examine the institution of slavery through its legal framework and the dynamics of the slave trade, this chapter will look at the way in which the fear of slave uprisings shaped the security complex of the islands and became a significant force for intercolonial integration. Although the microregion thus increasingly took on the state-like functions of an internal security guarantor, such practices did not completely supplant existing inter-imperial rivalries. Rather, these two dynamics – mutual security reliance and political rivalry over trade and territory – coexisted in an uneasy constellation, the balance between them often depending on the strength of local and imperial ties of centrally placed actors within the islands' intercolonial networks.

Approaching issues of war and uprisings in the Leeward Islands from the perspective of traditional nationally or imperially discrete histories can take one only so far. While well suited for providing domestic metropolitan context for events in the colonies and for analyzing political and strategic decision-making by imperial governments, these approaches tend to lose sight of intercolonial entanglements at the periphery. Even an interpolity perspective, focusing on the relations and interactions between imperial actors, obfuscates many of the actual dynamics at the local level, so crucial for the way violence and security were constituted and practiced on the ground. Adopting a trans-imperial and microregional perspective, in contrast, helps illuminate these otherwise obscure aspects of the violent decades at the turn of the century and thus provides a useful addition to existing accounts. This perspective allows us to illuminate key intercolonial

[1] Goveia, *Slave Society in the British Leeward Islands*, 65.
[2] See, in particular, Ada Ferrer, *Freedom's Mirror: Cuba and Haiti in the Age of Revolution* (Cambridge: Cambridge University Press, 2014), chapter 4.

dynamics in the Caribbean, including the relative lack of violent clashes between colonial powers; the stability in the colonial social order, despite the seemingly constant threat of slave revolutions; and continued intercolonial integration in the face of sustained imperial rivalries.

The invasions and temporary occupations of islands in the region during the eighteenth and early nineteenth centuries were almost always carried out by the major imperial powers, namely, France and Britain. The smaller empires of Denmark and Sweden, and even the Dutch Republic – hardly a minor player from a global perspective – were rarely perpetrators, and often were victims of such events. Part of the explanation for this relates to the relative power distribution among the empires and particular alliances and declarations of neutrality during these decades. But another part lies in the way in which the smaller, neutral colonies functioned. Denmark and Sweden in particular exercised a distinct form of thin sovereignty over their colonial possessions. They certainly laid claim to the territories and installed official representatives, but the actual exercise of imperial power and control was limited. Much of the day-to-day administration was left to colonial governors and magistrates, even more so than in the colonies of larger empires, and the territories were seen as more distant than was the case of French, British, or Spanish overseas possessions, leading to a certain hands-off approach being taken by the imperial capitals. The fact that the free populations of these small colonies were never predominantly from the metropole only amplified the pattern and meant that local merchants and planters were highly unlikely to identify predominantly as Scandinavian subjects, let alone to lay down their lives for the defense of the Danish or Swedish crowns. In the words of historian Neville Hall, Denmark's Caribbean colonies were ruled by "an empire without dominion."[3] This particular relationship between colony and metropole in the Scandinavian empires had important consequences for the region at large, making their colonies convenient buffer zones between larger rival empires. The relatively laissez-faire approach to colonial administration also led to a high degree of continuity in the islands' governance and the daily lives of their residents, even during prolonged periods of foreign occupation as was the case during the Napoleonic Wars.

Internal Security: Revolts and Paranoia

While other disruptions to colonial security, including those of war and piracy, ultimately did little to interrupt the flow of Caribbean commerce

---

[3] Hall, *Slave Society in the Danish West Indies*, 6.

or to truly endanger the safety of white elites, the specter of large-scale slave uprisings not only put the lives of individual planters in danger but promised to destabilize the entire system on which their societies were based. White fears coexisted with a deeply paternalistic view among planter elites of a societal ordering based on race as well as a more narrowly economic acknowledgment of the centrality of the slave population as the foundation of the entire West Indian plantation complex.[4]

The military infrastructure of the Leeward Islands was primarily focused on internal rather than external threats, with more resources devoted to militias and prisons than to defenses aimed at hostile vessels or invading forces. While most islands had some type of coastal defenses, the cannons were often kept in such a state that they were near-unusable in practice, and stocks of projectiles tended to be very low. The fortifications on the smaller western islands were especially understaffed and dilapidated, and even as safeguards against uprisings rather than invasions, the military forces were in a sorry state. Not only was the number of soldiers stationed on these islands generally low, but their lack of experience and a high susceptibility to local diseases meant that very few of them were prepared to engage potential threats at any given time.[5]

Garrisons and fortifications were most often located at the outskirts of the main port cities, such as Fort Christian in Charlotte Amalie or Fort Oscar in Gustavia, while other islands were in effect left entirely without military defenses. Fort Recovery on Tortola, which had been built in the 1620s when the island was in Dutch hands, was largely left as a ruin until the outbreak of the French Revolutionary Wars, when the local assembly passed a number of acts in order to raise money to rebuild and expand the fort.[6] Slaves performed much of the actual work on the fort, since an act passed in 1797 obligated any and all owners of slaves on Tortola to send "a proportion thereof to work on the forts and fortifications of these islands."[7] Already two decades later, at the end of the Napoleonic Wars, imperial administrators saw little use for such

---

[4] Richard S. Dunn, *Sugar and Slaves: The Rise of the Planter Class in the English West Indies, 1624–1713* (Chapel Hill: University of North Carolina Press, 1972); Mintz, *Sweetness and Power*, 19–73; Philip D. Curtin, *The Rise and Fall of the Plantation Complex: Essays in Atlantic History* (2nd edition) (Cambridge: Cambridge University Press, 1998), 129–43.

[5] For more on the role of disease in Caribbean military affairs in general, see McNeill, *Mosquito Empires*, 15–62. For more on yellow fever in the Danish West Indies in particular, see Torben Geill, "Den Gule Feber i Dansk Vestindien," *Dansk Vestindisk Selskab* XVI (1981).

[6] Contained in TNA, CO 315/2, 88–112.   [7] TNA, CO 315/3, 3.

defenses, and Fort Recovery was once again left to crumble on the beach. This trend of diverting resources away from local security continued, and by 1834 the total expenditure on the militia and garrisons on Tortola was minuscule.[8]

The defense situation on the Danish islands was little better. From the mid-1700s to the mid-1800s the overall military budget for the Danish West Indies was generally modest, with a noticeable spike in the number of soldiers temporarily garrisoned there during the volatile decade of the 1790s.[9] Not until the arrival of Governor-General Peter von Scholten in the1830s were serious attempts made at improving the security of the colonies through organizational reforms and increased funds, and even then only half-heartedly.[10] During an investigation of an alleged slave conspiracy on St. Croix in 1759, an official report mentioned the derelict condition of one of the island's main military fortifications. It was seen as "an easy matter to take the West-End fort, which indeed at that time was with ten men ... since there was no gate to the fort. There were, to be sure, a cannon, but no *rapperter*. The soldiers were half demoralized and entirely starved, and the fort not half built."[11]

This situation was not much of an improvement from the state of affairs on neighboring St. John, where a few decades earlier the dozen or so members of the local garrison had faced a full-scale slave rebellion. In late November of 1733 a group of slaves rose up in an organized revolt, captured the nearby military fortification, took control of the majority of the colony's estates, and forced a large part of the white population off the island. The rebels, who identified themselves as Aminas and hailed in large proportion from the western coast of Africa, proceeded to declare the island their own. Faced with this significant challenge to imperial authority and local security, the Danish Governor, Philip Gardelin, did not appeal to the Danish government for assistance, nor did he turn to his superiors in the Danish West India and Guinea Company. Instead, he wrote a letter to his French counterpart in the nearby Windward Islands, pleading for military aid:

---

[8] "Blue book of statistics, 1834," TNA, CO 317/5.
[9] Reports and calculations concerning the West Indian military administration, 1764–1851," RA, COC 464.
[10] The royal ordinance from 1830 concerning organizational changes in the island defenses is contained in RA, COC 467. See also Kay Larsen, *Dansk Vestindien, 1666–1917* (Copenhagen: C. A. Reitzels Forlag, 1928), 226.
[11] Translated and printed in Waldemar Westergaard, "Account of the Negro Rebellion on St. Croix, Danish West Indies, 1759," *The Journal of Negro History* 11:1 (1926): 56. *Rapperter* is the commonly used early modern Scandinavian term for a gun carriage.

I feel that we are on the verge of some terrible happening unless you have the kindness to honour me with your assistance; I request it, Monsieur, in the name of the King my master. Not only are you bound to save us because we are allies, friends and neighbours, but also because, as Christians, you cannot allow slaves to triumph over our weakness and to render us victims to their rebellion.[12]

The French governor, Jacques-Charles Bochart de Champigny, obliged this request, acknowledging both the importance of regional stability and the personal obligations that connected the two officials:

[S]ince I know better than anyone all the regrettable consequences, which might arise if such crimes are committed with impunity by slaves against their masters, consequences which are of interest to all nations, I flatter myself greatly and give you many thanks for the preference that you have been kind enough to show me among all my neighbours by requesting that succour which I grant you with all the more pleasure since you have hereby provided me with the means to repay you, Monsieur, with the gratitude which I owed your predecessor.[13]

A few weeks later an imperial expeditionary force from Martinique consisting of 200 French and Swiss soldiers arrived on the island and put a violent stop to the rebellion over the next two months.[14] French concerns for regional stability were not unfounded, as part of the rebels' plan seems to have been to spread the uprising to neighboring islands, including both St. Thomas and Tortola, which themselves had large groups of Amina slaves and whose white colonists dreaded the potential spread of the St. John uprising.[15] It is worth noting that the French governor made his decision before having received approval or official word from Paris, a fact that underlines the autonomy of imperial agents in the region. In the words of Champigny: "I did not see the necessity to consult with the King, my master, who honored me with the command of all the Windward Islands; as long as I continue to hold this office, I will always represent him through my word and my actions and with the proper disinterest as the great King he is."[16]

A further dimension of the inter-imperial response to the uprising on St. John is to be found in the report of the governor of the British

[12] Letter from Gardelin to Champigny, March 21, 1734, printed in *The French Intervention in the St. John Slave Revolt of 1733–34*, ed. Aimery P. Caron and Arnold R. Highfield (Christiansted: Bureau of Libraries, Museums and Archeological Services, 1981), 26.
[13] Letter from Champigny to Gardelin, April 12, 1734, in ibid., 34.
[14] Letter from Champigny to Longueville, April 12, 1734, in ibid., 27–30. See also Letter from d'Orgueville to the French foreign minister, July 1, 1734, in ibid., 48–49.
[15] Pierre Joseph Pannet, *Report on the Execrable Conspiracy Carried out by the Amina Negroes on the Danish Island of St Jan in America 1733*, trans. Aimery P. Caron and Arnold R. Highfield (Christiansted: Antilles Press, 1984), 17.
[16] Letter from Champigny to Gardelin, April 12, 1734, in *The French Intervention*, 34.

Leeward Islands. The Danish governor had requested help not only from his French neighbor but also from the authorities of the British islands. In contrast to Champigny, the British governor, William Matthew, was a newcomer to the Caribbean, having served in the British Leewards for only a few years before the incident on St. John, and his ties to the elite networks of the region were far weaker than those of his French and Danish counterparts. Because of a long-standing dispute over the territorial rights to St. John, which both British and Danish empires had made claims to since the start of the century, Matthew flatly refused to assist the Danes.[17] More than that, he explicitly asked his superiors in London for clarification on whether or not he should seize the opportunity to finally rid the Virgin Islands of its Danish inhabitants: "Must I drive them [the Danes] out of St. Thomas and St. John's? I pray your Lordships will please to direct me herein."[18] It is unclear what the response from London was to this request, but in any case, by the time such orders could have arrived, the French forces had already reinstated Danish rule on St. John. For his part, Matthew continued to loathe the Danish presence in the West Indies throughout his reign as governor, seeing their presence in the Leewards as an affront to British imperial ambitions.

What this early case of intercolonial cooperation and competition in the face of a slave uprising tells us is just how strong a role intercolonial relations played in local governance. The primary reason the Danes requested assistance from their colonial neighbors, rather than from their nominal masters in Copenhagen, was no doubt practical. The time it would have taken to get the message across the Atlantic, let alone to equip, dispatch, and transport a group of armed men from Europe to the Caribbean in response, would have been far too long to resolve the situation on the ground. But the ease with which Champigny made his decision, and the way in which the French and Swiss soldiers secured the Danish colonies, underscores the robustness of the practice of intercolonial security and the priority given to handling threats to the white colonial order as a whole. It is also significant that while Matthew refused to send aid to his Danish counterparts, the magistrates and planters on nearby Tortola were more fearful of the insurrection than was their governor, located on faraway Antigua. While they would no doubt have cherished the opportunity to claim Danish colonial territory for their own, the looming threat of an uprising among British-owned slaves was

---

[17] Letter from Governor Matthew to Mr Popple, Antigua, November 26, 1734, *CSPC, 1734–1735*.

[18] Letter from Governor Matthew to the Council of Trade and Plantations, Montserrat, March 19, 1734, *CSPC, 1734–1735*.

more urgent. The lack of a local legislature until 1773, however, made it somewhat challenging for British Virgin Islanders to voice such on-the-record concerns directly to their governor.[19]

Fear of slave revolts did not subside during the following century, nor did the number of actual insurgencies. The Saint-Domingue revolution in particular, with its unprecedented scope and consequences for the French Atlantic Empire, sent shockwaves of fear and racial paranoia through the region's white population.[20] In a 1792 report to London, Governor William Woodley of the British Leeward Islands characterized the revolution as a "melancholy catastrophe" and described how refugees from the French colony were passing through the region in increasing numbers.[21] Throughout the 1790s, reports on the political situation in the French Empire were increasingly joined by anxious debates over the internal state of tranquility or unrest among the slave populations in the British colonies, and by recurring speculation over potential French spies and revolutionaries agitating for insurrection in foreign territories.[22]

One such alleged spy was M. Delosses, captured in 1794 in the Leewards and accused of traveling through British Caribbean ports, sowing seeds of discontent in order to spread the gospel of the French Republic, and no doubt weakening the British war effort in the process.[23] The following year, in 1795, a small vessel was seized off the coast of St. Christopher, carrying five black men including one Jean François de Catte. According to the acting governor of the island, John Stanley, de Catte was the commander of "a company of coloured people at Guadeloupe" and a member of the "Society of the Amis de la Liberté." His vessel arrived at St. Christopher from St. Eustatius, where he had been among the three hundred French troops who occupied that island earlier in the year. According to Stanley, de Catte and his four compatriots were planning to sow revolutionary fervor in the British Leewards: "There is every reason to believe that his Errand here was that of a spy from St. Eustatius,

[19] See Isaac Dookhan, *A History of the British Virgin Islands, 1672–1970* (Epping: Caribbean Universities Press, 1975), 28–26.

[20] For a detailed study of the reverberations of the Haitian Revolution in another Caribbean colony, Cuba, and the resulting anti-revolutionary measures taken, see Ferrer, *Freedom's Mirror*.

[21] Letter from W. Woodley to the Viscount of Melville, January 16, 1792, TNA, CO 152/72, 4. The number of refugees increased in the following year, especially after the declaration of war between France and Britain. See TNA, CO 152/73, 47.

[22] In 1792 alone, there were three reports on the "state of tranquility" of the slave population in the British Leewards. See letters from W. Woodley, January 2, 16, and May 28, 1792, TNA, CO 152/72, 1, 4, and 12.

[23] Letter from Whitehall to acting-governor John Stanley, January 17, 1794, TNA, CO 152/75.

and to excite a revolt amongst our Negroes."[24] The message from British authorities in both cases was clear: sources of instability such as Delosses and de Catte were to be dealt with swiftly and without mercy.

The perceived threat to the colonial order went deeper than foreign spies and agitators. A number of actual slave revolts and conspiracies were seen by officials as linked to or inspired by unrest in the French Empire, including a number of smaller uprisings in Dominica in 1791 and 1795. The Dominica slaves seem to have been at least in part inspired by events on nearby Guadeloupe, and John Orde, the governor of the British colony, feared that recently arrived Francophone refugees had republican agitators among them. He referred to these newcomers as "a swarm of people of the most desperate character, as well as an infinite number of slaves of a less exceptionable description who possibly may prove troublesome guests."[25] What made the situation in Dominica even more complicated was the long history of marronage and maroon communities on the island, perceived by some as a simmering internal threat just waiting to be ignited.[26] Slaves on the Pickering estate in Tortola likewise rose up in revolt in 1790, as rumors circulated among them that Britain had abolished slavery but local magistrates and planters refused to enact the law, thus keeping the slaves captive.[27] This rumor concerned an intra-imperial political event, but observers speculated that it actually sprung out of news about the French Revolution and its colonial Caribbean reverberations.[28]

An interesting window into British threat perceptions of the period can be found in the report of one Captain Berkeley, who traveled through the Leeward and Windward Islands in 1790 and 1791, evaluating the risk of

[24] Letter from John Stanley to William Cavendish-Bentinck, Duke of Portland, May 27, 1795, TNA, CO 152/77. f. 58. Stanley, a Member of Parliament for Kent, was born on Nevis and held several different offices in the Leeward Islands, including Solicitor-General of the British Leewards and President of the Council of St. Christopher, the seniority of the latter position making him acting-governor of the island following the death of Governor William Woodley in 1793.

[25] Quoted in Michael Craton, *Testing the Chains: Resistance to Slavery in the British West Indies* (Ithaca, NY: Cornell University Press, 1982), 226.

[26] Interestingly, a temporary reconciliation between the colonial regime and the Dominica maroons actually strengthened the island's defenses against potential French invaders, as the governor drafted both maroons and resident French royalists into the local militia. See Craton, *Testing the Chains*, 224–27. For more on the ongoing tensions between the government and the maroon communities, see Alan Burns, *History of the British West Indies* (revised edition) (New York: Barnes and Noble, 1965), 603–5.

[27] Goveia, *Slave Society in the British Leeward Islands*, 95–96. The Pickering estate would again be the site of an uprising in 1823, when slaves forcefully refused to be relocated to Trinidad by the estate's proprietor. See Dookhan, *History of the British Virgin Islands*, 85–93.

[28] Report attached to Shirley to Grenville, June 11, 1790, TNA, CO 152/69.

revolt in each of the British colonies.[29] St. Christopher was thus deemed relatively safe, due to its significant military presence, while Dominica was seen as most likely to face an uprising due to its natural geography, spread-out plantations, and the presence of numerous "sympathizers with the blacks."[30] Interestingly, Berkeley saw proximity to French colonies as an important factor in fostering instability among the slaves and increasing the odds of revolt, but did not necessarily see the presence of French planters within colonies like Grenada as a threat, because these individuals shared the British authorities' interest in preventing revolt and preserving stability. The perceived danger in all of the British Caribbean cases was not just insurrection – it was the threat of *black* insurrection, which was seen as especially contagious because it could so easily spread to other slave colonies. What is more, it was wrapped up in what was thought of as the revolutionary fervor of the times, springing out of the French and Haitian revolutions and carried across the waves by destabilizing agitators, infiltrators, and spies. Even when these outsiders were arrested or thrown out, the spread of information itself – whether news, speculation, or scuttlebutt – was seen as a source of instability. As one Danish governor put it decades later, in the midst of new fears of conspiracy on the eve of emancipation: "our only security against the effects of a [successful] revolt on Tortola will be the greatest alertness at sea, so that we may if necessary cut off all communication from that island."[31] In other words, if intercolonial security measures failed, the only way to contain an uprising would be to cut off contact to the affected node in the network.

St. Barthélemy was likewise hit hard by fear of insurrection, as abolitionist agents from neighboring French islands allegedly visited Gustavia on multiple occasions. Here they did their best to instill revolutionary fervor in the local French-speaking population, according to the reports of the Swedish governor, Carl Fredrik Bagge.[32] Rumors circulating in local elite networks told of a band of "free mulattoes, negroes, and 'white adventurers'" crisscrossing the islands, "holding meetings and speeches on the rights of man, irrespective of his color."[33] Whether true or not,

---

[29] Michael Duffy, "The French Revolution and British Attitudes to the West Indian Colonies," in *A Turbulent Time: The French Revolution and the Greater Caribbean*, ed. David Barry Gaspar and David Patrick Geggus (Bloomington: Indiana University Press, 1997), 82–83. The original report is kept in the collections of the British Library but has seemingly been lost or misplaced.

[30] Ibid., 82.

[31] Letter from Governor von Scholten to Frederick VI, March 15, 1834, RA, WILA 2.7.3.

[32] Letters from C. F. Bagge, September 20, 1791, and January 5, 1792, in RKA, SBS 2411/1/I B.

[33] Quoted in Ekman, "St. Barthélemy and the French Revolution," 23.

such rumors led to rampant paranoia and a renewed distrust toward the free people of color living in the colonies, especially those with French creole backgrounds.

These fears often led to actions and policies that further undermined colonial defenses. The number of black freedmen on the Danish islands was high, and the relatively open policy on intercolonial migration meant that there were many creoles of various linguistic and ethnic groups arriving in the bustling port of Charlotte Amalie. The local freedmen made up several racially categorized militia units, including one composed entirely of French creoles, some of whom hailed from Saint-Domingue. In 1801 the Danish Commandant of St. Thomas, Casimir von Scholten, observed this militia company with the utmost caution, deeming the soldiers as "untrustworthy French *gens de couleur*" and ultimately banishing several of them from St. Thomas out of fear of a conspiracy.[34] These specific concerns seem to have been baseless, and, considering what was to come for the Danish colony, the French creole militiamen would no doubt have been more valuable in defending the islands' sovereignty than were the white Englishmen serving with them.

The smaller French islands themselves saw several uprisings and accusations of conspiracy in the 1790s. Tensions were high in the wake of Saint-Domingue, and even rumors of revolt were often met with violence and a certain level of ferociousness among white inhabitants. A 1790 report from Martinique thus told how "a Plan was formed by the free Mulattoes (embodied as a Military Corps,) to destroy all the Inhabitants attending it [the Fête de Dieu parade], and to set fire to St. Pierre's, and indiscriminately to murder all the Inhabitants; sparing neither sex or age."[35] Confronted with this rumor by their commanding officers, violence erupted between the accused free people of color and the local white population. The skirmish was bloody and lasted the whole day: "so great was the rage at their Treachery, that the Inhabitants gave order to put all to Death. Their houses were searched, and many innocent People suffered with the Guilty – seventeen were hung the first day, and one hundred were to suffer the following Morning." The alleged plot was seen by locals to have originated among revolutionary elements within

---

[34] Report of Casimir von Scholten, January 11, 1801, in "The British Occupation of the West Indies 1801–1807," RA, COC 533. Despite these expulsions, free people of color continued to be an integral part of the Danish West Indian militia. Thus in 1807, the St. Croix militia was made up of approximately two-thirds whites and one-third free people of color. "St. Croix Militia, 1807–08," in the Caribbean Collection: Virgin Island Documents, the Florence Williams Library, Christiansted, St. Croix.

[35] Newspaper clipping dated June 8, 1790, attached to Shirley to Grenville, June 12, 1790, TNA, CO 152/69.

the military, and as a consequence "the Municipalities have come to a Resolution not to have a military force at all." The report, delivered by a white refugee from Martinique, ended on a note of profound regret over resultant white-on-white violence:

The lives of many white Persons have unfortunately been sacrificed in this dreadful affair. Among others a French Gentleman was killed in his Hamoc, when going to the Country for the benefit of his health; – his complexion rendered wan and fallow by disease, was mistaken for that of a coloured person, and he was shot dead by an inhabitant.[36]

Even as fear gripped white Caribbean societies, contemporary observers acknowledged with no small amount of dark humor the absurdity of letting such paranoid obsessions dictate all life in the colonies. As rumors of insurrection and conspiracy spread through the region like wildfire and fueled the growing atmosphere of paranoia, there is little reason to believe that colonial subjects accepted all of these stories as gospel truth, and many stories were no doubt dismissed as little more than untrustworthy hearsay or gossip. A telling parody appeared in a brief note printed in the newspaper *The Report of St. Bartholomew* under the title "Chronicle of Sayings of Hearsay":

Body Dicky has related in the Grog-Shop number 3 in this Town of Gustavia, that a black Girl, who used to see him at night has told him, that an American Sailor, who sees her now and then, had told her, that the Mate of the American Schooner, to which the Sailor belongs had told him, that he had heard his Captain say, that at the time the Schooner was at anchor at Point a Pitre, Guadeloupe, a coloured Girl, who used to come on board and see the Captain in the night, had related, that she had heard some talk of disturbances amongst the coloured people of Guadeloupe; but Body Dicky cannot tell, whether it had been of the disturbances of 1802, or any other.[37]

The events surrounding an alleged slave conspiracy on Tortola in the fall of 1831 show that the collective security regime in the Leewards lasted well into the nineteenth century, and that even the islands belonging to the British Empire relied on their neighbors in matters of internal security. According to magistrates on Tortola, the slaves' plan involved "the murder of all the white men and children of the island, the kidnapping of their wives, and a subsequent journey with the plunder to Saint-Domingue."[38] Since authorities on St. Christopher initially

---

[36] Ibid.   [37] *The Report of St. Bartholomew*, no. 28, November 1804.
[38] Letter from Governor von Scholten to the Frederick VI, September 30, 1831, RA, WILA 2.7.2. Post-revolutionary Haiti had at this point established itself in the imagination of Caribbean slaves as a beacon of freedom and black sovereignty, feeding both the hope of slaves and maroons and the anxieties of white slaveholders within the

responded to requests from the Tortola government with "no sympathy or aid," the government instead asked the Danish commander of St. Thomas for help.[39] Commander Rhodes responded favorably, dispatching a brig of war and a contingent of soldiers and ordering them to "afford every aid that the circumstances required" until "the local planters' fears ha[d] subsided."[40] Observing that the Danes had already sent troops to Tortola, the government of the British Leeward Islands reversed its dismissive stance. Already uncomfortable with the close ties between British and foreign colonies in the western Leewards, the British governor ordered the commander in chief, Sir James Lyon, to station a detachment of guards on Tortola, in order to satisfy the local council's request and see to it that "tranquility was restored."[41]

When the British soldiers arrived, the Danes had already been on Tortola for several weeks, in effect taking on the role of regional security guarantors. Their arrival had, according to a Danish report, caused "great joy and reassurance among the inhabitants, who lived in the most horrible fear of getting attacked at any moment by the slave population, as there was neither a regular military force nor a well-organized militia on the island."[42] As had been the case on St. John a century before, intercolonial concerns over regional stability ruled the day, and Danish colonial administrators showed little hesitation in supporting their British neighbors. When a robust imperial response proved absent or ineffective, microregional networks stepped in to fulfill the role of the state in securing the colonial social order. Once again, proximity and inter-island interdependence proved more reliable motivations for maintaining security within the microregion than did more formally established intra-imperial responsibilities.

External Security: Warfare and Occupation

In 1781 British warships delivered a pointed reminder to anyone who might have forgotten that seeking wealth and profits in the Caribbean was

region. See Ada Ferrer, "Haiti, Free Soil, and Antislavery in the Revolutionary Atlantic," *The American Historical Review* 117:1 (2012): 40–66.

[39] Florence Lewisohn, *Tales of Tortola and the British Virgin Islands* (Chicago: n.p., 1966), 57; Larsen, *Dansk Vestindien*, 232.

[40] Quoted in John P. Knox, *A Historical Account of St. Thomas* (New York: Charles Scribner, 1852).

[41] Letter from Governor Maxwell to Viscount Goderich, October 5, 1831, TNA, CO 239/25, 60. The order itself is contained in Papers of the Commander in Chief, 1830, TNA, CO 239/23.

[42] Letter from Governor von Scholten to the Frederick VI, September 30, 1831, RA, WILA 2.7.2.

a high-stakes game, not just for individuals but for colonies and empires as well. In retaliation for its regional role as a key supplier of both the French navy and the American revolutionary forces, British General John Vaughan and Admiral George Rodney attacked and captured the Dutch colony of St. Eustatius in an overwhelming display of naval force.

The capture of the island itself was relatively bloodless, and the only real clashes were between the British naval force and Dutch ships that had left the island shortly before the attack. The wealth of the Dutch colony was startling, however, and the two commanders took it upon themselves to oversee the seizure of all goods and property that were claimed as prizes for the British crown. This course of action led to a thorough and at times brutal search of the town of Oranjestad, during which the British forces confiscated all valuables belonging to the resident merchants.[43] Perhaps the most infamous event during the first weeks of occupation was the arrest and expulsion of some thirty heads of families from the local Jewish trading community, on the basis of their alleged failure to comply with the occupying force by hiding their property.[44]

The sacking of St. Eustatius had several major consequences. While many of the riches seized on the island never actually made it to England since French warships intercepted most of the British convoys, and despite the fact that Rodney and Vaughan held it for only ten months, the Dutch colony was nevertheless financially ruined and never regained the same centrality in the commercial networks of the microregion as it had held throughout previous decades.[45] The local Dutch traders were not alone in their outrage over British seizures but were joined by a number of resident English and British West Indian merchants whose property had similarly been taken as prizes by the occupying forces. The resulting legal battles, combined with accusations in parliament against Rodney and Vaughan for displaying excessive greed and neglecting their military duties, led to a drawn-out political aftermath in London, despite the fact that Rodney had by now been made a peer.[46] The political strife reached its peak with a 1785 petition to the king written by Rodney and Vaughan, in which they requested a commission be set up to investigate and reverse the decision by the Lord Commissioner of Appeals to award payments to the British merchants of St. Eustatius. In their appeal, the commanders argued that the claimants were not true British subjects,

---

[43] TNA, CO 318/8.

[44] Guido Abbattista, "Edmund Burke, the Atlantic American War and the 'Poor Jews at St. Eustatius.' Empire and the Law of Nations," *Cromohs* 13 (2008): 1–39.

[45] Jarvis, *In the Eye of All Trade*, 431–32. See also John Franklin Jameson, "St. Eustatius in the American Revolution," *American Historical Review* 8:4 (1903): 683–708.

[46] Many of the debates are contained in full or in part in TNA, PRO 30/20/26/7.

that seizure of their property was entirely warranted, and that it was in fact an "act of indispensible Duty" to attack and seize the enemy colony given the orders of the king.[47] On the other side of the channel, a broadside with the title "The Plundering of St. Eustatius" perhaps best captured contemporary Dutch views: "Britain bestows Vaughan and Rodney with the most beautiful names, in order to cover their wickedness. I, filled with horror at their vicious behavior, name Rodney Nero and Vaughan Caligula."[48]

The strong reactions to the sacking of St. Eustatius can be explained in part by the fact that such widespread seizures and destructive military actions went against the common intercolonial practices of a region where the mobility of merchants and the trade between different colonies were seen as close to sacred. Full-scale military clashes on this scale were particularly rare in the Leeward Islands. Even during the prolonged periods of inter-imperial warfare in the first two decades of the nineteenth century, most confrontations took place on the high seas, and the islands themselves were spared any large-scale destruction outside that inflicted by natural disasters or internal uprisings. A lack of bloodshed did not mean a lack of military confrontation, however, and both Danish and Swedish colonies found themselves under occupation multiple times during the two decades of the French Revolutionary and Napoleonic Wars, providing ample illustration of how inter-imperial skirmishes over the smaller Caribbean islands were typically carried out.

The French Revolutionary Wars saw several clashes between European powers spilling over into their Atlantic colonies, but it was not until the last years of the war that the British navy took to occupying the island colonies of neutral powers. In the spring of 1801, British forces invaded and occupied both St. Barthélemy and the Danish West Indies, in part as a reaction to the Swedish and Danish empires' involvement in the Second League of Armed Neutrality – a coalition of noncombatants that included Prussia and Russia and had as its aim the protection of neutral shipping in the face of the British navy's policy of searching all neutral vessels for French contraband. The Second League was inspired by the First League of Armed Neutrality, which had served a similar purpose during the last years of the American Revolutionary War and also included Portugal, the Netherlands, Sicily, and the Ottoman Empire.[49]

---

[47] Petition of Lord Rodney and General Vaughan to the Crown, 1785, in ibid., ff. 97–100.

[48] The print is held in the Atlas Van Stolk collection in Rotterdam and is available through their online repository, accessed May 27, 2014, www.atlasvanstolk.nl/en/collection.

[49] Isabel de Madariaga, *Britain, Russia, and the Armed Neutrality of 1780* (New Haven: Yale University Press, 1962).

Unlike its predecessor, the Second League was remarkably unsuccessful. Britain saw the declaration of armed neutrality as a de facto alliance with France and responded not only with the invasions of Swedish and Danish West Indian colonies, but also by hamstringing the Danish-Norwegian fleet anchored in the Copenhagen harbor and shelling the city into swift submission.[50]

"Invasion" might be a somewhat misleading term in the Caribbean context, however, as there was no real military confrontation to speak of. When British forces approached the Danish islands, they were met by ragtag bands of colonial soldiers and local militiamen. Not only was this defense force less than a fifth of the size of the British, it was also made up of a large percentage of British subjects living in the Danish colony.[51] These men could hardly be expected to take up arms against their countrymen in any serious manner, if not because of divided loyalties then because of the treason charges they would surely face if caught, as the British Empire was fully expected to execute any of its own subjects fighting against it.[52]

The Anglicization of the islands also influenced the political reaction to the British invasion, especially within the St. Thomas Burgher Council, at that point dominated by English-speaking merchants. The burghers' advice to the colonial War Council in 1801 amounted to little more than a call for unconditional capitulation.[53] This response was perhaps not unreasonable given the military superiority of the invasion forces, but it also seems clear that the priority of most local inhabitants was less a patriotic defense of the Danish imperial territory than a strong concern for their private property rights and their continued ability to trade freely with neighboring colonies and international sailors. Such demands were clearly put forth by the Burgher Council during subsequent negotiations, and the head of the British forces, Lieutenant-General Thomas Trigge, largely met them.[54] These concerns over free trade had characterized

---

[50] The latter event, known as the Battle of Copenhagen, not surprisingly has left a considerably deeper impression in Danish historiography than in British, where it is most often referenced in connection with the career of Vice Admiral Horatio Nelson. See, for example, Dudley Pope, *The Great Gamble: Nelson at Copenhagen* (London: Weidenfeld & Nicolson, 1972); Ole Feldbæk, *Slaget på Reden* (Copenhagen: Politikens Forlag, 1985).

[51] "Further Reports," in "The British Occupation of the West Indies 1801–1807," RA, COC 533.

[52] "Proceedings of the St Thomas Burgher Council," March 13, 1801, in "The British Occupation of the West Indies 1801–1807," RA, COC 533.

[53] Ibid.

[54] Ibid., Letter from Lieutenant-General Thomas Trigge to the Colonial Government of St Thomas, 1801. The obvious exemption was open trade with the enemies of Britain, namely, the French forces.

island politics since the early days of Danish colonization, and it should come as no surprise that they dominated much of the internal discussions over capitulation, despite the complaints of Governor General Lindemann. While Commandant von Scholten, stationed as he was on St. Thomas, was willing to go along with the recommendations of the Burgher Council – likely because he fully realized the military superiority of the British – Lindemann initially insisted on waiting for direct orders from Copenhagen before surrendering.[55] The fact that such orders were never registered as having been received, despite ostensibly having been drafted and sent across the Atlantic by the Danish government, puts the fragile link between Copenhagen and the West Indies on full display.

The British occupation of St. Barthélemy played out in a fairly similar manner. On March 21, 1801, a dozen British vessels arrived at the Swedish island, to inform the local government that the British government did not accept Swedish neutrality and that war had been declared between their two nations. In the words of the Swedish governor, Hans Henrik Ankarheim, the island's defenses were not up to the challenge of anything resembling an organized military threat, being nothing more than "18 weakened soldiers and barely 20 able Swedes, amongst a mob of disgruntled residents, with scarcely enough food to last 20 days and eight days worth of water, without any possibility of rescue in sight; threatened by an enemy, which in all the places they occupy act with an utmost cruelty and unfairness."[56] The unfortunate Ankarheim, who had been governor of the island for barely three full months, informed the Swedish authorities in Stockholm that he had little choice but to surrender to Lieutenant-General Trigge, negotiating the best terms possible in the process. This decision, he argued, was the only way to avoid a fate similar to that which had befallen St. Eustatius a few decades earlier.[57] The specter of the Dutch island's conquest still loomed large in the memory of local communities, serving equally well as an unspoken threat on the part of the British and as a carefully articulated excuse for bloodless surrender on the part of foreign governors.

The period of occupation on St. Barthélemy lasted just over a year. During this time, the British military authorities agreed to let "religion, laws and customs" remain unchanged, in essence leaving the majority of inhabitants to carry on their daily lives as normal. A notable exception was made in the case of legal administrative practice, as a general reluctance to cooperate with the British administrators on the part of local magistrates led to the occupying force seizing more direct control of the

---

[55] Vibæk, *Vore Gamle Tropekolonier*, 224–25.
[56] H. H. Ankarheim to Stockholm, March 21, 1801, RKA, SBS 2411/1/I C.   [57] Ibid.

legal process. Trigge declared that in order to "render the attainment of public justice more certain and effectual, and to afford that vigour and energy to the laws, which may the better tend to prevent them being violated with impunity," all cases that involved a death sentencing of the accused were to be transmitted to the commander in chief directly, suspending "the practice of appealing to the Mother-Country and waiting the confirmation of such sentence from thence."[58]

Despite the strong British reaction to the League of Armed Neutrality, a distinction between neutral and enemy powers was carefully maintained in the legal aftermath of the handover, as evidenced by the records of the High Court of Admiralty in London. Goods and capital held by French agents operating out of St. Barthélemy were readily claimed as prizes, whereas the property of the Swedish Crown and its subjects was either left alone or, as in the case of Swedish arms and armament, compensated following the end of the occupation.[59] While the British Empire reacted strongly to neutral parties trading with her enemies, officials nonetheless went quite far to preserve the status of neutrality as a legal and political category after the fact, perhaps as a reaction to the aftermath of the St. Eustatius affair two decades earlier.

Where the occupations at the end of the Revolutionary War had been rather brief and undramatic events, occupations of neutral territory during the subsequent Napoleonic Wars were more sustained and costly affairs. As an exception to this rule, St. Barthélemy went through the war years relatively unscathed, having been occupied for a mere fifteen hours in 1807 by French forces, allegedly as retaliation for having traded with now-independent Haiti – a misdeed that Napoleonic France could not let pass without retribution, especially when the culprit itself was a former French colony.[60] The Danish colonies, in contrast, went through a considerably longer military occupation, as British forces took the three islands in 1807 and did not return them to Danish hands until 1815, following the ratification of the Treaty of Kiel by the Congress of Vienna.

Once again it was Denmark-Norway's insistence on carrying out trade with France that led to British occupation of the Caribbean colonies.

---

[58] Minutes from St. Barthélemy cabinet meeting, July 7, 1801, RKA, LC 2414/18.
[59] Records of the High Court of Admiralty, September 30, 1803, TNA, HCA 32/859/544; Transcription of letter to Lord Hankesbury, May 20, 1802, RKA, LC 2414/12. There is good reason to believe that the picture painted by the court records is accurate, as the Swedish magistrates did not in other situations have any qualms about pursuing British naval or military authorities via legal channels, as seen in the next chapter, and would surely have done so had a significant portion of Swedish property in fact been confiscated.
[60] Axel Goes, *Några Minnen från St. Barthelemy* (Stockholm: P. A. Norstedt & Söner, 1878).

The surrender of the islands took place in much the same manner as it had done in 1801, with local authorities acknowledging the superiority of force on the part of their British foe. What followed was a period of occupation characterized in equal parts by continuity and opportunism. The British authorities kept the majority of minor officials on the Danish islands in office, with the exception of military personnel and the magistrates involved with customs and revenue.[61]

Finding new customs officers proved a difficult matter, however, and the posts of harbormaster and comptroller of customs on St. Thomas were often replaced following a number of unfortunate incidents and accusations.[62] The merchants of St. Thomas wrote several petitions to the governor requesting increasingly expansive privileges of free trade, especially pertaining to the neighboring Spanish colonies. Imperial authorities in London denied these requests, deeming it unnecessary to grant the petitioners any privileges beyond those held by other British free ports in the region.[63] There were frequent breaches of the revenue and navigation laws, as local traders continued to participate in the illicit commercial networks of the region despite the British occupation, but such breaches proved challenging to prosecute, as the lack of a local British court on the islands during the first years of occupation meant that the majority of cases had to be resolved in Britain.[64] It is worth noting that Governor McLean, the British commander of St. Thomas and St. John, seemed quite reluctant to process any of these cases in neighboring British colonial courts, perhaps because of the close ties between merchants there and the Danish smugglers.[65]

Governor McLean's reluctance seems prudent when considering some of the challenges posed to British colonial authority by activities on the neighboring islands. British privateers in 1810 seized two Danish vessels close to the harbor of St. Thomas, going by the colorful names of *John Smith Junior* and *Revolution*, carried them to Tortola, and sold off their cargoes without ever bringing them to the local prize court to properly claim them. After having been sold, the cargoes were then shipped back into Charlotte Amalie "in a clandestine and illegal manner."[66] The governor described these events with exasperation, concluding that "the whole of the proceedings at Tortola were irregular, and a manifest

---

[61] List of offices and duties on St. Thomas and St. John, 1808, TNA, WO 1/121, ff. 97–114.

[62] TNA, WO 1/124, ff. 16–18.   [63] TNA, WO 1/121, ff. 151–90.

[64] TNA, WO 1/122.

[65] See Chapter 6 for more on the relationship between the Tortola Court of Vice Admiralty and the St. Thomas merchant community.

[66] Letter from McLean to the Earl of Liverpool, January 25, 1811, TNA, WO 1/125, f. 28.

breach of the Revenue and Navigation Laws."[67] Such practices were commonplace in the Virgin Islands, and they were often carried out with the cooperation of local colonial agents, few of whom were as diligent in their duties as McLean.

Despite these administrative and jurisdictional challenges, the occupation did not face any serious or vehement opposition from the local population. According to the diary of Claus "Langhaar" Smidt, a member of the colonial council on St. Croix, the free people of color were especially welcoming of the military administrators, throwing several large balls in their honor and hoping perhaps that the rights and privileges of free people would be expanded under the new colonial leadership.[68] Such was hardly the case, however, and with the exception of the administrative and legislative reforms described in the previous chapter, the eight years of foreign rule left daily life in the Danish West Indies largely untouched.

These periods of occupation were part of a broader pattern involving neutral islands in regional Caribbean networks. The island colonies of neutral European powers played an important role in eighteenth- and nineteenth-century inter-imperial relations, acting as buffer zones of a sort between the larger empires of the region. Not only did these colonies occupy territory that might otherwise be held by larger rival empires, but they also provided sources of neutral trade during periods of war between the European great powers. As frustrating as this could be for some imperial players, as evidenced by the frequent British retaliation against neutral empires in the early 1800s, it was also a crucial component of the supply chains and regional markets operating during the frequent periods of conflict around the turn of the century. This role was explicitly acknowledged by British and French elites, and was among the chief reasons for granting Sweden territorial sovereignty over St. Barthélemy in the first place.[69]

The importance of keeping neutral territory in the region was apparent again in 1813, when Britain ceded the occupied island of Guadeloupe to

---

[67] Ibid. This was not a singular event, as evidenced by the similar fate of the Danish vessel *Sirius* the following year. TNA, T/3953.

[68] Quoted in Vibæk, *Vore Gamle Tropekolonier*, 132–33. See also RA, WIG 3/57/1.

[69] Hildebrand, *Den Svenska Kolonin S:t Barthélemy*, 24–33. Interestingly, the French government had entertained the idea of giving St. Barthélemy to the Dutch in exchange for Sint Marteen, the Dutch colony on the island of St. Martin, rather than give the territory to Sweden. This did not sit well with the British, however, who pushed for a Swedish acquisition in treaty negotiations. See "Projet de décision relative à un éventuel échange des îles de Saint-Martin et Saint-Barthélemy avec la Hollande," April 7, 1784, ANOM, Secrétariat d'État à la Marine COL C8B, 15, f. 133.

the Swedish crown.[70] While there were other reasons for this transfer, including personal ties and commercial interests, the importance of maintaining small imperial powers within the inter-imperial regional framework no doubt played a part. Guadeloupe was a larger undertaking than St. Barthélemy, however, and Sweden did not seem particularly disappointed when France reclaimed the island at the Treaty of Paris negotiations in 1814.[71]

The thin sovereignty that the Danish and Swedish crowns held over their Caribbean territories contributed to making these spaces especially vulnerable to foreign imperial invasions. This type of laissez-faire sovereignty also led to a peculiar phenomenon of business as usual during prolonged periods of military occupation. The bonds that bound the subjects of these colonies to their metropoles were for the most part not ties of loyalty or any sort of civil duty. Indeed, the majority of white inhabitants felt few if any obligations to the Scandinavian empires, since their relationships to them were contingent, based on opportunities for profit more than anything else. Even those plantation families that had been on the islands for generations often arrived during earlier periods, when the colonies were in the hands of other imperial powers, and had thus seen colonial administrations come and go, with little apparent impact on the daily experience of their subjects. While such situations were common for many people and regions across the early nineteenth-century world, they were especially apparent in the trade ports of the Caribbean. Here claims to sovereignty were often fleeting and the mobility of individuals was high, making formal imperial borders particularly fluid. On the whole, the focus on profit, freedom of movement, and partial interchangeability of governments did not lead to widespread political upheavals and intercolonial tensions, but resulted instead in a much more stable environment than that found in the continental Americas.[72]

---

[70] "Treaty of Concert and Subsidy between His Britannic Majesty and the King of Sweden," March 3, 1813, printed in *British and Foreign State Papers*, vol. 1 (London: HMSO, 1841), 296–303. Initially, the Swedish government saw this acquisition as both a political and economic gain, as expressed by Gustaf Wetterstedt in an early report to the king. See "Wetterstedt Apostilla," March 27, 1812, RKA, LC 2424/12.

[71] "Definitive Treaty of Peace and Amity between His Britannic Majesty and His Most Christian Majesty," May 30, 1814, in *British and Foreign State Papers*, vol. 1, 151–70. See also Reinhard H. Luthin, "St. Bartholomew: Sweden's Colonial and Diplomatic Adventure in the Caribbean," *The Hispanic American Historical Review* 14:3 (1934): 307–24.

[72] For a comparison between North American and Caribbean colonies within the British Empire during the American Revolution, see Andrew Jackson O'Shaugnessy, *An Empire Divided: The American Revolution and the British Caribbean* (Philadelphia: University of Pennsylvania Press, 2000).

Conclusion

Throughout the eighteenth century the smaller islands in the Leewards functioned as integrated spaces in microregional networks of mobile actors, allowing all manner of activity to flow through them, especially in times of inter-imperial warfare. This pattern slowly began to change in the early decades of the nineteenth century, as the rise of British naval power combined with the decline of the French presence in the region generated new regional power dynamics. While neutral ports continued to function as important nodes in trans-imperial networks, shifts in inter-imperial relations and an altered balance of power between major empires left magistrates on neutral islands with fewer options and limited space for maneuvering in intercolonial political relations, in effect making the ports reliant on the dominant power in the region: the British Empire. The ties between individual islands belonging to different empires continued to be tightly knit, but in terms of military affairs there were few places to turn besides the regional hegemon in the decades following 1815.

Such military dependence did not lead to uncontested British hegemony in other spheres, however, and the relationship between the British Empire and neutral islands was more complex than that of a hegemon and its proxies. Microregional interests often trumped imperial loyalties in day-to-day practice, and even during periods of direct military occupation foreigners as well as British subjects challenged the authority of imperial agents. These challenges did not take the form of political subversion or revolt, but rather stemmed from widespread practices of legal legerdemain and opportunistic profit seeking. Moreover, in times of perceived existential crisis, British colonies themselves turned to their foreign neighbors for assistance, especially when the metropole and its representatives proved unresponsive or inefficient.

Whereas the early decades of the nineteenth century had seen a remarkable escalation of maritime violence in the Caribbean, more peaceful waters would characterize the latter part of the century. This development was in part due to the end of the Wars of Independence in South America and the emergent British naval hegemony in the region following the decline of both French and Spanish colonial power. Part of the explanation also lies in the broader and more gradual shift of imperial attentions away from the West Indies and toward other corners of the globe – a shift perhaps most clearly heralded by the outbreak of the First Opium War in 1839.

The reigning social order within the microregion changed little during this period. Despite attempts to influence intercolonial politics in a more revolutionary direction, most of the Leeward Islands remained staunchly conservative and a bastion of the values espoused by its merchant and planter elites – namely, free trade and unfree labor. Coordinated counterrevolutionary efforts, whether formal or informal, that cross national or imperial borders can be extremely successful in stifling potential uprisings. They are, in some sense, the mirror image of the type of transnational revolutionary movements frequently described in the literature.[73] There was a revolutionary current in the region during this period, to be sure, but the widespread paranoia over potential black uprisings among white elites meant that any gathering was seen as a conspiracy and any sign of defiance was taken as treason, to be struck down on the spot. The threat of black violence was one shared by all officials in the region, and the perseverance of the status quo was the overriding concern for local governments. If an insurgence on one island proved successful, there was little doubt in the mind of officials that it would spread to neighboring colonies. The policies and practices that came out of this paranoia made it exceedingly hard for bottom-up complaints to be heard, let alone for actual revolutionary movements to take hold. While imperial elites did not entirely succeed in preventing efforts to overthrow the colonial order, as evidenced by the continued uprisings in the nineteenth century, antirevolutionary practices no doubt contributed to the perseverance of this order in spite of its fragile underpinnings.

---

[73] See, for example, Fred Halliday, *Revolution and World Politics* (Durham, NC: Duke University Press, 1999), 192–206; Nader Sohrabi, "Global Waves, Local Actors: What the Young Turks Knew about Other Revolutions and Why It Mattered," *Comparative Studies in Society and History* 44:1 (2002): 45–79; Daniel Nexon, *The Struggle for Power in Early Modern Europe: Religious Conflict, Dynastic Empires and International Change* (Princeton: Princeton University Press, 2009), 99–134; Sidney Tarrow, *The New Transnational Activism* (Cambridge: Cambridge University Press, 2005); George Lawson, "Revolutions and the International," *Theory and Society* 44:4 (2015): 299–319.

4   Prize Courts and Privateers

The practice of privateering was a key element of Caribbean politics for as long as there were European colonies in the region. Many of the Leeward Islands, including the Virgin Islands, functioned as havens for pirates and privateers alike during much of the seventeenth century, and this early reputation continued to haunt them in later decades. Privateering and associated activities served both as a source of regional integration and as a means of pitting colonies against one another, creating in essence a dynamic of push and pull effects within the microregion.

Privateering – the participation of private vessels in maritime warfare under a commission – was one of several early modern practices that essentially sought to mobilize private initiative to achieve public goals. This tactic was crucial in a world of relatively weak polities that were constantly feuding with one another, and while European imperial states had grown considerably in strength and military capacity by the turn of the nineteenth century, the practice of privateering was still being used by the time of the Napoleonic Wars.[1] It became a favored tool employed by revolutionary governments across the Americas exactly because of its ability to support the war effort of relatively weak states by mobilizing forces outside the formal military apparatus. It is important to make clear the legal differences between the practices of piracy and privateering. While privateers were operating under a letter of marque or a commission from a state or sovereign, stipulating the nationality of ships they could target, pirates generally had few if any qualms about the vessels

---

[1] See Richard Pares, *Colonial Blockade and Neutral Rights 1739–1763* (Oxford: Oxford University Press, 1938); Janice E. Thomson, *Mercenaries, Pirates, and Sovereigns: State-Building and Extraterritorial Violence in Early Modern Europe* (Princeton: Princeton University Press, 1994); Alejandro Colás and Bryan Mabee, "The Flow and Ebb of Privatised Seaborne Violence in Global Politics: Lessons from the Atlantic World, 1689–1815," in *Mercenaries, Pirates, Bandits and Empires: Private Violence in Historical Context*, ed. Colás and Mabee (New York: Columbia University Press, 2010), 93–116.

they boarded.[2] Privateering was in this way limited to attacks on belligerent parties to an ongoing conflict, and the loot and vessels taken by privateering outfits had to be brought to imperially sanctioned prize courts in order to be formally acknowledged as lawfully obtained prizes.

Prize courts were thus an integral component of privateering, as well as of other maritime practices. The location of these courts was a continuing wellspring of intercolonial rivalry, as different islands competed over jurisdictional power and, naturally, the many opportunities for wealth accumulation that accompanied such power. The resulting legal skirmishes were important for intra-imperial dynamics, but the legal regime of prize law also bound together the colonies of different empires, creating networks based in equal parts on imperially sanctioned practices and locally driven legal legerdemain.

While privateering was a staple of inter-imperial warfare throughout the eighteenth century and into the Napoleonic Wars, the spread of revolutionary movements across the greater Caribbean at the turn of the century created a host of new opportunities for profit and maritime predation. Many of these activities worked to connect the microregion directly to the larger political and commercial world of the circum-Caribbean, as early nineteenth-century pirate and privateering vessels were increasingly connected to multiple regional centers at once – acquiring letters of marque in South America, capital in North America, and crews in the Caribbean. Even as the first decades of the nineteenth century saw a certain resurgence of the practice of privateering, as a means of claiming sovereignty and independence on the part of Latin American revolutionaries, it also spelled the beginning of the end for this particular form of privatized warfare.

The present chapter examines the resurgent privateering of the early nineteenth century in order to analyze the way in which trans-imperial networks of the Leeward Islands were connected to wider regional and oceanic networks. Privateering as a political and strategic tool was a thoroughly Atlantic phenomenon, with actors on either side of the ocean employing privateers in order to weaken the maritime sinews of their rivals or to project claims of sovereignty to foreign powers. But while the letters of marque were issued in cities like London and Buenos Aires and bought by businessmen in Baltimore and Paris, much of the actual privateering took place in a smaller theater: the Caribbean. The Caribbean was at the

---

[2] Lauren Benton, "Towards a New Legal History of Piracy: Maritime Legalities and the Myth of Universal Jurisdiction," *International Journal of Maritime History* 23:1 (2011): 225–40; Alfred P. Rubin, *The Law of Piracy* (Newport, RI: Naval War College Press, 1988), 29–30.

center of the practice, as the region provided fertile grounds for recruiting crews, outfitting vessels, and raiding rival ships. The black markets and trans-imperial networks of the Leeward Islands were particularly well suited for such activities, and a number of neutral islands, including St. Thomas and St. Barthélemy, proved to be convenient ports in which to offload the cargoes and valuables acquired in the course of privateering for the Latin American republics.

The chapter also delves into the specifics of the colonial prize court system, particularly the one in the British Empire, in order to illuminate the legal framework for privateering and the crucial role played by vice admiralty courts in imperial clashes over jurisdiction and politico-legal power. Many such conflicts were intimately tied to the dynamics of the region's intercolonial networks and the role of different colonies within these networks, including Tortola and the Virgin Islands. By examining the phenomena of privateering and prize courts from the Revolutionary and Napoleonic Wars to the Latin American Wars of Independence, the chapter illustrates concrete ways in which the Leeward Islands were tied into transatlantic politics and imperial legal regimes. The microregion never stood outside the wider oceanic circuits surrounding it, but it was also not a passive receptacle for imperial plans and high politics. The Leewards became an important staging ground for bigger geopolitical struggles. But as these struggles came crashing onto the shores of the islands, they were inevitably caught up in the local rivalries and clever schemes of the region's actors.

Revolutionary Currents and Opportunistic Privateers

Since the late sixteenth century, privateering had been a well-established practice and an integral part of European inter-imperial warfare, especially so in the West Indies. It played a crucial part in every major military conflict in the region during the eighteenth century, and practices related to privateering were essential to the rise and fall of microregional commercial and jurisdictional centers alike. Even when outright war had not been declared between European powers, privateering was often used as a tool of harassment and disruption aimed toward ostensibly neutral powers. While most of the actors directly engaged in these activities were primarily driven by the potential of prizes, it is important to see the practice of privateering as both opportunistic and strategic – as a means of acquiring wealth for individuals and also as a tool for polities to strike at their enemies economically and militarily.

The clashes between Britain and France at the end of the eighteenth century created plenty of opportunity for privateering. Two of the most important neutral free ports in the microregion, Gustavia and Charlotte Amalie, grew rich on the transshipment of captured cargoes and the clandestine outfitting of vessels, while British, French, and US sailors operating in the region were quick to seek out letters of marque from their respective colonial authorities. St. Barthélemy in particular became a shelter for French privateers, especially during the British occupation of Guadeloupe in 1794, and several privateering vessels were fitted out in Gustavia.[3] The establishment of a French prize court, one of the revolutionary *agences de prises*, in Gustavia spurred on this traffic, allowing privateers sailing with French commissions to bring their prizes to the Swedish colony.[4] In part as retaliation for the Swedish support of and trade with French privateers, British ships increasingly came to target Swedish vessels and went so far as to block St. Barthélemy's access to freshwater sources on neighboring islands – actions that, not surprisingly, led to a veritable barrage of legal and diplomatic complaints from the Swedish colonial authorities aimed at St. Christopher, London, and Stockholm.[5] Swedish shipping was once again targeted later in the decade, as skirmishes between French and US privateers became increasingly common during the relatively brief Quasi-War between the two powers, and the distinction between French and Swedish ships was of less and less concern to North American captains.[6] Privateers brought several Swedish vessels to Philadelphia and claimed them as prizes, while the Swedish consul to the US lobbied intensely to reclaim them, mostly to no avail.[7]

Magistrates frequently invoked the fragile state of defenses on the smaller Leeward Islands in debates over privateering in this period. In 1794 the Assembly of Tortola laid out the situation in a statement referring to the threat posed by French and US privateers:

---

[3] Hildebrand, *Den Svenska Kolonin S:t Barthélemy*, 259–64.

[4] For more on these French prize courts in foreign Caribbean colonies, which were also set up in St. Eustatius and Puerto Rico, see Anne Pérotin-Dumon, "Cabotage, Contraband, and Corsairs: The Port Cities of Guadeloupe and Their Inhabitants, 1650–1800," *Atlantic Port Cities: Economy, Culture, and Society in the Atlantic World, 1650–1850*, ed. Franklin W. Knight and Peggy K. Liss (Knoxville: University of Tennessee Press), 67–68; Pérotin-Dumon, *La ville aux îsles, la ville dans l'île*. After a brief interlude with no prize agent on St. Barthélemy in the late 1790s, France appointed a new one in 1800. "Nomination du citoyen Bigard, comme commissaire aux prises à Saint-Barthélemy," March 9, 1800, ANOM, Secrétariat d'État à la Marine C7A52, f. 79.

[5] Transcripts of correspondence with London, 1794–95, RKA, LC, 2414/2; TNA, PRO 30/42/9/7, f. 2; TNA, CO 152/74, f. 4; Hildebrand, *Den Svenska kolonin S:t Barthélemy*, 271–73.

[6] See Michael A. Palmer, *Stoddert's War: Naval Operations during the Quasi-War with France, 1798–1801* (Columbia: University of South Carolina Press, 1987).

[7] Hildebrand, *Den Svenska kolonin S:t Barthélemy*, 286–89.

Lamentable must be the state of a Colony (weak, defenseless and remote as this is) when it is so truly known to the Enemy – and when we have such a lawless Banditti, such Desperadoes of Anarch, to cope with, it must be evident to your Excellency that not a moment's time is to be lost in order to prevent this Colony from becoming the devoted object of their merciless vengeance.[8]

Despite such expressions of concern over foreign privateers, Tortola was itself the center of gravity for much British privateering in the microregion. This was in no small part due to the important prize court located in Road Town, discussed in further detail below.

The end of the protracted period of Anglo-French warfare in 1815 heralded a new shift in regional privateering. With the growing unrest in the greater Caribbean region stemming from the struggles for independence in the Spanish Americas came a host of opportunities for unaffiliated actors to make a profit. As Napoleon's forces occupied the seat of the Spanish Empire in Europe, a number of the Spanish Empire's Atlantic colonies established new governments, finding themselves center stage in the inter-imperial games of war and diplomacy. Newly declared republics such as Gran Colombia and the United Provinces of the Río de la Plata issued a large number of letters of marque, allowing their holders to conduct privateering in the name of the Latin American states.[9] This was both a political and military strategy. It led to numerous attacks on enemy ships, most prominently those of the Spanish Empire. At the same time, it forced other imperial actors to take Latin American claims of independence seriously when they were faced with privateering commissions issued by governments and presidents who forcefully laid claim to their own sovereignty and political legitimacy.[10]

While some of the holders of such commissions were likely to be genuine patriots and ideological revolutionaries, many were mercenaries and adventurers who needed little other incentive than that of profit.[11]

---

[8] Letter from President of the Virgin Islands Mr. Leonard and Speaker of the Virgin Island Assembly Mr. Dougan to Governor John Stanley, January 12, 1794, TNA, CO 152/75, f. 22.

[9] Blaufarb, "The Western Question"; Jeremy Adelman, *Sovereignty and Revolution in the Iberian Atlantic* (Princeton: Princeton University Press, 2009).

[10] Lauren Benton, *Law and Colonial Cultures: Legal Regimes in World History* (New York: Cambridge University Press, 2002), 210–52; Matthew McCarthy, "'A Delicate Question of a Political Nature': The Corso Insurgente and British Commercial Policy during the Spanish-American Wars of Independence, 1810–1824," *International Journal of Maritime History* 23:1 (2011): 277–92; Benton, "Una soberanía extraña: La Provincia Oriental en el mundo atlántico," *20/10: El Mundo Atlantico y la Modernidad Iberoamericana* 1 (November 2012).

[11] Certain republics and revolutionary regimes relied more heavily on genuine patriots to fight for their cause on the open seas than others, and many privateers fell somewhere on the scale between idealism and opportunism. See, in particular, the case of Cartagena, in

This point went double for the owners and outfitters of the privateering vessels, men with finances who often hailed from countries and colonies outside Latin America. While most crew members turned to privateering out of necessity in a world of limited options to earn a livelihood, the financiers who backed their ventures tended to see privateering as only part of a broader portfolio of activities – many of which straddled the boundary of legality. From 1817 to the early 1820s, commissions began to circulate among mariners in United States ports, especially in Baltimore but also in Savannah, Charleston, and Providence, and were here employed on cruises against Iberian shipping across the Caribbean.[12] In this time and place potential pirates almost always sought the mantle of sanctioned privateering, even if this was sometimes little more than a shallow attempt to justify opportunistic sea robbery through the veneer of legal political violence. The dissemination of Latin American commissions made such mantles exceptionally easy to obtain, increasing for a time the risks faced by any crew traversing the Greater Caribbean, and not just those sailing under Spanish or Portuguese flags – the belligerent nations in the Wars of Independence.

Local British magistrates faced with this new situation sought official advice from London but often received mixed responses.[13] The general policy toward the Latin American republics was one of official neutrality and informal tacit acceptance, culminating in outright support following an 1825 declaration formally recognizing the sovereignty of the new nations of Mexico, Gran Colombia, and the United Provinces of the Río de la Plata.[14] The issue of republican privateering was more complicated than that, however, especially in the second half of the 1820s, when opportunistic privateers became less discriminating in their choice of targets. The ripples of these practices were felt in European capitals, not just via the growing number of legal complaints lodged by affected

Edgardo Pérez Morales, *No Limits to Their Sway: Cartagena's Privateers and the Masterless Caribbean in the Age of Revolutions* (Nashville, TN: Vanderbilt University Press, 2018).

[12] David Head, "A Different Kind of Maritime Predation: South American Privateering from Baltimore, 1816–1820," *International Journal of Naval History* 7:2 (2008); Sean T. Perrone, "John Stoughton and the *Divina Pastora* Prize Case, 1816–1819," *Journal of the Early Republic* 28:2 (2008): 215–41; Kevin Arlyck, "Plaintiffs v. Privateers: Litigation and Foreign Affairs in the Federal Courts, 1816–1825," *Law & History Review* 30:1 (2012): 245–78.

[13] Several examples of such correspondence are contained in "Misc. papers and correspondence on British policy towards Spanish America," TNA, WO 1/164.

[14] Jay Kinsbruner, *Independence in Spanish America: Civil Wars, Revolutions, and Underdevelopment* (2nd edition) (Albuquerque: University of New Mexico Press, 2000), 105–6.

Caribbean merchants, but also in the markets for maritime insurance – the price of which rose rapidly in the 1820s.[15]

St. Barthélemy gained a particularly notorious reputation as a central hub in the regional network of outfitting and privateering under Governor Johan Norderling. According to the US consul on the island, Robert M. Harrison, St. Barthélemy was in 1821 the haven for a "horde of pirates and desperadoes, which I am sorry to say, have found an asylum, and protection in this island by the Governor." Harrison went on to describe how privateers sailing under "Artigas Colours" were regularly being outfitted in the port of Gustavia.[16] There was no love lost between Harrison and Norderling, the former describing the latter as having "conducted himself more like the chief of a band of Pirates than the head of a civilized colony," but Harrison's accusations did not differ too widely from those made by other observers in the region, including both Danish and Spanish officials.[17] Indeed, the image painted by foreign governors fit well with the image of the Swedish island as a central node in local contraband networks, described in the previous chapters.

Johan Norderling himself was an interesting example of a relatively high-ranking official in the Swedish imperial service. He came from a decidedly middle-class family in the Swedish heartland but made his government career moving from one overseas territory to another, beginning as a consular secretary in Tangiers in the early 1780s. Following the handover of St. Barthélemy to Sweden in 1784, Norderling jumped at the opportunity to serve in the new colony, and in 1787 he was appointed as magistrate on the island.[18] This posting lasted a decade before Norderling returned to Sweden in 1798. He then spent the next two decades serving as Swedish commercial agent in Algiers, frequently assisting in negotiations between the United States and the Algerian government, and forged substantial professional and personal connections to American, Russian, and Dutch diplomats in North Africa. When Sweden was briefly given control over Guadeloupe, Norderling lobbied unsuccessfully for the position as governor of that island. After another brief stint back in Stockholm, he was named Swedish Chargé d'Affaires in Washington in 1819, a promotion that lasted less than a month, as he was instead given the post as governor of St. Barthélemy later that year.[19] When Norderling

---

[15] Matthew McCarthy, *Privateering, Piracy and British Policy in Spanish America, 1810–1830* (Woodbridge: Boydell & Brewer, 2013), 61–63.

[16] Robert M. Harrison to John Quincy Adams, 1821, quoted in Ernst Ekman, "A Swedish Career in the Tropics: Johan Norderling (1760–1828)," *The Swedish Pioneer Historical Quarterly* 15:1 (1964): 25.

[17] Letter from Governor Rothe to the Frederick VI, April 30, 1821, RA, WILA 2.7.1.

[18] Ekman, "A Swedish Career," 4–6.   [19] Ibid., 14–20.

left the governorship in 1826, following considerable pressure from the Swedish government, the governance of St. Barthélemy was reorganized, in effect placing the power of the governor in the hands of a local council, which was then led by Norderling's two sons-in-law, James Haarlef Haasum and Lars Gustaf Morsing.[20] Over his relatively long career in the colonial service, Norderling had fostered a significant number of connections to other European imperial agents, as well as personal connections across the Leeward Islands. His daughters married local landowners and through these links he gained access to the political, social, and commercial networks of the microregion – access that he drew on frequently over his seven years as governor of St. Barthélemy.

In the early 1820s Stockholm received multiple complaints as well as a formal request from the Portuguese government to no longer tolerate the presence of Artigas's privateers in St. Barthélemy, and to put an end to the sale of Portuguese vessels and cargoes as prizes on the island.[21] These requests did not make much of an impression on local magistrates, however, and privateers continued to use Gustavia and the nearby uninhabited island of Île Fourchue for outfitting and offloading their vessels. Norderling himself had multiple excuses and explanations for the presence of Latin American privateers in and around St. Barthélemy. These included accusations against the magistrates of St. Eustatius for equipping the privateer captains with Dutch flags and papers, possession of which made it next to impossible to deny them access to Gustavia.[22] Most of these explanations came off as half-hearted, however, and not until Norderling was effectively fired in 1826 did the privateering activities quiet down. Even then St. Barthélemy continued to be known as a place one where could rather easily acquire forged letters of marque from any number of nations.[23]

The entrepreneurial traders, sailors, and moneylenders of St. Thomas also participated in these privateering activities as, at various times,

---

[20] "Regulation of the Government of St. Barthélemy," April 29, 1826, RKA, SBS 2411/2/IX.

[21] Letter from Marquis de Marisalva to Count Löwenhjelm, July 8, 1820, RKA, LC 2414/13.

[22] Reports from Johan Norderling, June 3 and October 11, 1821, RKA, SBS 2411/2/VII B. It is worth noting that St. Eustatius was often brought up as a particularly notorious haven for Latin American privateers. In his memoir about life in the Danish West Indies, Johan Peter Nissen thus described how "those which sailed under the Columbian and Brazilian flags" made "these two islands [St. Eustatius and St. Maarten] and the other neighboring islands, their abode, where they brought the articles which they had plundered." Nissen, *Reminiscences of a 46 Years' Residence in the Island of St. Thomas, in the West Indies* (Nazareth, PA: Senseman and Co., 1838), 127.

[23] Details of such forgeries are described in a number of reports by the US consul on the island in 1829. RKA, LC, 2414/41.

perpetrators, backers, or victims.[24] Local officials, in contrast, found themselves in a political tight spot. Denmark's membership in the Holy Alliance and its general policy of support of absolutism against republican revolutionaries meant that the government preferred not to take sides in the Latin American struggles directly. Instead, they largely left the actual decisions to local governors. These officials then had to try to maintain good relations with their Spanish counterparts in the neighboring colony of Puerto Rico, which was an important regional actor, while also favoring the private commercial interests of St. Thomas, which profited substantially off the continued conflict. The solution for local authorities was to stay neutral for the most part, while purposefully ignoring most instances of direct local involvement with the independence movements.[25]

In the summer of 1828 a case began to unravel that could not so easily be ignored. In that year a sailor named Jean Jayet de Beaupré was arrested in the port of Charlotte Amalie, after having flaunted a spectacular collection of gold and silver jewelry and other seemingly ill-gotten goods. He eventually confessed to having been a crew member of the schooner *Las Damas Argentinas*, a privateering vessel operating in and around the region. Over the next few days, local colonial authorities rounded up and arrested a number of his former shipmates who were also lying low in Charlotte Amalie. This turned out to be a motley crew of men of mostly Irish, French, and creole origin.[26] While *Las Damas* had ostensibly been sailing under the flag of the Republic of Buenos Aires and carried a commission from that young polity, the ship had never actually been to the country, nor did its crew seem to have shown much discrimination in their choice of vessels to board during the Wars of Independence.

While contemplating what to do with their prisoners, the Danish magistrates received news that British authorities on St. Christopher were holding *Las Damas*, her captain, and the remainder of her crew, who had been arrested after similar indiscretions on Dutch St. Eustatius a few weeks earlier.[27] In the eyes of the British, the line between politically questionable privateering and outright piracy was crossed when, two

[24] For an example of St. Thomas merchants in the role of victims of privateering, see the case of Captain Lang discussed in Chapter 2.
[25] A few examples of criminal investigations into piracy by local inhabitants can be found in "Proceedings of criminal cases, 1823–1826," RA, WILA 13/6/3.
[26] "The case against Jean Jayet de Beaupre and others concerning piracy, 1828–1829," RA, WILA 2/42.
[27] *The Annual Register, or a View of the History, Politics, and Literature of the Year 1828* (London: T. S. Hansard, 1829), 355–59.

hundred miles off the Canary Islands, the privateers had boarded and plundered a British brig from Liverpool named the *Carraboo*. Despite warnings from some crew members that targeting British vessels was not a sound strategy, Captain Joseph Buysan could not resist the temptation of claiming the ship, which carried a cargo worth close to 28,000 pounds sterling. Despite the stipulations of his commission, Buysan had never restricted himself to Spanish ships but had allegedly boarded a number of neutral vessels in the past.

What complicated the case further, and illustrates the complex web of formal and informal networks across the region, were the accusations made in the Leeward Islands *St. Kitts Advertiser*. Articles in this newspaper argued strongly that *Las Damas*, while she might have sailed under the flag of Buenos Aires, was in actuality backed by influential money-men on St. Thomas, namely, the merchant house Cabot, Bailey, & Co. This group of traders had alleged ties to local Danish officials, including, according to some sources, then-Governor General Peter von Scholten.[28] The commentators in the *Advertiser* claimed that financial support of such shady and illicit activities was neither surprising nor uncommon in the Danish colony.

The foreman of the grand jury on St. Christopher, M. R. Burke, subsequently raised similar allegations against Dutch colonial authorities, claiming that "various acts of piracy" had been committed "not only with encouragement from private individuals in the islands of Saint Thomas and Saint Eustatius, but under the sanction of the Public Authorities on the latter island."[29] The same note mentioned the merchant house of Cabot on St. Thomas as a private entity involved in the affair, and one Mr. Shaw, a partner in the house, was apparently even on board *Las Damas* at one point. Officials further alleged that Governor Willem Albert van Spengler of Dutch Saba received a bribe for letting piratical goods from the vessel be transshipped via his harbor and giving the vessel a Dutch register. Parenthetically, the governor's price seems to have been "500 dollars and some coffee and sugar" – a detail reinforcing van Spengler's reputation for being both corrupt and cheap to buy off. For the privateer's second cruise, Cabot paid between 1,200 and 1,500 dollars to finance the crew, but since St. Thomas authorities did not allow crews to openly board privateering vessels in their harbor, the crew was hidden on a smaller sloop that followed *Las Damas* out of the port. On this second cruise the vessel allegedly raided five Portuguese vessels, one

---

[28] Undated newspaper cutouts from the *St. Kitts Advertiser* located in RA, WILA 2/42.
[29] "Reports on the Piracy of the Carraboo," August–September 1828, TNA, CO 239/18, 7–20.

Spanish brig, an English schooner, and a French brig. Finally, the *Carra-boo* was taken, an act that ultimately proved the downfall of the pirates.[30]

While a court of law never tested the validity of the accusations made against the colonial authorities on St. Thomas, the allegations illustrate the way in which such issues were caught up in local politics. Sensational news stories and criminal cases quickly became new fodder for long-standing inter-island rivalries, such as those between the British Leewards and the neutral islands of the Dutch and Danish empires.

The merchant house of Cabot, Bailey, & Co. was a striking example of the expansiveness of illicit commercial networks within the micro-region, the dark underbelly of the intercolonial trade networks described in Chapter 2. Not only had the company sponsored other privateering vessels sailing under various Latin American flags; it also had an extensive history of involvement in the illegal slave trade to Cuba and Puerto Rico. The owners claimed both English and Danish sub-jecthood, depending on the needs of the situation, and they financed smuggling vessels sailing under Dutch, French, and Danish colors. While any personal connections to von Scholten are unproven, the merchants no doubt had some links to local magistrates on both the Danish and British Virgin Islands, and they were under investigation by imperial authorities on more than one occasion, but had thus far man-aged to stay in operation.[31]

The web of connections was not confined to the microregion. While Cabot, Bailey, & Co. was involved in the financing of the ship, the original owner was one John D. Quincy of Baltimore. In the United States, Quincy had bought and outfitted the schooner, at that time called *Bolivar*, acquiring the commission of privateering in the process, and had then sent the ship to the West Indies. Here the *Bolivar* arrived at St. Thomas, where the captain sought out willing financiers who could provide arms and a crew with the proper experience. This seems to be the point at which contact was made with Cabot and Bailey, drawing on their wide network of contacts within the Caribbean underworld. The original commission was passed on twice, first to one Mr. Stiles and then to Captain Buysan.[32] St. Thomas, together with St. Eustatius, also proved

---

[30] Ibid.

[31] On their involvement in the illegal slave trade to Cuba by the Dutch schooner *Zee Bloem*, see "Mr. Secretary George Canning to the Right Hon. Frederick Lamb, Foreign Office, April 4, 1825, Including 15 Enclosures," in *British and Foreign State Papers*, vol. 12 (London: HMSO, 1846), 242–51.

[32] *The Annual Register, 1828*, 358; "The United States v. John D. Quincy," in *Report of Cases Argued and Adjudged in the Supreme Court of the United States, January Term 1832* (Philadelphia: D. B. Canfield & Co., 1853), 445–69.

to be convenient ports in which to offload the cargoes and valuables acquired in the course of privateering.

While most of the men arrested and accused of piracy on St. Eustatius and St. Thomas were sentenced and hanged in the winter of 1828 and 1829, the financial backers of the enterprise fared better.[33] The owners of Cabot, Bailey, & Co. had left the island in the midst of the affair's unraveling and were now nowhere to be found. Their history of illicit activities and their prior run-ins with British imperial magistrates indicate that they might have fled for greener, and safer, pastures. Their partners in Baltimore were less adept at avoiding the consequences of their questionable entrepreneurship. US authorities arrested Quincy, accusing him of illegally arming and outfitting a vessel to participate in piratical activities. Since the schooner had specifically targeted at least one Brazilian ship, an ally of the United States at the time, this act was deemed a serious criminal offense. The legal ambiguity of the terms "arming and fitting out" made the case go all the way to the Supreme Court, which in 1834 ruled in favor of the state.[34] As for the schooner itself, its history continued, as the Royal Navy confiscated it, renamed it *Kangaroo*, and used it in the Caribbean for the next several years.[35] A similar fate awaited the three youngest members of the ship's crew, who were pardoned and made to serve in the navy for a period of ten years.[36]

Opportunistic privateering during the initial decades of Latin American independence was firmly anchored within regional networks. Not only were crews transnational in composition, but the entire process of securing letters of marque, financing cruises, outfitting privateering vessels, and ultimately offloading prizes took place within a context of trans-imperial connections and underground markets.

The case of the *Carraboo* and *Las Damas Argentinas* coincided with the end of an era for privateering in the Leewards, and indeed in the wider Caribbean. While there were later cases of piracy in the region, none captured the imagination and attention of contemporaries quite so much,

[33] Letter from Governor Maxwell to President Rawlins, March 26, 1829, TNA, CO 239/20, 7. De Beaupré and his accomplishes arrested on St. Thomas were hanged on February 6, 1829. Records contained in "Court Cases, 1806–1907," in the Caribbean Collection: Virgin Islands Documents, the Florence Williams Library, Christiansted, St. Croix.
[34] "The United States v. John D. Quincy," 465–69.
[35] J. J. Colledge and Ben Warlow, *Ships of the Royal Navy: A Complete Record of All Fighting Ships of the Royal Navy from the 15th Century to the Present* (Havertown: Casemate, 2010), 211. Such a fate was common for both smuggling and pirate vessels seized by the Royal Navy in this period, greatly increasing the number of fast and maneuverable vessels in British hands.
[36] *The Annual Register, 1828*, 359.

and in a way that so distinctly cast the deed as a case of sea robbery, rather than an at least quasi-legitimate act of privateering.[37] Following the trial of Buysan and his crew, privateering all but disappeared from the wider Atlantic region. This trend, combined with the French conquest of Algiers in 1830, which effectively put an end to privateering off the Barbary Coast, signaled a significant decline in the scale of privateering activities, two and a half decades before the signing of the Paris Declaration Respecting Maritime Law, which formally abolished the practice.[38]

Jurisdictional Politics and the Power of the Prize Courts

The prize courts of the Caribbean were integral to the practice of privateering and served as the primary arenas for many of the legal and political struggles surrounding this activity. Prize courts also played an important role in the implementation of the abolition of the slave trade. The seizure of slave trading vessels and confiscation of slaves had to go through local courts, which would then decide and in many cases administer the future of the confiscated property as well as of the human cargo. In both these areas, then, prize courts became the arbiters of disputes and the guarantors of the legality of seizures of property, placing in the hands of the marshals, judges, and magistrates of these courts the power to direct and legitimize the flow of significant fortunes.

In the British Empire, prize cases in the colonies fell under the jurisdiction of the vice admiralty courts, which also handled other maritime disputes as well as infringements of the Navigation Acts. The system of overseas vice admiralties developed alongside British incursions into the Atlantic, with the first court established in Newfoundland in 1583.[39] The early origins of the West Indian prize courts are somewhat

---

[37] Contemporary English-language printed accounts all describe the case in these terms. Besides the sources already quoted, see also John Malzac, *Piracy: Details of the Case of the Brig Carraboo of Liverpool, Together with an Account of the Capture of the Pirate-Vessel, the Schooner Las Damas Argentinas* (St. Christopher: J. A. Howe, 1828). This book was printed in multiple editions, examples of which are held in the New-York Historical Society's Patricia D. Klingenberg Library.

[38] For the full text of this declaration, see Thomas Gibson Bowles, *The Declaration of Paris of 1856* (London: Sampson Low, Marston and Co., 1900). The break with the practice of privateering was, of course, not as clean-cut as that. Multiple countries did not sign the declaration, and both the Confederate States of America, during the US Civil War, and Bolivia, during the War of the Pacific, continued issuing letters of marque. See also Jan Martin Lemnitzer, "The 1856 Declaration of Paris and the Abolition of Privateering: An International History," PhD thesis (London School of Economics and Political Science, 2010).

[39] Helen Josephine Crump, *Colonial Admiralty Jurisdiction in the Seventeenth Century* (London: Longmans, 1931).

murky, but they seem to have proliferated across the Atlantic empires in the second half of the seventeenth century. The first court in the British Leewards was established in 1677, when those islands were jurisdictionally separated from Barbados.[40] The system of prize courts became more ordered over the course of the early eighteenth century, although the practices of colonial prize courts remained highly tied to local concerns. Thus the Atlantic and Indian Oceans became increasingly distinct legal zones in the imagination of colonial agents as well as regional actors, leading to a specifically West Indian system of colonial vice admiralty courts, different in theory and practice from the company-operated courts of the East Indies.[41] Besides the permanent courts established in most British Atlantic colonies, temporary courts were set up in occupied territories during wartime, such as those of Martinique, St. Lucia, and Guadeloupe, operating at various times during the Revolutionary and Napoleonic Wars.[42]

Prize courts were not unique to Britain, and most other Atlantic empires established similar institutions in their own colonies. The French system of *agences de prises* mentioned above was a particularly expansive example of such an institution, placing representatives in neutral territories to act as extensions or satellites of the colonial French prize courts in Guadeloupe and Martinique.[43] Several neutral islands also had their own prize courts, as did the newly independent South American nations, to whom privateering was of particular importance. Many of the smaller empires did not rely on dedicated judges, but instead placed control of the prize adjudication directly under either the governor or the local military commander. This practice created its own set of problems of authority and potential conflicts of interest – problems that were somewhat different from the challenges posed by

[40] Michael John Craton, "The Caribbean Vice Admiralty Courts, 1763–1815; Indispensable Agents of an Imperial System," PhD dissertation (McMaster University, 1968), 23; A. P. Thornton, *West India Policy under the Restoration* (Oxford: Clarendon Press, 1956).
[41] Lauren Benton, *A Search for Sovereignty: Law and Geography in European Empires, 1400–1900* (New York: Cambridge University Press, 2010), 146–48.
[42] Craton, "The Caribbean Vice Admiralty Courts," 42–44. See also Craton, *Empire, Enslavement and Freedom in the Caribbean* (Kingston: Ian Randle, 1997), 104–16.
[43] Within the Leeward Islands there were agents from the court in Guadeloupe not only on St. Barthélemy but also, at various times, on St. Eustatius and Puerto Rico, as well as attempts at placing a representative on St. Thomas. When Guadeloupe was outside French control, either due to internal uprisings or British occupation, these *agences de prises* were directed either from Martinique or from Cuba. "Décret de Napoléon nommant un agent général à La Havane, avec un adjoint à Santiago de Cuba, à Porto Rico, à Caracas, à Saint-Thomas, à Saint-Barthélemy et à Curaçao," 1804, ANOM, Secrétariat d'État à la Marine COL C8B, 25, f. 80.

the British use of local magistrates, who were not always the most qualified arbiters of justice from a strictly legal standpoint.

The British vice admiralty courts were of central importance not just to issues of prizes and privateering but also to smuggling and maritime commerce in general. They served a key function in the implementation of trade policy, and their interpretation of commercial law could make or break the business of local traders as well as transient merchant mariners. Such power in the hands of the magistrates of the court brought with it significant opportunities for personal enrichment and politicking, and corruption was a perpetual problem in the administration of these courts, not least on the smaller Caribbean islands. While cases could be, and indeed often were, appealed to the High Court of Admiralty in England, the bureaucratic and physical logistics of this process were such that it could take months or even years before a local ruling was overturned, making the immediacy of rulings at the colonial level hugely important.

Other logistical and geographical issues played key roles in shaping the practices associated with prize courts in the microregion. In particular, the close proximity between courts, as illustrated in Figure 4.1, meant that individuals bringing prizes to the courts often had some choice in where to take their cases. This was particularly important due to the commonly perceived variety of legal standards followed at different courts, with some, including the British court at Tortola, being known as especially lax in their interpretation the letter of the law. There were frequent discrepancies between the way the law was interpreted in temporary wartime courts and in more permanent courts of vice admiralty in the British Empire, and the same was true between permanent courts, or *tribunals*, and more temporary *agences de prises* in the French Empire. While the British wartime courts were typically operated by naval officers, who at times had a better understanding of prize law than did the often untrained civilian magistrates of smaller local courts, the French *agences de prises* were run by imperial agents who functioned as much as informal ambassadors of the newly republican empire as they did judicial officials.[44] The fact that several islands in the region, including Guadeloupe, were hosts to the prize courts of different empires at various times at the turn of the century further complicated the image, with locals becoming implicated in a variety of legal regimes during times of military occupation. Such transitions were perhaps less severe than one might

---

[44] In St. Barthélemy the role of political representative was at one point handled by the local prize agent, who replaced the consul. "Suppression de la place de délégué des agents des consuls à Saint-Barthélemy, son remplacement par un commissaire aux prises," March 8, 1800, ANOM, Secrétariat d'État à la Marine C7A52, f. 79.

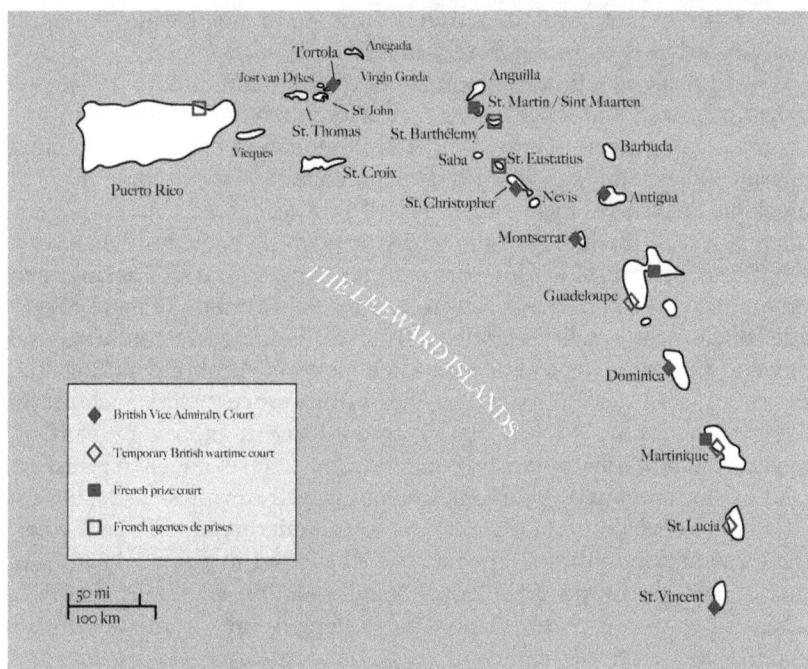

Figure 4.1 Prize courts in the Leewards and neighboring islands during the Revolutionary and Napoleonic Wars.

think, however, as many local actors in the microregion were already at least partially conversant in the maritime laws of multiple empires, so as to better protect their own property or potentially claim that of others. Regardless of who operated it, the presence of a prize court, whether temporary or more permanent, was often a boon to the local port economies, as the surge in maritime traffic led to a general increase in commercial activity, especially when visiting privateers had newly earned prize money to spend.

The proliferation of prize courts at the end of the eighteenth century led not just to decreased control from the metropole but also to a dearth of qualified men who could staff them. Most courts sat under judges who had little to no legal training and were chosen among the local white populations, often for personal or local political reasons rather than on the basis of any qualifications.[45] The 1790s were particularly untamed,

---

[45] Elsa V. Goveia, *Slave Society in the British Leeward Islands at the End of the Eighteenth Century* (New Haven: Yale University Press, 1965), 61–62.

as the bar for condemnation of ships and vessels had apparently been set extraordinarily low in many colonial courts, leading to a spate of seizures and growing frustration on the part of neutral and allied polities alike, including the United States. In 1806, Sir William Scott wrote of the practice of the courts during the French Revolutionary Wars: "It is a matter of publick notoriety, that during the last war the Prize Courts in the West Indies were, with very few Exceptions, administered in such a manner as to provoke great complaints from various foreign governments in Alliance with His Majesty." Scott singled out the courts of the British Leewards as especially irregular, and the one on Tortola in particular.[46]

Among the troublesome vice admiralty courts in the British Leewards, which also included those of Anguilla, Antigua, Montserrat, Nevis, and St. Christopher, the court on Tortola was notorious indeed. As early as 1781 the Tortola court was temporarily suspended, following widespread complaints over the conduct and abuse of power of its judges.[47] The prize court was back in operation in the 1790s, only to once again be suspended at the end of the decade because of more irregularities. Its closure led to several petitions to the Privy Council from local magistrates pleading for its reopening – requests that were eventually met in 1804 following the reforms of the prize system, but this time with a new judge appointed directly by London.[48]

Very few procedural documents from the Tortola court have been preserved for posterity, and historians have thus been able to say relatively little about the role of the island in the wider legal network of the British Atlantic.[49] Of those documents that do exist, a surprising number are located in the Danish National Archives. These records provide insights into the peculiar relationship between the British and the Danish Virgin Islands, and illustrate one of the ways in which microregional ties were used to circumvent imperial policies and regulations.

While relations between the St. Thomas merchant community and the Tortola prize court were fraught at the court's inception in the 1770s, leading to a large number of official and unofficial complaints, two decades later the two seemed to have formed a more mutually

---

[46] Quoted in Craton, "The Caribbean Vice Admiralty Courts," 302.
[47] George Germain to Thomas Shirley, September 1, 1781, TNA, CO 152/61.
[48] "Notes relative to resuming the prize jurisdiction of the court of Vice Admiralty on Tortola," December 15, 1803, TNA, PC 1/3605B; "Letter from His Majesty's Advocate General, respecting the establishment of a Prize Court at Tortola," January 4, 1804, TNA, PC 1/3587A.
[49] Those few documents that do exist in the British National Archives are kept in TNA, HCA 30/796, HCA 49/101, and HCA 49/106.

beneficial relationship.[50] A number of vessels sailing through the Danish West Indies from 1793 to 1798 were seized and taken to Tortola, where their captains or owners appeared before the local judge, who would either acquit them or condemn their vessels for carrying goods between the ports of belligerent powers. After condemnation, many of these vessels then seem to have been sold back, either to their original owners or to a middleman of some sort, registering them in the process in the neutral port of Charlotte Amalie.[51] Several such vessels were later caught by British privateers or the Royal Navy and by them brought to the larger prize court on Jamaica, only to present their notes of acquittal or decrees of condemnation and accompanying bills of sale in an attempt to avoid seizures.[52]

The fact that so many of these vessels were not subsequently acquitted in Jamaica, but rather condemned there for blockade running, indicates the illicitness of the activity in the Virgin Islands. The relationship between St. Thomas and Tortola and the practice of using the two islands as clearing houses for otherwise illegal transshipments during the Revolutionary Wars were seemingly common knowledge among merchant mariners operating in the microregion. In a 1798 letter to a business partner, merchant and ship-owner Jesse Pritchett of Philadelphia stated: "I have been out and carried into Tortola ... where Vessell and Cargo had been acquitted and now can ensue the Voyage Freely. I have become a Danish Burger and am Respected in that Capacity what I venture I get Insured here. If I make out to return Safe the Voyage will be very productive to me."[53] Despite such hopes, his vessel was captured by a British naval ship later that year and condemned as French property in 1799.[54]

The practices of the 1790s and the growing autonomy of the Caribbean prize courts led to calls for reforms in London and the eventual passing of a new Prize Court Act in July 1801.[55] This new act restricted

---

[50] A number of complaints from Danish and Norwegian subjects, including over the cases of the vessels *Elizabeth Christina*, *The Dorothia*, and *The Delight*, all from 1777, are contained in "Tortola Privateering, 1777–1788," RA, DFA 1290.

[51] These records are located in RA, DFA 1291 and 1292.

[52] Statistics and summaries of the records of the Jamaican court of vice admiralty, including the preponderance of cases previously cleared in Tortola, are presented in Craton, "The Caribbean Vice Admiralty Courts," 292–98.

[53] Quoted in ibid., 293.

[54] Pritchett and his partner Isaac Starr were unfortunate men indeed. Only two years earlier a French privateer had captured their vessel, at that time named *Abby*, for sailing to British-occupied Martinique with food and provisions. This gave them the dubious accomplishment of being condemned in both French and British prize courts over the span of a few years. For the French seizure, see Greg H. Williams, *The French Assault on American Shipping, 1793–1813* (Jefferson, NC: McFarland, 2009), 43.

[55] "Prize Act," 41 Geo. III, c. 96.

the powers of colonial vice admiralty courts somewhat, granting the privileges of prize commissions and the ability to write letters of marque to only a few of them; it also changed the salary structure of the magistrates of the court, increasing the salaries and pensions of judges but placing an upper limit on the fees they could claim for themselves from adjudicating seizures and condemnations; finally, it limited the other engagements a judge could have, decreeing that no judge could also be a prize agent, own any shares in privateering enterprises, or in any way be "concerned in the Care, Management, or Superintendance of any Estates in any Island of the West Indies or the Continent of America."[56] While these new regulations did not succeed in reining in all the irregular activities of local courts, they did seem to have some effect in increasing centralized imperial control of their general practices. The larger courts on Jamaica and Halifax, and later Barbados, were now to be the primary arbiters in cases regarding outright piracy or in cases that could not be handled on a local level; appeals to the High Court of Admiralty were handled somewhat more expediently; and all local courts generally adhered to a docket of fees and regulations sent out from London.[57] While only the vice admiralty courts on Jamaica and Halifax were initially granted the privileges of adjudicating prize cases, these courts proliferated quickly at the outbreak of the Napoleonic Wars, leading to prize courts returning to Antigua, Bermuda, Bahamas, Barbados, and Tortola.

At the end of the Napoleonic Wars, Antigua and Tortola were the only vice admiralty courts in the British Leewards left with prize commissions. This led to a political skirmish over jurisdiction between authorities on Tortola and St. Christopher, the latter arguing vehemently to London that all parties would be better served if the prize court currently residing in the Virgin Islands be transferred to St. Christopher on a permanent basis.[58] The Secretary of State for War and the Colonies, Earl Bathurst, granted this request, and agreed that "steps may be taken on a renewal of hostilities, for having the prize commission transferred from the vice admiralty court at the island of Tortola, to the vice admiralty court at St. Christopher."[59] For colonial magistrates the prize courts remained

---

[56] Quoted in Craton, "The Caribbean Vice Admiralty Courts," 309.

[57] When commissioners from England visited Tortola in 1823, the court was still using the docket of fees sent to them by London a decade earlier. TNA, CO 318/65, f. 84.

[58] Governor Maxwell to the Lords of the Admiralty, December 10, 1823, TNA, CO 239/9 93.

[59] The Admiralty Office to Governor Maxwell, February 12, 1824, TNA, CO 239/11. Although no hostilities broke out between imperial powers in the region immediately following this decision, the Tortola prize court seems to have processed its last case, the seizure of an illegally transported slave, in July of 1825. TNA, HCA/796 f. 34.

important sources of power well into the 1820s, and in the imagination of authorities in London Tortola remained a place of dubious passions and questionable interests – not a colony one wished to rely on in times of crisis. This impression was cemented by the court's activities related to the abolition of the slave trade and the subsequent auctions of prize slaves from seized slave trading vessels, a topic that I return to in some detail in Chapter 6.

Conclusion

While privateering had been a part of colonial Caribbean societies since the late sixteenth century, the period from the 1790s to the 1820s witnessed a remarkable resurgence of the practice. The changing political dynamics of the region, namely, the emergence of new polities and the plurality of imperial actors, combined with the increased focus on tightening imperial jurisdiction and control, led to a particularly complex situation surrounding privateering. The shift in practices was particularly noticeable between the last decade of the eighteenth century, with clashes between American, British, and French privateers, and the years following the end of the Napoleonic Wars, which saw a new wave of privateering and piracy caused by the internal conflicts within the Iberian empires. Whereas privateering in the earlier period was fairly consistent with previous practice and driven by large imperial powers and their regional proxies, a messier and more challenging set of political dynamics characterized the later period. Political recognition had always been an important component of privateering, but as letters of marque signed by Bolívar and Artigas became increasingly common across the Caribbean, the legal distinction between privateering and piracy gained ever more serious implications for regional politics and claims to sovereignty. Profit-seeking captains and financiers, on the one hand, and Latin American politicians, on the other, used each other strategically in a high-stakes game of maritime predation, which, as the case of *Las Damas Argentinas* shows, lasted only for as long as both written and unwritten rules were followed, and as long as other regional players deemed it prudent. At the end of the 1820s privateering in the Caribbean was already becoming more of a sensationalist fiction than an accepted practice, as the last remaining privateers were branded as pirates, as much a result of their own actions as of a changing attitude in their would-be judges.

Within the Leeward Islands persistent political turmoil alongside relatively durable social and economic networks led local entrepreneurs to profit handsomely from the continued inter-imperial struggles at the turn of the century, and the situation spurred on cooperation as well as competition between the different colonies of the microregion. Competing centers of jurisdictional authority in disputes over prizes became exceedingly important for the inter-imperial rivalries of the region and for the relationship between different colonies within the British Empire. The location of courts had deep economic and political consequences, and depending on time and place, these could be either positive or negative for local actors and networks. While the internal struggle for prize courts in the British Leeward Islands was a matter of both financial opportunity and political prestige, the placement of a French *agence de prises* on St. Barthélemy brought with it as many political challenges for local administrators as it did economic opportunities for merchants and sailors.

The Leeward Islands played an important role in Latin American privateering as well, as neutral ports such as Gustavia and Charlotte Amalie proved useful havens for entrepreneurial captains cruising for Artigas or Bolivar, at least for a time. While the flags and seals were new, there were important continuities between the maritime predation of this period and the activities of previous decades. Locally anchored trans-imperial networks saw the newfound interest in privateering as another opportunity to make profit, and many of the people involved drew on their experience shipping smuggled goods or enslaved Africans. Local and global concerns came together, altering both the geopolitical struggles and the local politicking as a consequence.

5   Slave Laws and Free Communities

There can be little doubt that slavery was the central institution in the colonial Caribbean, seeping into all aspects of social, economic, and political life within the region. In the Leeward Islands, the specifics of slavery looked different depending on the island and economic system in question. The slave societies found here spanned the gamut from full-blown plantation complexes, such as those of cotton- and sugar-producing St. Croix and Dominica, to the significantly less cultivated and more urban entrepôts of St. Thomas, St. Eustatius, and St. Barthélemy. In between these two extremes were a number of islands with agricultural production that in one way or another diverged from the standard models of plantation-based slave societies, including those of smaller islands such as St. John and Jost Van Dyke where enslaved individuals engaged in economic practices with a considerable degree of autonomy. Despite the variations among individual colonies, the fundamental underlying structure and tenets of Caribbean slave society were common to all of the Leewards.

In many ways, the Leeward Islands functioned as one integrated slave system. Scholars of the transatlantic slave trade have pointed out that the entire Atlantic region became entangled in a transoceanic plantation complex built on slave labor; on the microregional scale the integration between slave societies was even more apparent.[1] Even though not all islands were equally involved in the direct process of agricultural production that drew on the majority of slave labor, the smaller urbanized islands played roles closely related to these plantation practices. Flourishing slave markets developed on islands that were not themselves the primary recipients of enslaved Africans, but rather served as convenient ports for the transshipment of captives. Entrepôts such as Charlotte Amalie on St. Thomas primarily drew intercolonial and inter-imperial trade because of their convenient location amid the larger islands of other

---

[1] Philip D. Curtin, *The Rise and Fall of the Plantation Complex: Essays in Atlantic History* (2nd edition) (Cambridge: Cambridge University Press, 1998), 129–43; David Eltis, *The Rise of African Slavery in the Americas* (Cambridge: Cambridge University Press, 2000).

empires. As described in previous chapters, the threats to colonial order posed by enslaved Africans and Afro-Caribbeans were a key factor in increased intercolonial integration within the microregion, but so were other institutions and practices of slavery. Such institutions included legal codes associated with slavery, which, if not outright copied from one colony to another, were at least easily translatable between empires; the production processes associated with plantation economies themselves, which were closely mirrored between islands; and, crucially, the social bonds formed between the black communities of different colonies, despite the best attempts of white elites to prevent such inter-island networks.

Some of the fiercest struggles between colonial autonomy and imperial authority in the Leeward Islands were waged in the arena of slave law. As imperial administrators at the metropolitan level attempted to tighten their jurisdictional control and rein in the actions of colonial magistrates, local actors pushed back and strained to assert their autonomy, not least when it came to the governance of plantations and the treatment of slaves. The topic of slave conditions became increasingly contentious as abolitionist sentiment grew at home and a number of high-profile cases of murder and mistreatment of slaves caused outrage and controversy in European capitals as well as within the colonies themselves. This story has often been told as a British one, linked either to shifts in the balance of power within the British Empire or to changing moral sentiments in British public and political life, but the struggle over slavery between colonies and metropoles was in fact one shared across colonial powers in the Caribbean.

Meanwhile, as one group of white elites clashed with another, the subjects over whom their legal and political duels were allegedly fought – the region's African and Afro-Caribbean population – increasingly came to utilize the letter of the law to their own advantage within the colonial and imperial systems. Free people of color waged their own fights over political and economic rights, including rights of inheritance and landownership, and enslaved individuals stood up against their white masters at court, either directly or through legal proxies. Thus, the jurisdictional and political disputes at the heart of turn-of-the-century slave law in the colonial Caribbean were not just clashes between metropolitan and local interests. They were indicative of a layered and complex network of groups and actors, sometimes working with each other in the pursuit of different goals and sometimes opposed to one another on contested issues.

While many slaves and free people of color were working to change their conditions within the structures of colonial law, others existed outside this system entirely, at least for a time. These were the maroon societies found throughout the Caribbean, on small and otherwise sparsely populated islands such as Jost Van Dyke or in the inhospitable mountains and forests of larger islands. Escaped slaves formed these small societies, which also included runaway convicts and African survivors from some of the many wrecked slave ships washed ashore in the region – an increasingly common phenomenon in the years after the 1807 British slave trade abolition. Maroons were not the only founders of free black communities. In the first half of the nineteenth century, imperial authorities established a number of small villages and townships specifically for previously enslaved Africans freed as a consequence of abolition. Such officially sanctioned free towns proved controversial within colonial society, and they often faced nearly as many challenges as the maroon communities that they sometimes resembled.

The legal and social dimensions of slavery outlined above, when viewed through a microregional lens, look quite different from when they are seen through other historical perspectives. The connections between colonies were paramount to the way in which slave codes were drawn up in the territories of smaller empires, without their own long histories of legislating unfreedom to draw on. The close proximity of different, often rival, jurisdictions had important implications for enslaved and slave owner alike, and it led to a number of clashes between magistrates accusing each other of using legal loopholes to enrich their own colonies. This proximity of islands to one another also led to increased integration between communities of color at the transimperial level. Pathways to freedom emerged that were not as readily available in other parts of the Caribbean, and the density of networks caused information to move swiftly across the polyglot colonies of the Leeward Islands. As in every other case where the supremacy of slave-owning whites seemed threatened, such subversions of the slave system – and in particular the practice of maritime marronage – led to intercolonial countermeasures, as local elites scrambled to protect their social and economic order.

Legal Codes and Intercolonial Imitation

In the area of slave law, the intercolonial integration of the Leeward Islands took place through the imitation of legal codes and the adoption of perceived best practices across imperial borders. In this sense the French and British approaches to policing their Afro-Caribbean slave populations and free subjects became a sort of legal template for the colonies of smaller empires, even as these approaches themselves faced serious internal and external challenges and ruptures around the turn of the century.[2] Legal practices were not just disseminated from large to small powers, but also circulated between the colonies of smaller imperial players, as Swedish magistrates looked to their Danish neighbors in order to fashion an adequate legal system through which to govern their new colony.

When St. Barthélemy was initially handed over to the Swedish Empire in 1784, Stockholm proclaimed that the civil law of Sweden would be fully applicable in the new colonial territory.[3] This was hardly congruent with a Caribbean slave society, however, and it became obvious to local magistrates that a comprehensive set of laws governing slaves and the growing population of free people of color was needed in order to govern the island.[4] Thus in 1787 Governor Pehr Herman Rosenstein introduced a specific slave code for St. Barthélemy that was by and large an adaptation of the preexisting French Code Noir.[5] This ordinance would be the primary judicial framework for the treatment and governance of African and Afro-Caribbean subjects on St. Barthélemy for the next several decades, but it proved hard to convey its relevance to local planters and slave owners who preferred a more ad hoc and autonomous approach to the policing of their slaves. The ordinance was reprinted several times in the following years, including in the 1804 *Report of St. Bartholomew*, with the following remarks: "As the following Ordinance is of a very old Date, but Still a Standing Law of the Island, We think it usefull, if not necessary, to make the same a little better known, than daily experience proves it to be."[6] The very next year the ordinance appeared in the *Report* once again, this time with a slightly different introduction: "We have inserted this Ordinance long before divided on two different numbers; as we think it of more importance to the Country than the inhabitants seem

---

[2] For a comparative analysis of British and French slave law in the region, see Elsa V. Goveia, *The West Indian Slave Laws of the Eighteenth Century* (Mona: Caribbean Universities Press, 1970).

[3] Slave law was not the only area in which St. Barthélemy relied on the best practice of other empires. The governing council set up in the colony in 1785 and reimplemented in 1811 was itself borrowed from the model used in nearby St. Eustatius. See Wilson, *Commerce in Disguise*, 81–82; Hildebrand, *Den Svenska Kolonin* S:t Barthélemy, 110–20.

[4] Fredrik Thomasson, "Thirty-Two Lashes at Quatre Piquets: Slave Laws and Justice in the Swedish Colony of St. Barthélemy ca. 1800," in *Ports of Globalisation, Places of Creolisation: Nordic Possessions in the Atlantic World during the Era of the Slave Trade*, ed. Holder Weiss (Leiden: Brill, 2016), 280–85.

[5] "Ordinance concerning the Police of Slaves and free Coloured People," July 30, 1787, transcribed in RKA, LC 2424/22. For one of the best historical treatments of the Code Noir, see Malick W. Ghachem, *The Old Regime and the Haitian Revolution* (New York: Cambridge University Press, 2012).

[6] *The Report of St. Bartholomew*, April 30, 1804, National Library of Sweden.

to believe, We have thought proper to give it a new and full length in one Number to facilitate reading of same."[7]

In the first decades of the nineteenth century, the Swedish ordinance was supplemented by a number of royal decrees, leading to a fairly complicated set of laws regarding the treatment and rights of slaves in the colony. Moreover, the slow lines of communication between Stockholm and St. Barthélemy combined with the recurring theme of Swedish disinterest in the daily governing of the colony resulted in local magistrates being given extensive freedom in their interpretation of the law. Thus, the Swedish colony was saddled not only with a complex set of rules governing the lives of slaves and free people of color but also with a certain level of unpredictability in the daily administration of these rules. As everywhere else in the Caribbean, St. Barthélemy had a paucity of legally trained subjects to place on juries and tribunals, and the large number of French merchants and planters serving as jurors and magistrates functioned to further enshrine the continued importance of the Code Noir in daily practice. Local Swedish administrators looked to their neighboring Dutch and Danish colonies for inspiration of how to successfully police a slave society, despite the fact that these colonies themselves were ruled by rather piecemeal legal codes.[8] The Danish West Indies proved particularly interesting to Swedish administrators. In 1802 colonial authorities compiled a list of sixty-seven questions regarding the governance of their Danish neighbors, many of which dealt with the specifics of slave law.[9] Among the key concerns behind this inquiry was how to effectively administer a slave colony and, in particular, how to categorize the legal status of the free and enslaved black population, something that proved a lasting challenge for Swedish magistrates.

The legal situation on the Danish islands was somewhat different from that of the Swedish colony, however, as Danish administrators had not inherited a preexisting set of colonial legal codes, having held most of the territory since the seventeenth century. Instead, they came to rely on a ragtag system of disparate and sometimes contradictory laws that imitated many of the practices of other empires in the region, while adding their own peculiar characteristics. The first fifty years of Danish rule took place with no formally written slave law on the islands. In the wake of the

---

[7] *The Report of St. Bartholomew*, July 20, 1805, National Library of Sweden.
[8] Fredrik Thomasson, "'Contre la Loi mas en considérant les Circonstances dangereuses du moment.' Le tribunal suédois de l'île de Saint-Barthélemy pendant la période révolutionnaire," in *Les colonies, la Révolution française, la loi*, ed. Frédéric Régent, Jean-François Niort, and Pierre Serna (Rennes: Presses Universitaires de Rennes, 2014), 231–49.
[9] Thomasson, "Thirty-Two Lashes at Quatre Piquets," 287–88.

1733 slave rebellion on St. John, a leading Danish magistrate proposed that a set of laws concerning slaves be codified, following the examples of neighboring colonies: "Could the Negro codes of the French, English, and Dutch islands, be collected by a competent man, and then worked over not only by the burgher councils on St. Croix and St. Thomas, but also by the wisest of the planters, it would be possible in my opinion to produce in that way a permanent law."[10] Even by the mid-eighteenth century, such laws had yet to be institutionalized in the Danish territories, and the process of codification took several more years. Indeed, the sort of comprehensive slave code envisioned in 1733 never fully materialized, but it is telling that the solution perceived by colonial magistrates was to adopt the best practices of other empires. This suggestion shows the ways in which foreign colonies were often seen as the most obvious place to look for inspiration in designing the local legal framework of governance, since magistrates and white settlers could not rely on Copenhagen to provide such institutions.

In principle, the civil law of Denmark, Danske Lov, was applicable to all Danish territories, including the Caribbean colonies, but these laws were superseded by both local regulations and royal decrees specific to the colonies, of which there were many.[11] Thus, rather than operate within a system of specific Danish imperial law, the Caribbean colonies had cobbled together over time a set of laws and practices that combined Danish civil law, metropolitan decrees, ad hoc additions by local magistrates, and the perceived best practices of other imperial actors within the region in a matrix of laws and customs that were nearly impenetrable for subjects and outsiders alike, especially since many of the local additions were never made widely available in print.

The relationship between Danish metropolitan and colonial law was especially important when it came to slavery, since the very core of the Caribbean colonial system relied on not granting enslaved persons the same set of privileges as other subjects of the crown.[12] In this sense, slaves were first and foremost subordinate to their masters, and the question of how to govern them was an issue of the owner's prerogative to establish his own rules and mete out his own punishment vis-à-vis the

[10] Translated and printed in Westergaard, "Account of the Negro Rebellion on St. Croix," 58.
[11] See Poul Erik Olsen, "Danske Lov på de vestindiske øer," in *Danske og norske lov i 300 år*, ed. Ditlev Tamm (Copenhagen: Djøf Forlag, 1983), 301–2.
[12] See Gunvor Simonsen, "Skin Colour as a Tool of Regulation and Power in the Danish West Indies in the Eighteenth Century," *Journal of Caribbean History* 37:2 (2003): 256–76; Simonsen, "Magic, Obeah and Law in the Danish West Indies, 1750s–1840s," in *Ports of Globalisation, Places of Creolisation*, ed. Weiss, 245–79.

guidelines set out in royal decrees and colonial regulations, much as was the case in the British, French, and Swedish colonial territories.[13] For the vast majority of the period of colonial rule, the question of slaves' *rights*, in the modern sense of the word, was essentially a nonissue.[14] Rather, the issues at stake in legal and reformist debates were concerns over the proper treatment of slaves in a paternalistic and humanitarian sense, rather than in a rights-based sense. African and Afro-Caribbean enslaved people were seen as property, as labor, and, increasingly, as risks, but never as full subjects. In the eyes of colonial as well as imperial law, rights were something belonging to slaveholders – not to slaves.

Amelioration and the Planters' Prerogative

While magistrates in the British colonies had been given considerable leeway in their handling of slave laws during the eighteenth century, imperial policies began to change at the turn of the century. This trend toward more centralized control and uniformity in legal codes began as early as the 1780 and culminated at the turn of the century. Two factors in particular led to this increased focus on slave law. The first was the growing momentum of metropolitan abolitionist movement, which had gained strength in London and other European metropoles, increasing the pressure on decision makers to enforce a more humane treatment of plantation slaves.[15] The second factor was the wider global trend of imperial consolidation and the desire for more centralized control over colonial peripheries. In the case of the British Empire, such tensions were caused in no small part by the events of the American Revolution.[16] Legal codes concerning slavery became central concerns for both these

---

[13] On the prerogative of slave owners to police and punish their slaves in the colonial Caribbean legal context, see, in particular, Diana Paton, *No Bond but the Law: Punishment, Race, and Gender in Jamaican State Formation, 1780–1870* (Durham, NC: Duke University Press, 2004); Ghachem, *The Old Regime and the Haitian*, 63–74; Lauren Benton, "This Melancholy Labyrinth: The Trial of Arthur Hodge and the Boundaries of Imperial Law," *Alabama Law Review* 64:1 (2012): 93–96.

[14] For an illuminating take on the very recent origins of modern notions of universal human rights discourse, see Samuel Moyn, *The Last Utopia: Human Rights in History* (Cambridge, MA: Belknap Press, 2010). For an opposing view, see Robin Blackburn, *The American Crucible: Slavery, Emancipation and Human Rights* (New York: Verso, 2013).

[15] See Christopher L. Brown, "The Politics of Slavery," in *The British Atlantic World, 1500–1800* (2nd edition), ed. David Armitage and Michael J. Braddick (New York: Palgrave Macmillan, 2009), 214–32.

[16] See, for example, Bayly, *Imperial Meridian*; Lauren Benton and Lisa Ford, "Magistrates in Empire: Convicts, Slaves, and the Remaking of the Plural Order in the British Empire," in *Legal Pluralism and Empires, 1500–1800*, ed. Lauren Benton and Richard Ross (New York: New York University Press, 2013), 173–98.

movements and formed, together with the slave trade abolition, one of the main arenas of political contestation between local elites and imperial agents.

A major addition to slave codes of the Leeward Islands came in the form of the Amelioration Act of 1798.[17] This ordinance pertained to the treatment and governance of slaves, and was in part an attempt at limiting the unrestricted rights of planters to punish their slaves as they saw fit. Though the council of the British Leeward Islands on St. Christopher approved the act, the impetus for it came from London rather than from the colonies themselves.[18] The contents of the act were primarily focused on preserving the general health and well-being of slaves and on preventing the worst excesses of planter violence, but such concerns were never couched in a language of slaves' rights. Rather, the main motivation behind the act seems to have been a concern for building a more stable and sustainable system of slavery in the Leeward Islands, a notable concern in the decade leading up to the abolition of the slave trade. Only by securing the basic conditions for survival could the high mortality rates among slaves be brought down. By curbing the wicked behavior of West Indian planters, imperial authorities might have hoped to combat the rise in slave insurrections sweeping the region. Such concerns, pragmatic as they might have been, had little purchase in the colonial Caribbean where any attempt to rein in the autonomy of slave owners was seen by white colonial elites as a serious infringement of the planters' prerogatives, and despite the symbolic and political shift brought about by the passing of the Amelioration Act, little seemed to change in the day-to-day treatment of slaves during the first decade of the nineteenth century. Despite of this recalcitrance, the British Leewards witnessed a number of high-profile cases of violence against slaves in the years following the passage of the act, bringing renewed attention to the issue.

Of the many scandals painting the British Virgin Islands as a zone of anarchy and corruption, few were as controversial as the 1811 trial of Arthur William Hodge on Tortola, well documented in both British and Caribbean pamphlets and newspapers of the period.[19] Hodge stood accused of the murder of Prosper, one of his own slaves, who in 1807

---

[17] A printed copy of the act is preserved as *An Act More Effectually to Provide for the Support and to Extend Certain Regulations for the Protection of Slaves; to Promote and Encourage Their Increase, and Generally to Meliorate Their Condition* (Basseterre: Richard Cable, 1799).

[18] The act was likely part of an attempt by the council to preemptively stave off further intervention from London by showing that the colonies themselves were capable of policing the treatment of slaves.

[19] The most comprehensive scholarly analysis of the Hodge case is Benton, "This Melancholy Labyrinth."

had been beaten so badly and repeatedly that he died of his injuries.[20] While the murder of Prosper was the initial reason for Hodge's trial, it quickly emerged that it was far from the only crime, or even the only murder, committed by the Tortolan planter. As the proceedings progressed, a number of witnesses, including free people of color and three white men, conveyed increasingly disturbing tales of maltreatment and outright torture on the Hodge estate, including the brutal treatment of a number of children of color, some of whom were allegedly his own, and the killing of two enslaved women, who had boiling water poured down their throats.[21] After a brief consideration the jury returned with a guilty verdict but recommended mercy rather than execution for the accused.[22]

The presiding judge declined to follow the recommendation of the jury and instead ruled that Hodge was to be hanged for his crimes a week after the end of the trial, making him the first slave owner to hang in the British Caribbean for the murder of one of his own slaves.[23] This verdict caused a stir in the white community, as the immunity of planters had thus been dealt a serious blow by the judge as well as by the governor of the Leeward Islands who had appointed him, the experienced diplomat and noted abolitionist Hugh Elliott. Local unrest among angry Tortolan whites was deemed so likely by colonial authorities that both the militia and forces from the Royal Navy were called in to keep order, and Elliott ordered martial law from sunrise to sunset in the days leading up to the execution.[24] The fact that Hodge was brought to trial at this time seems to have had relatively little to do with his crimes themselves – vile as they were – since these had been going on for years. Rather, the timing of the trial was likely the result of a number of factors, including interpersonal rivalries within the local elite on Tortola, pitting Hodge and his lawyer William Musgrave against powerful magistrates with ties to the intercolonial networks associated with the illegal trade in prize slaves, and a mounting political pressure in the metropole to act against the autonomy of cruel planters who publicly flaunted imperial decorum.[25] In its report of 1826, the Commission of Legal Enquiry commented on the Hodge trial, concluding, with the benefit of fifteen years of hindsight, that

[20] A. M Belisario, *A Report of the Trial of Arthur Hodge, Esquire (Late One of the Members of His Majesty's Council for the Virgin Islands), at the Island of Tortola, on the 25th April, 1811, and Adjourned to the 29th of the Same Month; for the Murder of His Negro Man Slave Named Prosper* (Middletown, CT: Tertius Dunning, 1812), 94–96.

[21] Ibid., 10–12, 96–150.   [22] Burns, *History of the British West Indies*, 603.

[23] Belisario, *Report of the Trial*, 185–86.

[24] John Andrew, *The Hanging of Arthur Hodge: A Caribbean Anti-slavery Milestone* (Bloomington: Xlibris, 2000), 175.

[25] Benton, "This Melancholic Labyrinth," 98–103.

"it cannot be a matter of wonder, nor, except upon the sternest and most unbending principles of justice, of regret, that Arthur Hodge should have been convicted, condemned, and executed, upon evidence slight, doubtful, and suspected."[26]

The crimes and trial of Hodge lingered as a specter over the Leeward Islands for many years and continued to be a point of reference for debates about both colonial law and the treatment of slaves. It was, however, far from the only controversial trial over the mistreatment of slaves taking place in the British Leewards during this period, and the 1810 case of the Nevis planter Edward Huggins provides a good example of how an island with a different power dynamic between magistrates and governor handled such cases. Mr. Huggins stood accused of having publicly flogged a number of his slaves with undue severity, administering upward of several hundred lashes, which was well above the legal limit of fifty lashes. Elliott, the newly appointed governor of the British Leewards Islands, had been bedridden and thus been removed from much of the legal proceedings against Huggins. In a process seemingly tainted by corruption and favoritism, a jury largely composed of friends and acquaintances of Huggins found the man not guilty and acquitted him of all charges, leading to political uproar and a prolonged debate in both local and imperial assemblies and the regional public sphere.[27] This debate mirrored the one surrounding the execution of Hodge, but with the two sides switched. Advocates of increased metropolitan control and of improved conditions for slaves accused the magistrates on Nevis of circumventing justice and flouting imperial law, while local planters and politicians did their best to defend Huggins's character and the rights and privileges of slave owners. In a widely distributed 1811 pamphlet, Thomas John Cottle, president of the assembly and collector of customs on Nevis, spent several pages justifying the jury's verdict.[28] This justification included a strong reaffirmation of the rights of slave owners that managed to thoroughly ignore the amelioration act:

Mr. Huggins has certainly not transgressed against this custom, as we have shown, neither has he outraged any law in existence, for none of our laws forbids that to be done, by the order of the Master, which Mr. Huggins in this

---

[26] *Third Report of the Commission of Legal Enquiry in the West Indies*, 1826, in TNA, CO 318/65, 94.

[27] TNA, CO 152/100, ff. 17–19. See also Goveia, *Slave Society in the British Leeward Islands*, 200–201.

[28] T. J. Cottle, "A Plain Statement of the Motives, which gave rise to the public punishment of several negroes, belonging to the estate called Pinnet's, on the 23 January 1810, and of the serious consequences resulting from it, with a sketch of the characters of Mr. Huggins & Mr. Tobin," 1811, in TNA, CO 152/100, miscellaneous.

instance did; our laws only require the intervention of the Magistracy between Master and Slave, in cases of Life or Limb; in all other cases the power of Punishment is lodged with the Master; they suppose no body can be more alive to the protection and preservation of the slave, than the Owner.[29]

The planters' prerogative was thus at the heart of the legal and political discussion of Huggins's trial. Responding directly to Cottle's pamphlet in the pages of the *St. Christopher Gazette*, one of the most widely distributed publications in the microregion, J. W. Tobin, among the fiercest critics of Huggins's acquittal, pointedly remarked on the potential consequences of such claims for colonial law: "Were the doctrine you have laid down, that the Magistrate has no right to interfere but in cases of Life or Limb, once to be admitted, it would follow, that a Slave in the *West-Indies*, is not entitled to that protection which, in *Great-Britain*, is afforded to a Horse or a Dog."[30] In an even sharper, if subtly worded, critique, Tobin summoned the specter of Hodge in a way that was sure to resonate with West Indian readers:

But it would seem that your Honor thinks Law unnecessary, when you say, that "there can be no one really more interested in the good treatment and well being of the Slave than the Master; and that this interest will always have a more active effect than Law; than all the writings of Philosophic Society." Have you, then, so soon forgotten the Tyrant of *Tortola*?[31]

Both the Hodge and Huggins trials are indicative of the persistent tensions between central authority and local elites within colonial society in the Leewards and the related conflict between the principles of amelioration and the planters' prerogative. They also highlight the fact that such tensions did not align entirely with a center–periphery dichotomy, since fierce debate raged within the microregion itself over the social and legal issues at hand. Not all colonial elites were advocates of upholding the authority of slave owners, and not every imperial magistrate stationed on the islands had much interest in enforcing metropolitan decrees or upholding imperial law.

The issues over slave laws on Tortola were not just related to politics and ideology but also to more deeply entrenched colonial institutions. Since there were few incentives for local authorities to reform and alter legal frameworks concerning slaves, the daily interpretation of the law in colonies such as Tortola was left up to individual magistrates to carry out more or less as they saw fit. The considerable autonomy of practice that

---

[29] Ibid., 17.
[30] Letter in the *St. Christopher Gazette*, January 1812. Clipping contained in TNA, CO 152/100, miscellaneous. Emphasis in original.
[31] Ibid. Emphasis in original.

the entire region had operated under during the decades surrounding the turn of the century began to change, however, as British imperial authorities embarked on a new course of tightening institutional control over their overseas colonies in the late 1810s. In the case of Caribbean jurisdictional issues, this process gained momentum with the British Commission of Legal Enquiry of 1826, which set out to examine legal codes and jurisdictional practices across the British Caribbean.[32] On arriving in Tortola from St. Christopher in 1823, the King's Commissioners noted their surprise in their report on learning that "in this island the laws all remain in manuscript, and are as might be expected, many of them in an imperfect state." They further noted that the island's Slave Act, from 1783, appeared both "crude and barbarous."[33] The local Crown Officer met these concerns with assurances of a speedy reform of the Act: "'I would propose,' said the crown officer, 'a trial by a jury of twelve men for all capital offences committed by slaves; the present slave law will speedily undergo a complete revision, as a committee from the council and assembly has been appointed for the purpose.'"[34]

Despite the promise of reform, legal and political criticism of the Tortola slave laws persisted for another decade. The 1783 Slave Act still formed the basis for legal practice in the colony almost half a century later, with no signs of the promised 1823 assembly overhauling it. In an 1832 report related to the case of five slaves accused of mutiny on Tortola, Attorney General Thomas Denman, "with a view to the future administration of criminal law in Tortola, and in other colonies where similar laws may have been made," expressed "serious doubts whether the Law of 1783 is not in its own nature too vague, indefinite and unintelligible, to be capable of enforcement in any case."[35] Furthermore, Denman argued, "this law may well be challenged, as being contrary to natural law," since the 1783 acts in effect made it possible to punish alleged crimes, such as mutiny, without "even requiring [these crimes] to be evinced by any overt act."[36] A major revision of the Tortola slave laws was never implemented, however, since the 1834 abolition of slavery in the British West Indies in effect made any concerns over outdated slave codes irrelevant.

Tortola might have been an extreme example, but it was hardly alone among the British Leeward Islands in pushing back against the

---

[32] The relevant manuscripts of the Commission's report are contained in TNA, CO 318/62–64. The final report is held in TNA, CO 318/65.

[33] *Commission of Legal Enquiry in the West Indies, 1826, Third Report*, TNA, CO 318/65, f. 81.

[34] Ibid., f. 87.

[35] Thomas Denman to Viscount Goderich, January 24, 1832, in TNA, CO 239/31.

[36] Ibid.

ameliorating initiatives coming from London. In his memoir, the abolitionist and Member of Parliament Thomas Fowell Buxton wrote of the
overwhelming resentment among white planters in the region, following
a series of resolutions introduced by foreign secretary George Canning in
1823 to ameliorate the condition of slaves: "Thoughts were openly
entertained of resisting the innovations of the government by force of
arms. It was even proposed to throw off the yoke of the mother country,
and place themselves under the protection of America."[37]

The jurisdictional tensions and legal–political struggles over slave
codes were not limited to the British Caribbean but were a region-wide
phenomenon in the early nineteenth century. Even the generally more
laissez-faire Scandinavian empires saw similar attempts to rein in the
autonomy of colonial elites, if not by metropolitan governments themselves, then by their direct representatives on the ground. In the early
1830s the balance of power between imperial representatives and
colonial interests shifted significantly in the Danish colonies. Governor
General of the Danish West Indies Peter von Scholten, appointed to this
post in 1827, had several clashes with a number of local magistrates over
jurisdictional issues throughout his career in office. The son of former
governor and commandant Casimir von Scholten, the younger von
Scholten had previously served as first collector of customs and then
governor on St. Thomas after the end of the British occupation,
following a successful military career in Europe during the Napoleonic
Wars. He was thus tied to imperial as well as regional networks, and had
strong personal connections to local colonial society.[38] He was also
involved in a well-known affair with a prominent woman of color on
St. Croix, Anna Heegaard, who lived with him following 1829 and might
have provided the first direct connection between the governor and the
growing community of prominent people of color in Charlotte Amalie
and Christiansted.[39]

An example of the jurisdictional conflicts provoked by the governor's
active approach to government can be seen in the Kierulff, Fulg, and
Sarauw case in the early 1830s. The incident took place during a routine
inspection of the administrative facilities on nearby St. John, where von
Scholten found a young black man by the name of Michel shackled in

[37] Charles Buxton (ed.), *Memoirs of Sir Thomas Fowell Buxton, Baronet* (3rd edition) (London: John Murray, 1849), 120.
[38] The premier biographical history of von Scholten is Herman Lawaetz, *Peter v. Scholten: Vestindiske Tidsbilleder fra den sidste Generalguvernørs Dage* (Copenhagen: Gyldendal, 1940).
[39] H. F. Garde, "Anna Heegaard og Peter von Scholten," *Personalhistorisk Tidsskrift* 78 (1958): 25–37.

a cell.[40] After some investigation, the governor learned that Michel had been arrested after a violent fight had broken out in the street between him and a white local by the name of Dumerque, who had subsequently been released on bail. Von Scholten saw the release of Dumerque as a politically insensitive and extraordinarily unfortunate action, since the black community on St. John and St. Thomas was likely to see it as unjust that a white man was released for attacking a black freedman while the latter remained imprisoned – an assessment with which the governor himself tended to agree. Von Scholten thus suggested that the district bailiff, Kierulff, release Michel as well in order to cool tempers.[41]

This course of action on behalf of the governor did not sit well with the two lawyers involved in the case, prosecutor Sarauw and defense attorney Fugl, both twenty-five years of age and newly graduated from the University of Copenhagen. They loudly and publicly accused von Scholten of violating the freedom of the courts and overstepping his jurisdictional boundaries.[42] The governor reacted by ordering the two men to appear before him on St. Croix, where he, when they finally responded to his order, proceeded to lecture them sternly and threaten to suspend them in the case of any further public airing of grievances on their part. If they had a problem with his administration, the lawyers were told, they were welcome to lodge an official complaint. They promptly did so a few days after their appearance before the governor.[43] At the local level, the West Indian governing council initially sided with Fugl, Sarauw, and Kierulff, who had joined in the complaint, arguing that von Scholten had misunderstood his own authority vis-à-vis that of the government, overstepping his bounds and acting on his own political motivations. It was not the fact that he had interfered in a legal proceeding that so irked the local government, but rather that he had done so without consulting them, doubly troubling since he had seemingly taken the side of a black man in a case of public violence. On the imperial level, the Chamber of Customs in Copenhagen, the highest authority besides the king in matters of colonial governance, sided with the governor and, while arguing that clearer lines should be drawn up between the different jurisdictions of colonial government, indicated that social stability was indeed a valid concern.[44] Implicit in this decision on the part of the imperial authority in Copenhagen was perhaps also a certain disdain for the autonomy of

---

[40] "The case against Kierulff, Fugl, and Sarauw concerning maltreatment of a black youth, 1833," RA, WIL 2.39.1.
[41] Ibid.   [42] Lawaetz, *Peter v. Scholten*, 75.
[43] "The case against Kierulff, Fugl, and Sarauw concerning maltreatment of a black youth, 1833."
[44] Ibid.; Lawaetz, *Peter v. Scholten*, 78–79.

local magistrate rule, personified by the entitled government council, and for the overzealous lawyers, who showed so little understanding of what kept the colonial social order in place.

The case, and particularly its ultimate outcome, was indicative of a new trend on the Danish islands in the following decade: increased control in the hands of the governor and the rise of an unspoken and perhaps even accidental alliance between von Scholten, the local black elites, and the largely disinterested Chamber of Customs. This coalition of political forces began to gradually rein in the power and influence of the network of white magistrates who had enjoyed their position of privilege in Danish colonial society for decades. It was not a coincidence that the issue over which magistrates and governor clashed in 1833 was a case of racialized violence and the unjust treatment of a black man by the local justice system. In an account of his travels in the Caribbean, the famous Quaker and abolitionist Joseph John Gurney observed that acts of amelioration on St. Croix were often "no matter of law, but the simple result of the imperative benevolence of the governor-general, von Scholten."[45] Gurney wrote the following general observation of amelioration in the Danish and the British colonies:

I cannot, however, refrain from observing, that legal provisions for the amelioration of slavery, are in general of little use. In the British Colonies, the measures of this kind which were enacted by Parliament at home were constantly frustrated by local influence; and, in spite of law or reason, man will often be found, in the hour of temptation, to abuse arbitrary power over his fellow man. I consider it therefore highly probable, that even in Santa Cruz [St. Croix], where the ameliorating laws are enforced by a local government, at once vigilant and despotic, acts of oppression and cruelty may at times take place, which are wholly unknown to the government.[46]

Freed People and Free Communities

The first decades of the nineteenth century witnessed a significant growth in the population of free black people across the Leeward Islands. These free people of color, whether African or Afro-Caribbean, born into freedom or enslavement, were becoming a rising social force in colonial societies in Danish, Swedish, Dutch, French, and British islands in the region. The ways in which slaves obtained their freedom were many and varied. They included the act of buying one's own freedom and being

---

[45] Joseph John Gurney, *A Winter in the West Indies, Described in Familial Letters to Henry Clay, of Kentucky* (London: John Murray, 1840), 20. The benevolence identified by Gurney was no doubt mixed with a certain dose of pragmatism and self-preservation.
[46] Ibid., 21.

granted it by an owner or even by a court of law. While the social status gained by free people of color in the early nineteenth-century Caribbean did not grant access to the same privileges or rights as were enjoyed by free whites, the shift from enslavement to freedom was nonetheless a significant transformation with a number of implications, perhaps the most important of which was that one's children would not be born into slavery. Freedom from enslavement was never intended by imperial governments to lead to the kind of liberty enjoyed by white subjects. And yet, as Natasha Lightfoot has shown in her study of Antigua, free people of color found myriad ways to challenge the constraints they faced by a system fundamentally oriented toward limiting their possibilities.[47]

In the Danish West Indies, the percentage of free people of color among all free subjects of the colonies rose from just over 30 percent in 1797 to more than 70 percent in 1835, with the biggest growth happening in and around Charlotte Amalie (see Table 5.1). Similar demographic shifts took place on St. Barthélemy and in the British Virgin Islands, again concentrated around the port cities (see Tables 5.2 and 5.3).[48] Meanwhile, the enslaved populations did not fall as dramatically, despite the fact that many freedmen were former slaves, indicating that either the import of slaves continued to a significant extent or the high mortality rates of pre-abolition days had fallen drastically.

While still decidedly second-class citizens when compared with their white neighbors, free people of color in the Leeward Islands were carving out a spot for themselves in colonial society. Given their limited opportunities to acquire land, they often engaged in commercial activities and with time became integral parts of the trade-based networks of the microregion. Others became seamen, joining the crews of vessels passing through Charlotte Amalie or Gustavia, actions that also served to widen the networks of free people of color across the region, further increasing communication and integration across imperial borders.

For their part, colonial legislatures were scrambling to put together rules concerning the growing communities of free blacks in an effort to ensure that their own privileges would remain untouched. This process often led to a heightened control of the movement and actions of people of color, as on St. Barthélemy, where any sort of gathering or festivities among black people required the prior approval of colonial authorities.

---

[47] Natasha Lightfoot, *Troubling Freedom: Antigua and the Aftermath of British Emancipation* (Durham, NC: Duke University Press, 2015).

[48] It is worth noting that many of the "free" people of color in the British colonies were in fact part of the apprenticeship system, and thus in practice closer to bondage than freedom. See the following chapter for more on apprenticeships.

Table 5.1 *Free and enslaved populations in the Danish West Indies, 1797, 1815, and 1835*[a]

Island	1797			1815			1835		
	Whites	Free people of color	Slaves	Whites	Free people of color	Slaves	Whites	Free people of color	Slaves
St. Thomas	726 (13%)	239 (4%)	4,769 (83%)	2,122 (24%)	2,284 (26%)	4,393 (50%)	1,977 (16%)	5,204 (42%)	5,315 (42%)
St. Croix	2,223 (8%)	1,164 (4%)	25,425 (88%)	1,840 (6%)	2,480 (9%)	24,330 (85%)	1,892 (7%)	4,913 (18%)	19,876 (75%)
St. John	113 (5%)	15 (1%)	1,992 (94%)	157 (6%)	271 (10%)	2,306 (84%)	208 (9%)	202 (9%)	1,943 (82%)
Total	3,062 (8%)	1,418 (4%)	32,186 (88%)	4,119 (10%)	5,035 (13%)	31,029 (77%)	4,077 (10%)	10,319 (25%)	27,134 (65%)

[a] These numbers are compiled in Hall, *Slave Society in the Danish West Indies*, 5 and 180.

Table 5.2 *Free and enslaved populations on St. Barthélemy, 1787 and 1812*[a]

Location	1787			1812		
	Whites	Free people of color	Slaves	Whites	Free people of color	Slaves
Gustavia	294 (45%)	83 (13%)	279 (42%)	1,025 (26%)	1,038 (27%)	1,818 (47%)
Countryside	533 (53%)	8 (1%)	464 (46%)	933 (58%)	90 (6%)	588 (36%)
Total	827 (50%)	91 (5%)	743 (45%)	1,958 (36%)	1,128 (20%)	2,406 (44%)

[a] These numbers are compiled in Lavoie, Fick, and Mayer, "A Particular Study of Slavery in the Caribbean Island of Saint Barthélemy," 382–84. The population of Gustavia reached its zenith in 1812 and fell steadily over the following three decades.

Table 5.3 Free and enslaved populations in the British Virgin Islands, 1815 and 1823[a]

Location	1815				1823			
	Whites	Free people of color	Slaves	African apprentices	Whites	Free people of color	Slaves	African apprentices
Towns	207 (11%)	482 (26%)	778 (42%)	377 (2%)	252 (15%)	508 (31%)	684 (41%)	215 (13%)
Countryside	279 (4%)	456 (6%)	6507 (88%)	157 (2%)	281 (4%)	940 (13%)	5,940 (82%)	80 (1%)
Total	486 (5%)	938 (10%)	7,285 (79%)	534 (6%)	533 (6%)	1,448 (16%)	6,624 (75%)	295 (3%)

[a] These numbers are taken from "Statistical tables of the British Virgin Islands at two periods," in TNA, CO 239/9.

Among the questions posed by the Swedish inquiry to the Danish colonial authorities in 1802 was the issue of whether or not "a free colored can in any way forfeit his freedom and be sold as a slave."[49] This idea of reenslavement of free blacks, while never widely practiced in the Leewards, was indicative of the thin line between freedom and bondage in the region, both in practice and in the eyes of white elites.[50] In practice, the law tended to assume any black person to be a slave unless proven otherwise, both in the Scandinavian and in the Dutch and British colonies. The British Commission of Legal Enquiry, mentioned above, noted the following exchange with the Chief Justice of Tortola in 1823:

The law, said the chief justice, does certainly presume every negro to be a slave, unless the contrary shall be made apparent; that presumption has not, however, in any instance, to my knowledge, interfered with the rights of free persons, or persons passing for free persons, who are never molested if they conduct themselves with propriety; and after a very short time, unless the contrary shall appear, they are considered from their reputation of freedom, entitled to all the privileges that other persons enjoy. The same gentleman "would, in most cases, consider that twelve months time would be sufficient to establish a reputation of freedom." So, if a "negro is known to be a slave, he may pass, by good conduct unmolested, as a free person, there being no proof to the contrary; until he acquires the reputation of freedom."[51]

As many free people of color found themselves coming up against the entrenched antagonism or stubborn indifference of local magistrates, these individuals increasingly came to utilize an alternative approach to achieving their goals: writing directly to imperial authorities in Europe, thereby bypassing the local colonial level altogether. By engaging with the imperial level directly and using the letter of the law to their own advantage, free people of color came to play a direct part in the ongoing intra-imperial tensions between local and metropolitan governments. Much as had been the case when some Native American polities lodged their claims to land and legal complaints directly to London a century and a half earlier, the direct interaction between marginalized groups in the colonies and imperial authorities in Europe led to a potential loss of influence by colonial elites.[52]

---

[49] Quoted in Thomasson, "Thirty-Two Lashes at Quatre Piquets," 287.

[50] For the continued distinction between white and black freedom after emancipation, see Lightfoot, *Troubling Freedom*, 224–32.

[51] *Commission of Legal Enquiry in the West Indies, 1826, Third Report*, TNA, CO 318/65, 86.

[52] For examples of Native Americans utilizing imperial law for their own benefit, see Jenny Hale Pulsipher, *Subjects unto the Same King: Indians, English and the Contest of Authority in Colonial New England* (Philadelphia: University of Philadelphia Press, 2005). For an example of a similar dynamic in the context of the late Russian Empire, see Jane

An example of this dynamic was in the handling of the wills and property rights of free people of color by the government of the British Leeward Islands. One case in particular is worth examining – that of George Martin of Tortola. When Martin, the owner of a relatively small plantation on the island, died in November of 1818, he left behind him several children of manumitted slaves. The children of Martin had the status of free people of color and all took their father's last name, but local men of influence were reluctant to grant them their rightful inheritance. Since the only one of Martin's children who was of age, George, had himself passed away before the inheritance could be settled, one Mr. Hanley had been appointed by local authorities as caretaker of the estate and land. Hanley proved a poor caretaker as he allegedly stated that if he "met any opposition from them [the inheritors] in accomplishing his wishes ... he would neglect the estates and let them go to ruin and he would not pay any more money to the Inheritors."[53]

The family's issues went beyond that of a poor caretaker, however, since the local court system proved remarkably hard to persuade of the Martins' distress, doing its best to make the process of judicial hearing as difficult as possible. Faced with a magistracy that was at best indifferent and at worst predatory, the inheritors instead turned to imperial authorities. When the Commission of Legal Enquiry visited Tortola in 1823, its members met with Bice Martin, the mother of the oldest heirs, and assured her that they would bring news of the case to London. When this action did not seem to bring about any immediate results, the Martins hired the writing clerk Henry J. Dryer and with his assistance sent several petitions directly to Lord Bathurst, Secretary of State for the Colonies. In the first of these petitions, Bice Martin called on the government to consider her children as full and proper subjects: "That these Children of Mr. Martin though distinguished by color have been tenderly reared and we humbly conceive Your Lordship will consider them as fairly constituted to the enjoyment of a Property so honestly acquired and so indisputably bequeathed to them by their Parent as the fairest and most exalted of His Majesty's Subjects would be ..."[54] These petitions were met with considerably more receptiveness than the initial legal proceedings had been on Tortola. By bypassing the colonial level of authority and instead going directly to metropolitan authorities in

Burbank, *Russian Peasants Go to Court: Legal Culture in the Countryside, 1905–1917* (Bloomington: Indiana University Press, 2004).
[53] "Petition from Bice Martin and other persons of colour to the Earl of Bathurst," August 1, 1824, Tortola, in TNA, CO 239/11.
[54] Ibid.

London, the Martins finally succeeded in securing their inheritance, despite the best attempts by local agents to sabotage their efforts.

St. Barthélemy's population of free people of color filed their own share of petitions to Stockholm, especially when they found a less receptive audience in the local colonial administration. Ale Pålsson has shown how groups of free people came together on several occasions to petition for the right to vote for the colonial governing council, something that had been denied them by Governor Norderling. While a petition filed by 1812 was initially rejected, another filed in 1821 was approved rather expediently by the Colonial Department in Sweden – despite the objections of Norderling, who accused the people of color living in the colony of being untrustworthy and generally "guilty of indecent conduct."[55]

In 1816 Frederick VI, the Danish monarch, received similar petitions from his West Indian subjects. That year a delegation of freedmen arrived in Copenhagen to petition the king on behalf of 331 free people of color living in the Danish West Indies, demanding that he extend to them "the rights and privileges of rational creatures."[56] The petitioners requested that the equality nominally existing between white and colored free subjects in Denmark be extended to the Caribbean colonies and protested the excessive violence employed by the colonial administration to punish free people of color. While the response in Copenhagen was mixed, with members of government arguing both for and against the validity of the petitions, it is interesting to note that the representatives for the Chamber of Customs, who had the most direct links to authorities in the colonies, were in favor of suppression, while the Chancellery argued for a closer integration between white and colored subjects.[57] No immediate concessions were made as a consequence of the 1816 delegation's efforts, but it became an important stepping-stone for future struggles over rights in the Danish colonies.

In these varied ways, free people of color, and frequently free women of color, used the imperial legal apparatus to seek what was rightfully theirs within the confines of colonial law, even when local jurisdictions effectively denied them their claims and property. Whether it was by exercising their right as subjects of the crown to petition their monarch or by circumventing local jurisdictions by taking legal suits directly to the

[55] Ale Pålsson, "Smugglers before the Swedish Throne: Political Activity of Free People of Color in Early Nineteenth-Century St. Barthélemy," *Atlantic Studies* 14:3 (2017): 322–23.

[56] Quoted in Christian Damm Pedersen, "The Question of Rights in a Colour-Conscious Empire: The Danish West Indies and the Global Age of Revolutions (1800–1850)," in *Ports of Globalisation, Places of Creolisation*, ed. Weiss, 166.

[57] Ibid., 168–69.

metropole, these groups and individuals exploited the tensions existing between imperial and colonial authorities. While imperial metropoles were far from beacons of tolerance in an otherwise racially intolerant colonial system, they did have a somewhat different conception of the purpose of the law than did the local networks of white planters and magistrates tasked with upholding it on a daily basis – especially if enforcing it meant reining in colonial judicial power in the process.

Maritime Marronage

Not all freedom was granted, and many slaves threw off their shackles entirely by their own efforts. The western part of the Leeward archipelago is particularly dense, with many of the Virgin Islands being within just a few miles of each other, including the western islands of Vieques and Culebra off the coast of Puerto Rico. This geographical proximity made it particularly easy, if still exceedingly dangerous, for escaped slaves to traverse the sea and travel from one island to another with the use of very simple crafts or rafts, crossing imperial borders in the process and sometimes escaping the reach of vengeful masters and colonial jurisdictions.[58] Maritime hubs such as Danish Charlotte Amalie, Oranjestad on St. Eustatius, and St. John on Antigua were particularly attractive destinations for maroons, since the islands' transient populations and heavy traffic of small craft and people made it relatively easy for runaways to slip between the cracks and eventually escape into the wider world of Atlantic crossings.[59]

Many owners who lost slaves posted notices and promised monetary rewards for information leading to their capture in regional newspapers. On August 2, 1798, a notice appeared in the *Antigua Gazette*, paid for by one Campbell Brown. The notice alerted readers that a "stout young Creole Negro Man named Alexis, well known at the Privateers-Men's haunts," had fled captivity as a slave at the estate of Thomas Montgomery. Alexis, according to Brown, had boarded a privateering vessel "as a free man" and ostensibly attempted to join the crew of the American ship. The notice ended with a stern warning: "All Masters, in particular of Privateers and armed Vessels, are therefore caution'd against

---

[58] According to the 1802–7 St. Croix police reports, marronage was the single most common violation of the slave law, making up about one-third of total registered crimes committed by slaves on the island. Notably, this was the case for men as well as women. Quoted in Hall, *Slave Society in the Danish West Indies*, 103.

[59] Reports on the difficulties caused by slaves fleeing to the Dutch and Danish islands from the British Leewards were frequent. See, for example, "Report from St. Christopher on Fugitive Slaves," August 29, 1827, in TNA, CO 239/17, f. 118.

employing him as they will be prosecuted with rigour if detected."[60] The notice appeared several more times in the paper over the course of August and September, with no indication that Alexis had been caught or returned to the plantation. The young man's fate is unknown, but it is likely that he was successful in leaving the island as a crew member on one of the many vessels passing through the harbor of St. John's, despite Mr. Brown's printed plea to captains and masters.

A different notice, this one posted in the *Saint Thomas Gazette* in 1810, illustrates some of the key factors driving maritime marronage in the western Leewards.[61] According to their former master, George Martin of Tortola (the very same as above), three enslaved men going by the names of Jack Spot, London, and Atrix had "run away from Tortola in a small boat," arriving recently in St. Thomas. Between them the three men spoke "very good English, Spanish well ... Creole and a little French," and the youngest, London, was trained as a cooper. A significant reward of 120 dollars total was promised "to any person or persons who will apprehend and lodge in the Fort of this Island the said three Negroes."[62] The fate of the three men is again unknown, but their actions are indicative of a wider pattern. The escape by boat from Tortola to St. Thomas was an exceedingly common route taken by maroons, and their impressive linguistic skills, reflecting the polyglot nature of the region itself, would have made a transition to most any other colony in the Caribbean quite easy. Much as with Alexis, mentioned above, it is doubtful that St. Thomas was their final destination, and once out of the Danish port it would have been very difficult indeed to track them down. The heavily trafficked free ports of the Leeward Islands served as gateways to the wider Atlantic world beyond the microregion, not just for merchants and captains but also for those seeking freedom and refuge from vengeful masters.[63]

---

[60] *Antigua Gazette*, August 2, 1798, front page. Available in the Caribbean Newspapers collection, AAS.

[61] The term "maritime marronage" was coined by Neville Hall in his pioneering work on the Danish colonies. See "Maritime Maroons: 'Grand Marronage' from the Danish West Indies," *The William and Mary Quarterly* 42:4 (1985): 476–98; *Slave Society in the Danish West Indies*, chapter 7. For a more recent overview of marronage across the Atlantic, see Simon P. Newman, "Rethinking Runaways in the British Atlantic World: Britain, the Caribbean, West Africa, and North America," *Slavery and Abolition* 38:1 (2017): 49–75.

[62] *St. Thomas Gazette*, August 23, 1810, 3, in AAS. It is worth noting that forty dollars per man was significantly higher than the normal rate promised for the return of maroons, which was closer to ten dollars judging by a number of contemporaneous notices posted on August 23 and September 25, 1810, in the *St. Thomas Gazette* and *St. Thomas Monday's Advertiser*, respectively, both in AAS.

[63] For more on the mobility offered to people of color by this maritime traffic, see Scott, *The Common Wind*; Bolster, *Black Jacks*.

This is not to say that the port towns of the region were always safe harbors for black Caribbeans. In fact, overzealous officials attempting to catch escaped slaves often mistook for maroons the free people of color passing through these maritime hubs. Jan Simons, a free man from Curaçao, was thus apprehended in Christiansted on St. Croix in September 1805 while visiting a local tavern.[64] The sheriff questioned him repeatedly, suspecting him of being a maroon looking for passage aboard one of the many vessels passing through the port, despite Simons's repeated claims of being a free person already employed as a crew member on the brig of one Captain Groth. After two days of questioning, Groth finally appeared, compelling the sheriff to reluctantly release Simons.[65] This was far from a unique case, as free people of color traveling through the region frequently had to endure the suspicion and hostility of local officers of the law. The challenges facing slave owners notwithstanding, many maroons were ultimately apprehended. At times this came about because colonial governments stepped in directly, as in one 1825 case where British Virgin Island authorities made a concerted, and largely successful, effort to restitute a number of slaves who had escaped plantations on St. Eustatius and St. Barthélemy.[66]

Despite such instances of intercolonial cooperation, it often proved challenging to reclaim slaves once they had made their way to another island, especially one belonging to a different empire. While there was substantial collaboration in bringing back fugitive slaves between colonial elites within the Leeward Islands, Spanish colonies were generally more hesitant to engage with such intercolonial cooperation. This was especially true in the case of Puerto Rico, a frequent destination for escaped slaves as local Spanish authorities proved reluctant to return maroons to neighboring colonies based on a long history of sanctuary decrees. Some of these decrees were specifically tied to conversion to Catholicism, essentially promising freedom at the cost of baptism, while others had little to say about religious faith.[67] A certain shift in the attitude toward

---

[64] Police Journal, Sheriff of Christiansted, September 19, 1805, RA, WILA 38.31.2.
[65] Police Journal, Sheriff of Christiansted, September 21, 1805, RA, WILA 38.31.2.
[66] TNA CO 239/12, f. 180.
[67] See Linda Rupert, "'Seeking the Waters of Baptism': Fugitive Slaves and Imperial Jurisdiction in the Early Modern Caribbean," in *Legal Pluralism and Empire, 1500–1850*, ed. Richard J. Ross and Lauren Benton (New York: New York University Press, 2013), 201–6; Jorge L. Chinea, "A Quest for Freedom: The Immigration of Maritime Maroons into Puerto Rico, 1656–1800," *The Journal of Caribbean History* 31:1–2 (1997): 51–87. For similar sanctuary policies in a different part of the Spanish Atlantic, see Matthew Restall, "Crossing to Safety? Frontier Flight in Eighteenth Century Belize and Yucatan," *Hispanic American Historical Review* 94:3 (2014): 381–419.

foreign maroons took place during the middle decades of the eighteenth century, as the island's authorities realized the usefulness of the potential workforce arriving on their shores. According to magistrates on Tortola, the maroons who fled to Puerto Rico were increasingly put to use as laborers there and were "essentially serviceable to the colonisation of a large and spacious island."[68] Following the emancipation of slaves in the British colonies in 1834, Tortola and other British colonies in the Leewards became increasingly popular destinations for escaped slaves in the microregion.[69] A number of cases of maritime marronage from the Danish West Indies created regional headlines amid a steady stream of individual escapes during the years leading up to the Danish emancipation in 1848.[70] In an 1841 report to Copenhagen, Governor von Scholten made it clear that when visiting the island of St. John "the frequent flight of Negroes to Tortola was an issue, that very much attracted my attention. It must be regarded as the highest necessity to expend the necessary resources to quell this rampant evil."[71] In the same report, von Scholten also pointed out that the Danish territories were used as stopovers by maroons making the journey to Tortola from the Spanish island of Vieques, off the coast of Puerto Rico.[72]

The continuities in colonial practices before and after the abolition of slavery were remarkable. In the British Empire, the institution of slavery was replaced with a new system of indentured servitude – the so-called apprentice system – requiring the continued labor and servitude of emancipated slaves for a period of four to six years, depending on the classification of their apprenticeship.[73] This situation of, at best, quasi-free labor led not to a cessation of marronage but rather to a new wave of escapes in the mid-1830s, accompanied by renewed efforts toward capturing these "runaway apprentices." When escaped apprentices were apprehended, they were typically delivered back to their masters to serve out the remainder of their contracts. However, if no notices had been

---

[68] Quoted in Goveia, *Slave Society in the British Leeward Islands*, 255.
[69] For a discussion of maritime marronage from the Dutch Leewards during this period, see Jessica V. Roitman, "Land of Hope and Dreams: Slavery and Abolition in the Dutch Leeward Islands," *Slavery and Abolition* 37:2 (2016): 375–98.
[70] "Expelled and wanted persons, 1818–1828," in the Caribbean Collection: Virgin Island Documents, The Florence Williams Library, Christiansted, St. Croix. Some of these are described in more detail in Hall, *Slave Society in the Danish West Indies*, 136–38.
[71] Governor von Scholten to Christian VIII, January 15, 1841, RA, WILA 2.7.3.
[72] Ibid.
[73] "Slavery Abolition Act of 1833," Section IV. For a broader discussion of the issue of post-emancipation labor in the Caribbean, see, in particular, Thomas C. Holt, *The Problem of Freedom: Race, Labor, and Politics in Jamaica and Britain, 1832–1938* (Baltimore: Johns Hopkins University Press, 1992); Craton, *Empire, Enslavement and Freedom*, 356–438.

posted or no claims had been made, they would instead be auctioned off to the highest bidder, in a process eerily similar to the slave auctions taking place in prior decades. In 1835 constables in Castries, Saint Lucia, arrested a black man named Charlerie on suspicion of being a "runaway apprenticed laborer." The following week a public notice was posted in the *Saint Lucia Gazette*, declaring that "the apprenticeship of said Charlerie, will be sold at Auction to cover Gaol Fees, unless he be immediately claimed by his Employers, and those fees paid."[74]

While many escaped slaves settled down in other ports and cities across the region in order to forge new destinies for themselves, others chose a life more deliberately outside the sphere of imperial rule. They banded together in villages that were largely self-sustaining, typically located on remote islands, in dense jungles, or on isolated mountainsides. Such maroon societies could be found across the rim of the western Atlantic throughout the eighteenth and early nineteenth centuries, and many of them have been well documented in the historical literature.[75] They represented a different aspect of maroon life, explicitly seeking the security and safety of a community existing outside the realm of colonial society and shaped by the shared experience of enslavement and escape.

The Leeward Islands were hosts to many such maroon communities. While the smaller islands of the western Leewards had fewer remote places for such communities to settle down without drawing unwanted attention from officials, some of the otherwise uninhabited islands in the archipelago became hosts to a diverse group of inhabitants living outside the bounds of colonial society. The small Salt Island, just five miles off the coast of Tortola, was one example of this type of maroon society. The island, just one mile long and one mile wide, was uninhabited for most of the eighteenth century, but at some point in the second half of the century it became home to a small community of former slaves, either escapees from regional plantations or survivors of a wrecked slave ship. Very few records of this community remain, but there seem to have been few if any attempts to evict the inhabitants or bring any of them back into slavery. In late 1813 the British government was reminded of the island's existence through reports from naval officers patrolling the area, and in an effort to determine the territorial rights and production potential of

---

[74] *Saint Lucia Gazette*, March 18, 1835, p. 2, in AAS.
[75] See, for example, Richard Price, ed., *Maroon Societies: Rebel Slave Communities in the Americas* (3rd edition) (Baltimore: Johns Hopkins University Press, 1996); Alvin O. Thompson, *Flight to Freedom: African Runaways and Maroons in the Americas* (Mona: University of the West Indies Press, 2006); Sylviane A. Diouf, *Slavery's Exiles: The Story of the American Maroons* (New York: New York University Press, 2014).

the land they sent a request for information to John Julius, commander in chief of the British Leeward Islands.[76] Responding to the inquiry, the president of the Virgin Islands, Richard Hetherington, informed his superiors that Salt Island was an altogether inhospitable piece of land, being both "small and poor in soil," with "4 or 5 white poor people living on it, and some poor free people who endeavor to support themselves by fishing, and by such things as they plant being subject to dry weather, and they get their water from Tortola."[77]

Whether the Salt Island inhabitants in 1814 were indeed free people of color having relocated there from Tortola or rather the remnants of the earlier maroon community living there is unknown, but it is clear that authorities in Road Town had very little interest in the island or its inhabitants. Officials in London did not like the idea of a salt-producing community existing outside the reach of imperial authority, and, through Commander Julius, they sent Tortola magistrates scrambling to dig up an old declaration that officially declared Salt Island as part of the British Virgin Islands, divided the land and salt ponds on the island between the existing inhabitants, and proclaimed a tax on the production of salt and cotton.[78] This declaration certified that no other empire could claim the patch of land for itself, but by the very act of delivering the document to London, the local government had accepted a certain level of responsibility for actually policing this particular frontier. While local magistrates in the microregion cared relatively little for monitoring the outer bounds of their territories when such duties held little or no possibility of profit, the view from imperial capitals was quite different, and the existence of spaces outside colonial control was repugnant to the very idea of imperial order.

Kingstown and the Fate of Liberated Africans

A different type of free black society, existing entirely within the sphere of colonial jurisdiction, emerged in the Leewards following the British slave trade abolition. As British naval ships seized vessels engaged in the illegal transatlantic slave trade, they found themselves with hundreds of confiscated or, as they were commonly termed in official documents, liberated Africans. These men and women were ostensibly to be given their

---

[76] John Julius to the Earl of Bathurst, January 20, 1814, TNA, CO 152/104, f. 4.

[77] Richard Hetherington to John Julius, January 17, 1814, TNA, CO 152/104, f. 5.

[78] Despite the date on the document, it is unclear whether this memorial was indeed authored in 1811 or rather made for the occasion in 1814 in order to avoid any competing territorial claims. "Memorial of the Council and Commons House of Assembly of the Virgin Islands," September 17, 1811, TNA, CO 152/104, f. 5.

freedom, but only after having served a fourteen-year period of apprenticeship, similar to the institution established with the Slavery Abolition Act a few decades later. Apprenticeships were essentially a form of indentured servitude that could take place on plantations, in towns, or in local militias.[79] A new class of people of color in the Caribbean was thus created, a middle category of sorts between the binaries of freedom and enslavement that in practice, if not legally, often had more in common with contemporary slaves than with the white indentured laborers imported from Europe. The system of apprenticeship meant that the challenge of settling and integrating the new freedmen into colonial society did not emerge until more than a decade after their initial liberation, and since freedom was granted to most, if not all, slaves in the British Leewards following the commencement of abolition in 1834, it became part of the broader issue of freedom in the post-emancipation colonies.[80]

There were, however, exceptions, and the early seizures of slaves in the 1810s led to a number of Africans leaving their indentured service in the late 1820s. Some of these individuals were given land by the crown and settled within British colonial territories, forming small villages in otherwise unused and hence often less than fertile areas of the various islands.[81] This was the case in the British Virgin Islands, where a number of very large slave ships had been seized in 1814 and 1815, including the *Venus*, the *Manuella*, the *Candelaria*, and the *Atrevido*. These ships, together with the wrecked Portuguese slave ship the *Donna Paula*, described in further detail in the next chapter, together had more than 1,500 Africans onboard, some of whom were eventually resettled on Tortola.[82] The large number of new freedmen on the island led to the

---

[79] See Chapter 6 for more on how these periods of apprenticeship were used as a way to de facto continue the intercolonial slave trade.

[80] For discussions of these issues, see Seymour Drescher, *Abolition: A History of Slavery and Antislavery* (New York: Cambridge University Press, 2009), 245–93; David Brion Davis, *The Problem of Slavery in the Age of Emancipation* (New York: Alfred A. Knopf, 2014). For the wider reverberations of abolitionism in the British Caribbean, see Edward Bartlett Rugemer, *The Problem of Emancipation: The Caribbean Roots of the American Civil War* (Baton Rouge: Louisiana State University Press, 2009); Richard Huzzey, *Freedom Burning: Anti-slavery and Empire in Victorian Britain* (Ithaca, NY: Cornell University Press, 2012).

[81] For an excellent comparative study of resettlement in Trinidad and the Bahamas, see Rosanne Marion Adderley, *"New Negroes from Africa": Slave Trade Abolition and Free African Settlement in the Nineteenth-Century Caribbean* (Bloomington: Indiana University Press, 2006), 23–91. For the establishment of such villages in Sierra Leone, see Padraic X. Scanlan, "The Colonial Rebirth of British Anti-slavery: The Liberated African Villages of Sierra Leone, 1815–1824," *The American Historical Review* 121:4 (2016): 1085–113.

[82] The inventories are reproduced in the notes of the Commission of Inquiry into the State of Captured Negroes in the West Indies, Tortola Schedules, TNA, CO 318/82, ff. 9–12.

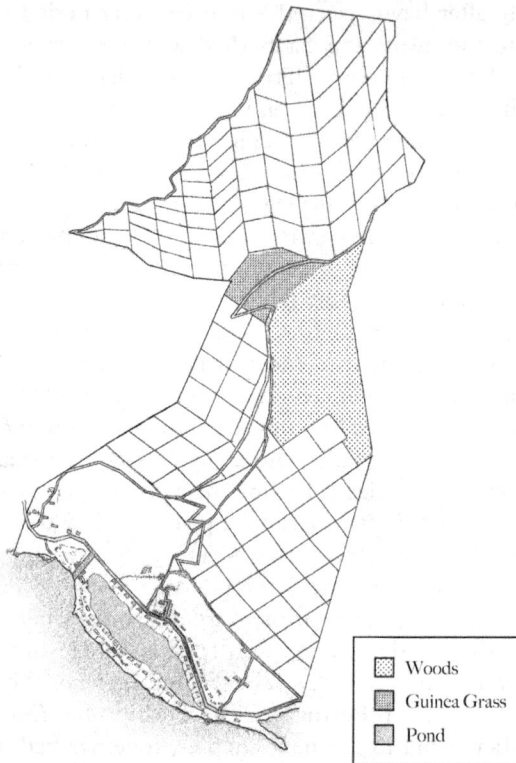

Figure 5.1 Plan of Kingstown, c. 1831.

establishment by imperial decree of the village of Kingstown on the
eastern part of Tortola in 1831.[83]

The initial population of Kingstown was around 350, half of whom
were children.[84] Under the supervision of the collector of customs,
Robert Claxton, each family was given a plot of land on which to build
their residence and grow crops, as shown on the initial plans of the town
depicted in Figure 5.1.[85] The village began with around seventy-five
allotments and grew slowly over the next decade, as the villagers themselves cleared out forested areas to make room for more lots.[86] While the

[83] "Proposal of location for liberated Africans at Tortola," 1831, TNA, T 4303.
[84] Lease of land on Tortola, July 6, 1831, in TNA, CO 239/25.
[85] Robert Claxton to Governor Maxwell, September 1831, in TNA, CO 239/26; "Plan of
    Kingstown," TNA, CO 700/Virgin Islands, f. 6.
[86] Land surveys of Kingstown from the 1830s and 1840s are contained in TNA, CO 700/
    Virgin Islands.

initial intention of the British government was to integrate Africans liberated from the illegal slave trade into colonial society, the construction of Kingstown and the reaction of white Tortolan society to the presence of more free blacks on the island made such integration increasingly difficult. In effect, the village functioned more as an officially sanctioned maroon community than as a part of the colonial social order. The liberated Africans made up a distinct social group, separate from both slaves and free people of color given their nominal freedom and limited access to employment as well as colonial social networks. These factors made it difficult for the inhabitants of Kingstown to sustain themselves, especially considering the poor conditions of the land granted to them, much of which was overgrown by Guinea grass, and the question of whether or not they were liable for the island-wide house and income taxes led to further friction within the colonial government. Claxton and others saw it as unreasonable that houses built from funds by the British government were to be taxed by a local colonial administration, an argument vehemently refuted by both the Assembly of the Virgin Islands and imperial authorities.[87]

The status of Kingstown as its own legal and political entity within the colony of the Virgin Islands was further solidified with the establishment of a small police force, made up of local Africans appointed by and under the supervision of Claxton, and both a school and a church, run primarily by local missionaries.[88] This growing separation led to even less engagement and assistance from colonial authorities, including in the aftermath of a devastating 1837 hurricane. It seems that in those first two decades of the village's existence, more inhabitants of Kingstown sought employment on neighboring St. Thomas than they did in Road Town on Tortola, strengthening trans-imperial ties as intra-colonial integration failed.[89]

Since several of the freedmen moving to villages such as Kingstown were coming from indentured service on other Caribbean islands, these new communities had the unintended consequence of furthering trans-imperial integration through the microregional networks of slaves and free people of color. The new residents on Tortola brought with them a

---

[87] Robert Nickle to Viscount Goderich, September 26, 1832, in TNA, CO 239/30, f. 29.

[88] Following damages wrought by the 1837 hurricane, the initial church would eventually be replaced by St. Phillip's Anglican Church in 1840, built and operated by the local African and Afro-Caribbean community with some support from the colonial government. See Patricia G. Turnbull, *Can These Stones Talk? St. Philip's Church Ruins at the Liberated African Settlement in Kingstown, Tortola* (Tortola: Rainwater Institute, 2012).

[89] See Dookhan, *A History of the British Virgin Islands*, 110–11.

range of connections from their past lives, and even though their new positions did not offer them much in terms of resources beyond the mere necessities of survival, many nonetheless stayed in contact with friends and family in other colonial territories.

The same was true for the scattered maroon communities within the Leeward Islands. While their inhabitants were arguably more limited than freedmen in their ability to traverse the region freely, these communities did bring together a range of individuals from various colonial and imperial territories, resulting in a type of trans-imperial and intercolonial society that in some aspects mirrored and even surpassed the linguistic and ethnic diversity of white societies in towns such as Charlotte Amalie and Gustavia.

While white elites in the Leeward Islands were happy to utilize the de facto slave labor of African apprentices, they were much more reluctant to accept the resettlement of apprentices-turned-freedmen, as illustrated by the local reactions to Kingstown on Tortola. The existence of growing groups of free people of color was already destabilizing the colonial social order as perceived by white planters, and the introduction of more black people living outside the shackles of slavery was far from a welcome addition to white communities dominated by racial paranoia and the fear of black uprisings. These communities were in many respects unprepared for the coming winds of emancipation.

Conclusion

In the microregion of the Leeward Islands, slave laws and free communities brought together different colonies in different ways. New trans-imperial networks formed on the basis of the growing population of free people of color traversing the region, forming connections across colonial and imperial borders and strengthening the integration and communication between nonwhite communities. At the institutional level, legal codes became a crucial arena for contesting authority between imperial capitals and colonial territories. Such laws were also prime examples of the adaptation and translation of codes and practices taking place across different colonies, ultimately creating a number of legal norms that spanned imperial borders.

Colonial legal codes functioned both as a force of institutional oppression and, with time, as an arena for pushing back against such oppression. Even when legal reforms were enacted, it was often difficult to change the actual legal practices on the ground, as white colonial elites were reluctant to give up their position of privilege and dominance in the legal system. The Caribbean colonial system was built on racial hierarchies and systematic oppression, and the growing population of free people of color in the early nineteenth century did relatively little to change this in the short term. Even as the institution of slavery was losing political legitimacy at home, the line between freedom and enslavement in the colonies was thin and easily erased.

Despite these reactionary tendencies, Africans and Afro-Caribbeans managed in many and varied ways to throw off their shackles and carve out their own lives in the region. Maritime marronage was one obvious way to achieve freedom from slavery, even if it was a risky and sometimes short-lived endeavor. Others were able through their labor to buy freedom – that of their children if not always their own. Another way to challenge the colonial order within the framework of empire was to bypass the level of colonial intermediaries entirely by going directly to imperial administrators with petitions and complaints, in this way utilizing and sometimes fanning the flames of intra-imperial jurisdictional conflict.

Such jurisdictional conflicts often took place over legal codes that were more like haphazard patchworks of foreign laws and outdated remnants than fully formed and internally consistent legal frameworks. Much was left up to the interpretation of individual judges and magistrates, in effect creating a system that was driven more by established norms and practices than by written laws. When legislation designed to improve the conditions of enslaved populations was adopted, such as the Amelioration Acts in the British Leewards, it was slow to filter into daily practice and typically did so only after a prolonged period of time or the uncovering of shocking scandals, which brought renewed attention to the otherwise politically distant colonies. The issues at stake to most contemporaries in these conflicts were not those of human rights, but rather those of imperial authority, colonial autonomy, and the proper treatment of enslaved black bodies.

6   Abolition and the Illegal Slave Trade

Perhaps no event in the nineteenth-century Caribbean more clearly illustrates the tensions between imperial policy and local interests than the abolition of the slave trade. While decision makers at the imperial level in Northern Europe decided to ban the trade in slaves across the Atlantic, local actors were much more reluctant to give up the buying and selling of African slave labor, and the illegal trade continued well after its nominal abolition in the first decade of the century. Enforcement of abolitionist policies took different forms in different places, but common to most of them were their intimate linkage to British imperialism and, in particular, their role in demonstrating and enforcing the growing British hegemony in the post-Napoleonic Atlantic world.

Prior to its abolition, the transatlantic slave trade was a crucial component of the inter-imperial system of the Leeward Islands. All empires with colonies in the region were implicated in the trade, both as buyers and as suppliers of slave labor, and the majority of Caribbean imperial powers also laid claim to colonial territory on the African coast.[1] Even those empires with little presence in Africa still had numerous vessels and individuals participating in the trade, and islands such as St. Thomas and St. Barthélemy were significant regional slave markets in the late eighteenth century, popular among Caribbean planters and slavers who were more than willing to visit a foreign colony if it meant paying a lower price for their human wares.

This chapter begins with an analysis of the inter-imperial political context within which the abolition of the slave trade was enacted, focusing in particular on the Danish and British edicts outlawing the trade in 1803 and 1807, respectively. It continues with an examination of the practical implementation of the ban and ends with a more detailed treatment of the continuation of the illicit intercolonial trade as carried out within the microregion of the Leeward Islands.

---

[1] The one exception in the Leeward Islands was Sweden, which lost its last fort on the African Gold Coast in 1663 to Dutch competitors.

The history of the abolition of the slave trade has most often been told from the perspective of imperial legislators and advocates of abolition. When the implementation of the abolition has been treated with serious effort, it has typically been done either through a top-down analysis of diplomacy and international politics or via studies of the places most notably evading the abolition, namely, Cuba and Brazil.[2] Employing a microregional perspective and using the Leeward Islands as the historical case reveals a different side of the story of abolition. This analysis largely confirms the hierarchical dimension of the slave trade abolition in an inter-imperial context, but it also illustrates the vast gaps between imperial policy and colonial practice by showcasing the myriad ways in which local actors and networks circumvented official decrees and continued trading in slaves. The continuation of the trade was not limited to Spanish, French, and Portuguese merchants and planters, but was carried out to an extensive degree within the very empires that were the first to champion its abolition – namely, those of Britain and Denmark. What is more, a not insignificant portion of the slave trade in the Leeward Islands took place within the legal framework of the abolitionist project itself via the buying and selling of confiscated prize slaves.

Abolishing the Trade

While the political trajectory toward the abolition of the transatlantic slave trade can be traced further back, the first concrete legislative action came with the Danish edict of 1792 to abolish that empire's slave trade, effective on January 1, 1803. The reason for the ten-year delay was the perceived necessity for planters in the Danish West Indies to increase the number of enslaved Africans employed on their plantations before the implementation of the ban. A careful, if rather incomplete, demographic analysis lay behind this estimate, and administrators built into the edict incentives for improving working and living conditions, in order to increase the average life span of slaves, and for importing more female slaves.[3] The final edict stated:

---

[2] See, for example, David Murray, *Odious Commerce: Britain, Spain and the Abolition of the Cuban Slave Trade* (Cambridge: Cambridge University Press, 1980); Beatriz Mamigonian, "In the Name of Freedom: Slave Trade Abolition, the Law, and the Brazilian Branch of the African Emigration Scheme," *Slavery and Abolition* 30:1 (2009): 41–66.

[3] For the debate over demographic considerations, see Svend Erik Green-Pedersen, "Slave Demography in the Danish West Indies and the Abolition of the Danish Slave Trade," in *The Abolition of the Atlantic Slave Trade: Origins and Effects in Europe, Africa, and the Americas*, ed. David Eltis and James Walvin (Madison: University of Wisconsin Press, 1981), 231–58; Hans Christian Johansen, "The Reality behind the Demographic

From the result of these enquiries, We are convinced, that it is possible, and will be advantageous to our West India Islands, to desist from the further purchase of new Negroes, when once the Plantations are stocked with a sufficient number for propagation and the cultivation of the lands; when the pecuniary assistance can be given to those who want to purchase Negroes for their estates; and if proper encouragement was to be given to marriage amongst the Negroes; and due attention paid to their instruction and morals.[4]

The "enquiries" referred to in the decree were primarily those conducted by the Commission for Improvement and Abolition of the Slave Trade, formed in 1791 by the crown in order to investigate the financial and political feasibility of a potential abolition of the trade. The commission was composed of a number of influential men in Danish politics, including several Copenhagen-based Caribbean landholders, perhaps the most prominent being the powerful Minister of Finance Ernst Schimmelmann. Judging from their report, and from the Danish political deliberations surrounding it, three main motives for the abolition for the Danish slave trade seem discernible.

First, the trade was regarded as a rather poor commercial enterprise for both the Danish state and the Danish Baltic and Guinea Trading Company, which held a national monopoly on shipping slaves across the Atlantic. Since the number of Danish vessels and merchants involved in the direct trade had been dwindling for several years, to the point where only a few ships per year transported slaves from the African coast under a Danish flag, the resources expended in manning and maintaining the forts along the Danish Gold Coast did not match the revenue earned, and the commission report's characterization of the trade as "insignificant to Denmark's trade and shipping" hardly seemed controversial.[5] This statement did not imply that slavery itself was seen as a bad economic venture, but rather reflected the view that the slave population on the plantations should move toward self-sustainability, thereby making the constant flow of African slave labor unnecessary.

Arguments to Abolish the Danish Slave Trade," in *The Abolition of the Slave Trade*, ed. Eltis and Walvin, 221–30.

[4] This translation of the Danish edict appeared in *The Times*, April 21, 1792. The full text is printed in Erik Gøbel, "The Danish Edict of 16th March 1792 to Abolish the Slave Trade," in *Orbis in Orbem: Liber amicorum John Everaert*, ed. Jan Parmentier and Sander Spanoghe (Ghent: Academia Press, 2001), 259–64.

[5] Ibid., 256. Green-Pedersen points out that the number of slaves sold from the Danish forts in Africa to foreign ships was, however, quite considerable. Svend Erik Green-Pedersen, "The History of the Danish Negro Slave Trade, 1733–1807," *Revue française d'histoire d'outre-mer* 69 (1975): 199. On the topic of other potential uses for the Danish fortifications and trading posts on the African coast, see Daniel P. Hopkins, "The Danish Ban on the Atlantic Slave Trade and Denmark's African Colonial Ambitions, 1787–1807," *Itinerario* 25 (2003): 154–84.

Second, a humanitarian or ideological concern over the nature of the slave trade and the conditions of the African slaves certainly seems to have played at least some role in the work of the commission. While the majority of such language was removed from the final edict, in part because of concerns over a potential backlash from West Indian planters and their political allies, many of the members of the commission, including Schimmelmann himself, were proponents of a complete abolition of slavery to be carried out at a later date.[6] It is worth noting that Schimmelmann was one of the largest plantation owners in the Danish West Indies, as well as a major shareholder in the Guinea Company, illustrating the complexities of both planter and abolitionist networks in Danish politics and the entanglement of one in the other.

Finally, the commission and the Danish government had a very real political concern over the contemporary developments in the British parliament. The government fully expected a British ban on the slave trade, potentially in conjunction with a similar ban by revolutionary France, and it was seen as a likely consequence that the two great powers would "agree to exert pressure on the smaller slave trading nations to do the same."[7] Thus, in the eyes of legislators, a Danish abolition, prior to a potential British act, not only preempted a forceful diplomatic concession but also cast the smaller empire as a prestigious example of morality in the European political landscape, at the cost of what was already a dubiously viable commercial institution.[8]

Not surprisingly, reality proved more complicated than it looked from Copenhagen, and the British abolition came a decade later than expected.[9] Despite the growing strength of the Committee for the Abolition of the Slave Trade, the primary abolitionist lobby group formed in London in 1787, the political process of abolishing the trade in Britain faced a number of serious obstacles. These obstacles included

---

[6] Green-Pedersen, "The History of the Danish Trade," 216; Gøbel, "The Danish Edict," 253.

[7] Ibid., 254. This concern over inter-imperial hegemonic pressures would prove to be particularly prescient.

[8] On the topic of abolition as a project of international prestige, see Matthew Mason, "Keeping up Appearances: The International Politics of Slave Trade Abolition in the Nineteenth-Century Atlantic World," *The William and Mary Quarterly* 66:4 (2009): 809–32. For more on the Danish context, see Pernille Røge, "Why the Danes Got There First: A Trans-Imperial Study of the Abolition of the Danish Slave Trade in 1792," *Slavery and Abolition* 35:4 (2014): 576–92.

[9] The Danish government kept a close eye on the political process in Britain, and the Danish ministers in London delivered frequent reports on the topic of abolition as well as copious amounts of printed material from both abolitionists and their opponents. Much of this material is kept in "Printed matter from the English Parliament," RA, COC 425, and in "Matters Related to the Suppression of the Slave Trade," RA, DFA 1208.

strong domestic political opposition, including from the West Indian lobby, which, in contrast to their counterparts in Copenhagen, had very little overlap with the abolitionist faction.[10] A number of unforeseen events on the international scene also played a part in delaying abolition, especially the revolution in Saint-Domingue. While the shift in political discourse in Britain following the American Revolution had highlighted the necessity of limiting settler sovereignty and strengthening imperial authority, the shift following the revolutions in France and in Saint-Domingue cast abolitionism in a darker light, associating it more with revolutionary fervor, the Reign of Terror, and black revolts than with an assertion of metropolitan power.[11] This shift in political and popular sentiment pushed abolition off the agenda for almost a decade, and not until a renewed effort on the part of the abolitionist lobby in parliament in 1804 did the process regain its momentum, culminating in the passing of the Abolition of the Slave Trade Act in March 1807.[12]

There was nothing inevitable about the early nineteenth-century abolition in Denmark, Britain, or indeed in the United States, which saw its own Act Prohibiting Importation of Slaves passed in 1807.[13] A multitude of political factors came together to create the necessary momentum for domestic actors, be they abolitionist movements or foresighted politicians, to pass the legislation that would ban the trade. Such imperial bans, combined with a rather different kind of abolition in the case of the newly independent Haitian state, meant that the slave trade in the North Atlantic and the Caribbean changed dramatically in the first decade of the new century.[14] Legislation was not enough, however, and the British Empire became a major agent for further and broader change, involving the rest of the imperial actors in the Atlantic.

---

[10] For a careful treatment of the declining influence of planters and the growth of abolitionist sentiments in Britain, see Christopher L. Brown, *Moral Capital: Foundations of British Abolitionism* (Chapel Hill: University of North Carolina Press, 2006), 391–450; Brown, "The Politics of Slavery," in *The British Atlantic World, 1500–1800* (2nd edition), ed. Armitage and Braddick, 214–32.

[11] See Philip D. Morgan, "Ending the Slave Trade: A Caribbean and Atlantic Context," in *Abolitionism and Imperialism in Britain, Africa, and the Atlantic*, ed. Derek R. Peterson (Athens: Ohio University Press, 2010), 103–4.

[12] "An Act for the Abolition of the Slave Trade," 47 Geo. III, c. 36.

[13] This piece of legislation followed the Slave Trade Act of 1794, which had already imposed limits on US involvement in the trade. See, for example, the pioneering work of W. E. B. Du Bois, *The Suppression of the African Slave-Trade to the United States of America, 1638–1870* (New York: Longmans, 1896).

[14] For more on the role of the young Haitian state in this context, see Ferrer, "Haiti, Free Soil, and Antislavery"; Du Bois, *The Suppression of the African Slave-Trade*, 74–96.

Enforcement and Regional Hegemony

While a number of polities had been active in pushing forward the new abolitionist regime across the Atlantic, the enforcement of this regime was first and foremost a British enterprise. The British Empire employed three key tools used in their active suppression of the slave trade: diplomacy, law, and naval superiority. Diplomatically, Britain engaged in a committed policy of signing bilateral agreements with any and all rival empires, regardless of how tangentially they were connected to the transoceanic shipping of slaves, persuading or forcing them into agreeing to work toward a comprehensive abolition. Flowing in part from this policy, Britain began the legal project of creating mixed commissions in foreign colonies, setting up courts with both British and host judges and magistrates in order to try captured slave ships. In order to apprehend these ships and their crew, the Royal Navy created the West African antislavery squadron, tasked with patrolling the African shore and seizing any and all ships thought to be engaged in the illicit slave trade. While this squadron started out on an ad hoc basis and became nearly inoperable due to limited resources during the War of 1812, it began operating on a permanent basis from 1816 onward. The antislavery squadron greatly expanded the presence of British naval forces in both Caribbean and African waters, and while many of the officers engaged in the task of patrolling these waters saw their work as a step down from the navy's other activities, the searches and seizures of foreign as well as British vessels served to effectively communicate the growing military superiority of the empire across the region.[15]

The diplomatic tools used in the suppression of the slave trade were closely tied to growing British imperial naval hegemony, both in the greater Caribbean region and in the Indian Ocean. Besides bilateral agreements of cooperation with Denmark, the United States, the Netherlands, and even Sweden in 1813 and 1814, the British Empire used the Congress of Vienna, convened at the end of the Napoleonic Wars, to include a multilateral condemnation of the slave trade in the Final Act. This condemnation opened with the remarkable statement that "having taken into consideration that the commerce, known by the name of 'the Slave Trade,' has been considered, by just and enlightened men of all ages, as repugnant to the principles of humanity and universal morality," and it signaled to the wider public that all signed parties shared the "wish

---

[15] The most comprehensive examination of the West Africa Squadron and the role of the navy remains Christopher Lloyd, *The Navy and the Slave Trade: The Suppression of the African Slave Trade in the Nineteenth Century* (London: Frank Cass and Company, 1968).

of putting an end to a scourge, which has so long desolated Africa, degraded Europe, and afflicted humanity."[16] Despite such moral flourishes, the timeline of an actual implementation of the ban was left vague, as the signatories "acknowledge that this general Declaration cannot prejudge the period that each particular Power may consider as most advisable for the definitive Abolition of the Slave Trade."[17]

Britain persuaded or coerced the other European empires to sign treaties granting mutual rights to search and seize ships in violation of the ban and to try offenders at mixed commission courts. Such treaties were signed with Spain in 1817 (coming into effect in 1820), with Portugal in 1817, and even with France in 1831, following a rather ambiguous and shifting French policy toward abolition after the fall of the First Republic.[18] The Swedish Empire also committed to a ban on the trade after some pressure from British officials, with the first official decree taking effect in 1813 and reiterated on several subsequent occasions.[19] While such decrees primarily pertained to the slave markets on St. Barthélemy, their effectiveness seems to have been partial at best.

The abolitionist treaty regimes created a peculiar legal situation, since most of the other empires had not themselves ratified abolitionist legislation but instead agreed to give up a small part of their sovereignty, specifically that of jurisdiction over suspected slave traders sailing under their flags. In the case of Portugal, the treaty made slave trade illegal only north of the equator, and when Brazil declared independence in 1822 the British Empire had to make deals with both Lusophone states.[20] The Anglo-Brazilian treaty, in which Britain recognized the independence of Brazil in return for, among other stipulations, the promise of a national abolition of the slave trade, did not prove particularly effective. While there was a significant but momentary drop in the slave trade from 1829 to 1831, the newly independent Brazilian government was largely unwilling to enforce abolition, and the British Empire lacked the naval resources necessary to patrol the massive coastlines of Brazil and its

---

[16] Contained in the *Final Act of the Congress of Vienna* as Act XV under the title "The Declaration of the Powers on the Abolition of the Slave Trade, of the 8th February, 1815."

[17] Ibid.

[18] See Serge Daget, "France, Suppression of the Illegal Trade, and England, 1817–1850," in *The Abolition of the Atlantic Slave Trade: Origins and Effects in Europe, Africa, and the Americas*, ed. David Eltis and James Walvin (Madison: University of Wisconsin Press, 1981), 193–217.

[19] See, for example, the Royal Declaration of 1830, reproduced in "Letters and Proclamations from His Majesty's Government," RKA LC 2424/13.

[20] Mason, "Keeping up Appearances," 813–14.

African trading partners.[21] Regardless of such practical limitations to its enforcement, the treaty regime emerging from the concerted effort of British diplomats and politicians was a remarkable example of a hierarchical legal–political order between polities, in which the British Empire created an image of international unity through the use of more or less coercive means.[22]

Turning to the judicial tools, the mixed commission courts provide an interesting historical example of the messiness of inter-imperial jurisdiction. The exact nature and historical significance of the mixed commissions within the larger framework of inter-imperial negotiations and intra-imperial jurisdiction is a hotly debated topic in the historiography, with some scholars of international law arguing that they functioned as examples of proto-human rights courts.[23] Other scholars, namely, Padraic Scanlan and Lauren Benton, have problematized this position by placing the mixed commissions within the longer perspective of the consolidation of imperial authority and the challenge to intra-imperial jurisdiction, and to abolitionist policies, posed by slaveholder rights and resistance from local elites.[24] Perhaps the main problem with seeing the commissions as early precedents for either international law or human rights regimes was the unilateral nature of their implementation and practice. In terms of both legal foundation and practical implementation, the courts were clearly dominated by Britain, and the majority of judges at any one time were almost always of British origin.[25] This British

---

[21] David Eltis, "Was Abolition of the U.S. and British Slave Trade Significant in the Broader Atlantic Context?," *The William and Mary Quarterly* 66:4 (2009): 729–30.

[22] For more on the slave trade treaties as an expression of interpolity hierarchy, see Edward Keene, "A Case Study of the Construction of International Hierarchy: British Treaty-Making against the Slave Trade in the Early Nineteenth Century," *International Organization* 61:2 (2007): 311–39.

[23] See Jenny Martinez , "Antislavery Courts and the Dawn of International Human Rights Law," *Yale Law Journal* 117 (2008): 550–64; Tara Helfman, "The Court of Vice Admiralty at Sierra Leone and the Abolition of the West African Slave Trade," *Yale Law Journal* 115 (2006): 1122–56. Other common interpretations focus on the mixed commissions as indicators of an emergent positivist international legal order. See, for example, Allain, "The Nineteenth Century Law of the Sea and British Abolition," 342–88.

[24] Benton, "Abolition and Imperial Law," 355–74; Padraic X. Scanlan, *Freedom's Debtors: British Antislavery in Sierra Leone in the Age of Revolution* (New Haven: Yale University Press, 2017).

[25] For a discussion of the problematic issues of international law vis-à-vis the mixed commissions later in the nineteenth century, see Robin Law, "Abolitionism and Imperialism: International Law and the British Suppression of the Atlantic Slave Trade," in *Abolitionism and Imperialism in Britain, Africa, and the Atlantic*, ed. Derek R. Peterson (Athens: Ohio University Press, 2010), 150–74. See also Jake C. Richards, "Anti-slave-trade Law, 'Liberated Africans' and the State in the South Atlantic World, c. 1839–1852," *Past and Present* 241:1 (2018): 179–219.

unilateralism in the suppression of the slave trade thus extended to the political, military, and legal aspects of the effort, and as Seymour Drescher has pointed out, abolition and British imperialism were intimately tied together in the nineteenth century.[26] In the case of the courts, British prize law, as previously discussed in this book, played a substantial role in the jurisdictional enforcement of abolitionist policies.

When viewed from within the inter-imperial microregion of the Leeward Islands, British enforcement of the abolition looked more like an application of imperial hierarchy than anything else, at both the intra- and inter-imperial levels. The moral arguments of abolitionists generally had little to no purchase among the Caribbean planter elites, and those landowners and policy makers who had directly advocated abolition tended to reside in faraway European capitals rather than on their West Indian plantations. For British imperial administrators, the ban on buying and selling slaves provided a convenient opportunity to tighten control over the empire's own colonies, to put local magistrates with ambitions of autonomy in their place, and not least to patrol the waters of foreign colonies – particularly in the years following the peace of 1815.

This was certainly the impression held by other colonial governors, for whom the growing presence of British naval power in the Caribbean during peacetime was cause for serious concern. There seemed little doubt among these men that whatever noble intentions might be proclaimed at the level of official politics, the primary purpose of having vessels equipped for war cruising Caribbean waters lay in their projection of British maritime power. It was interpreted as a less-than-subtle reminder to locals that what His Majesty's Empire had secured through legal and diplomatic channels could just as easily be obtained through sheer naval superiority. Some officials were not shy to call out displays of regional hegemony to their British counterparts when complaining about the conduct of British naval vessels. Governor Berndt Gustaf Stackelberg of St. Barthélemy, for example, sent a series of complaints to Governor Hugh Elliott of the British Leeward Islands over the conduct and "insolence" of British vessels boarding, inspecting, and sometimes seizing Swedish ships in the region.[27] These complaints are an interesting window into the intercolonial politics of the period, as they mixed criticism of British naval policy with outrage over the way in which the

---

[26] See Seymour Drescher, "Emperors of the World: British Abolitionism and Imperialism," in *Abolitionism and Imperialism in Britain, Africa, and the Atlantic*, ed. Peterson, 129–49; Drescher, "History's Engines: British Mobilization in the Age of Revolution," *The William and Mary Quarterly* 66:4 (2009): 737–56; Keene, "Case Study of the Construction of International Hierarchy."

[27] Most of these letters of complaint are contained in TNA, CO 152/101 and CO 152/102.

practical implementation of these policies threatened to destabilize the racial order of the region. Stackelberg thus combined a veiled attack on Britain's geopolitical dominance with "astonishment" over the fact that the British crews included armed "negroes and mulatoes" who dared to give orders to white sailors on board the Swedish vessels.[28]

The growing presence of British naval power did not elicit quite the same fearful response from landowners and merchants in the region. Rather than demonstrating respect for the new abolitionist regime, many of these local actors simply ignored the threat of naval patrols and sought new ways to carry slaves between the islands and from across the Atlantic, on smaller and swifter crafts and using many of those networks that had formed around earlier decades' intercolonial contraband trade. Thus, despite the fact that British naval ships often stopped and searched Danish, Dutch, and Swedish ships, the illegal slave trade hardly came to an end. In fact, the trade seems to have flourished in the late 1810s and early 1820s, particularly around the Danish and Swedish Caribbean territories. The enforcement of interpolity hierarchy that British imperial administrators engaged in did not resonate with most of the empire's subjects in the Leewards, since the interests of these actors were much closer aligned to that of their regional neighbors than to their European countrymen, at least when it came to the trade in African slaves.

The Impact of Abolition

Before venturing forth, it is worth briefly considering how impactful the multilayered attempt at enforcing abolition was on the wider Atlantic slave trade. In assessing this, it is fruitful to differentiate between different levels of measurement and distinct geographic spheres. Following the framework put forth by David Eltis, one can divide the transoceanic slave complex into two distinct realms: the northern and the southern Atlantic, divided by the equator and made up of largely separate shipping routes determined by regional winds and currents.[29]

The northern slave trade system was the one most significantly altered by the new abolitionist regime. Judging from the available data, this trade saw a marked overall decline following 1807, and Eltis points out that in the years immediately following this date the overall slave trade fell by approximately 60 percent, in no small part due to the fact that British slave ships disappeared almost entirely from the Atlantic Ocean. Already in the 1810s this trend changed, however, as the majority of slave trade

---

[28] Stackelberg to Elliott, January 5 and March 2, 1813, in TNA, CO 152/101, ff. 30 and 36.
[29] Eltis, "Was Abolition Significant?," 718–19.

shifted from the northern to the southern hemisphere.[30] If the British abolition of the slave trade was at least a partial success in the West Indies and the Atlantic region, the same was not true for British colonies in East Africa and the Indian Ocean. Richard Allen has shown how Madagascan illicit slave trade continued to be a major problem for imperial administrators in Mauritius and Seychelles well into the 1820s.[31]

In the case of the Danish abolition, the traffic of slaves on Danish ships saw a remarkable fall following 1803. This trend did not mean, however, that there were no slaves passing through the Danish overseas colonies. Historian Georg Nørregård has shown how the Guinea Coast fortifications continued to facilitate the traffic of African slaves, largely on board foreign vessels, but also on ships traveling to the Danish islands of St. Croix and St. Thomas, despite the official ban. According to Nørregård, this trade continued throughout the first quarter of the century, and as late as 1821 "the free mulattos maintained that the abolition of the slave trade had never been announced to them; so they knew nothing about it."[32] Not until well into the 1820s was any real effort made to put a stop to the trade on the Danish Gold Coast, in part because the African colonial territories were so far removed from metropolitan eyes and minds. The Danish West Indies also continued to be involved in the slave trade well past the 1803 abolition. Their role shifted, however, as the trade in which they partook was increasingly focused on local intercolonial and trans-imperial practices rather than on transoceanic shipping, as described in further detail below.

The Dutch case was similar to the Danish one, since the majority of the state-sponsored Dutch slave trade had in effect already come to an end by the mid-1790s.[33] This fact made it a relatively easy decision for the Dutch government to sign a bilateral treaty with Britain and to participate in the mixed commission courts at Freetown, Sierra Leone,

---

[30] Ibid., 721–22.

[31] Richard B. Allen, "Licentious and Unbridled Proceedings: The Illegal Slave Trade to Mauritius and the Seychelles during the Early Nineteenth Century," *The Journal of African History* 42:1 (2001): 91–116; Richard B. Allen, "Suppressing a Nefarious Traffic: Britain and the Abolition of Slave Trading in India and the Western Indian Ocean, 1770–1830," *The William and Mary Quarterly* 66:4 (2009): 873–94.

[32] Georg Nørregård, *Danish Settlements in West Africa, 1648–1850*, trans. Sigurd Mammen (Boston: Boston University Press, 1966), 182–84.

[33] The Dutch West India Company had lost its monopoly on the Dutch slave trade as early as the 1730s, and since then any Dutch subject could purchase a permit to participate in the trade as a free agent. Dutch state-sponsored slave trading ceased almost entirely following 1794. For a careful examination of the available data, see Johannes Postma, "A Reassessment of the Dutch Atlantic Slave Trade," in *Riches from Atlantic Commerce: Dutch Transatlantic Trade and Shipping, 1585–1817*, ed. Johannes Postma and Victor Enthoven, (Leiden: Brill, 2003), 115–38.

and Paramaribo, Surinam. As became clear in the proceedings of these courts, a number of ships of other nationalities, particularly French, continued to bring slaves into the Dutch territories under illegally obtained or forged Dutch papers. Many of these documents likely originated from corrupt Dutch colonial officials, including a large number being issued by a series of notoriously corrupt governors of St. Eustatius in the early 1820s.[34] According to historian Pieter Emmer, the shipping of slaves into Dutch colonies did not come to a real halt until 1826, when the Netherlands made it a priority to stop such corruption at the local level, in part because, as far as "the Dutch government was concerned, the bleak prospects of the Surinam plantation economy and the pressures from Britain, were sufficient stimuli to both stop the Dutch slave trade and to put an end to illegal slave imports into Surinam."[35]

The south Atlantic slave trade complex, for its part, saw a dramatic increase in volume after 1807. The bilateral treaties that the Spanish and Portuguese governments signed with the British were not perceived as being as binding or as important as the national legislative actions of Britain, Denmark, and the United States, and, as mentioned previously, there were often limits to the extent to which the Iberian empires were committed to outlawing their slave trade. When the trade north of the equator became more precarious for sailors and merchants, an increased shift to the south was a natural consequence. That the Brazilian government did not make good on their promises to Britain was also a major blow to abolition, and in the two decades after 1831 Brazil became one of the largest importers of slaves. In a similar vein, Spain saw slave imports as a crucial component of the Cuban economy, and, while tacitly agreeing to British demands, Spanish officials did their best to keep the flow of slaves to Cuba uninterrupted. According to Matthew Mason, Spanish officials succeeded by agreeing to cooperate with Britain on a diplomatic level while obstructing the legal process within the mixed commissions, and by manipulating the number of newly imported slaves to Cuba appearing in official demographic documents.[36]

In some ways the relative success of abolition north of the equator made it possible for the slave trade to increase so drastically in the southern Atlantic. One important factor in passing abolitionist legislation in Britain

---

[34] This is an oft-recurring point of complaint from other imperial officials in the Leewards. See, for example, British accusations against authorities on St. Eustatius in 1828, in TNA, CO 239/18, and similar Swedish complaints by Governor Norderling in 1821, in RKA, SBS 2411/2/VII B. See also Pieter C. Emmer, "Abolition of the Abolished: The Illegal Dutch Slave Trade and the Mixed Courts," in *The Abolition of the Atlantic Slave Trade*, ed. Eltis and Walvin, 181–82.

[35] Ibid., 187.   [36] Mason, "Keeping up Appearances," 818.

in the first place was reduced economic competition caused by the Haitian Revolution, which severely limited the French presence in the Caribbean and the Americas. A similar dynamic was playing out in the 1810s, as the sugar plantations owned by Northern European colonial powers gradually came to be less productive than those controlled by their Southern European competitors, despite the demographic measures taken prior to abolition. This fall in productivity, combined with the many French and American smugglers who were more than willing to ship slaves into the Iberian colonies, often sailing under Dutch or Swedish flags, created the grounds for Spanish and Brazilian territories to greatly expand their own plantation economies, eventually surpassing the former British, French, and Danish hubs in the production of sugar.[37]

Despite the differences in intensity between the northern and southern Atlantic, there was still a relatively large flow of illicit slave trade into and out of ports controlled by abolitionist empires or by powers that had partaken in the British treaty regime. This was certainly the case in the Leeward Islands, where informal and illicit slave markets continued to exist and even flourish during the two decades following abolition. A large part of the explanation behind this pattern should be sought in the limits of imperial authority and the recurring principal–agent problem existing between metropolitan legislators and colonial magistrates tasked with implementing imperial policy.

The Caribbean Slave Trade after Abolition

In general, the post-abolition slave trade in the Leeward Islands took three forms. The first was the direct and illicit transatlantic shipping of enslaved Africans, which continued to exist to some extent and even expanded in the first decade after abolition. The second was the illegal but widespread trade in slaves across and between colonies within the Caribbean. The third form, unlike the prior two types, was operating at least halfway within the realm of imperially sanctioned practice. This trade took place around the auctions of Africans confiscated as part of the British effort to enforce the slave trade ban.

The transportation of enslaved Africans across the Atlantic Ocean did not cease with the British abolition of the slave trade. Rather, it continued in somewhat altered forms and often under different flags over the next several decades. Much of this post-abolition trade originated in the

---

[37] As a point of comparison, in the middle decades of the eighteenth century, St. Croix produced more sugarcane than Puerto Rico and possibly even rivaled Cuba. See Dookhan, *A History of the Virgin Islands*, 79–82.

African colonies of imperial powers that either had not implemented the abolition or had retained some specific exceptions to their ban on the trade, such as the Spanish clause of keeping Cuba open to the importation of slave labor, but it was not limited to these territories. Both British and Danish entrepôts on the African coast continued to supply merchants and captains with slaves for almost two decades following abolition in each empire, and many of the ships engaged in the trade were owned or helmed by the subjects of abolitionist nations. When confronted by imperial officials, some colonial agents claimed that they had little choice but to continue to purchase slaves from their African contacts lest the local polities would decide that the Europeans had outstayed their welcome on the coast.[38] That these colonial agents collected substantial profits from the trade no doubt also played a role.

While the most significant markets for slaves shipped across the Atlantic in this period were the larger islands of the Spanish Empire, the Leeward Islands were not infrequent ports of call. This was especially true for the Danish colonies, which served as popular ports for transshipment of slaves to nearby Puerto Rico.[39] Tortola also saw the arrival of a few larger vessels carrying slaves directly from Africa, but these were often cases of captains either having been lost in the treacherous waters or being forced to lay anchor at a local port due to some unforeseen circumstance, and they almost inevitably led to seizure of the Africans on board.[40] A particularly notorious example was the Spanish ship *Venus Havannera*, which was seized by a British brig while off the coast of Tortola in 1814 and brought to the prize court there. The ship was ostensibly sailing from Africa to Havana but was waylaid by a storm en route and found itself in the Virgin Islands. It carried 530 enslaved Africans, 120 of whom either died on the voyage or shortly after being brought into Tortola.[41] Even if the ports of the Leewards were not at the center of the transatlantic trade after 1807, individuals from islands such as St. Thomas, St. Eustatius, and St. Barthélemy often participated in the trade in more conspicuous ways, supplying funds, crews, or flags and registries.

[38] Nørregård, *Danish Settlements in West Africa*, 175–95.
[39] While no exact numbers exist after the Danish abolition of 1803, Svend Erik Green-Pedersen has shown the centrality of St. Thomas and St. Croix as ports of regional transshipment prior to this date. See Green-Pedersen, "The Scope and Structure of the Danish Negro Slave Trade," *Scandinavian Economic History Review* 19:2 (1971): 149–97.
[40] For overviews of some of these cases, see "Tortola: Seizures 1829–1835," in TNA, CUST 34/818; Tortola Schedules from the Commissioners of Inquiry, in TNA, CO 318/82.
[41] The death toll of this voyage was so staggering that it was frequently invoked by British abolitionists. See *Papers Relative to the Slave Trade Presented to Parliament in 1819*, vol. 1 (London: R. G. Clarke, 1820), 191.

The practice of sailing under different flags became so prevalent in the illegal slave trade that blaming non-subjects for misusing one's flag was a convenient and increasingly common retort to inter-imperial complaints. In 1825 the Swedish government issued a proclamation as a response to the growing problem of slave vessels leaving the coast of Africa under Swedish colors. In it, the government made clear that any Swedish subjects found to have chartered or financed a vessel engaged in the slave trade would be considered "principals to this inhuman trade" and would be "prosecuted accordingly."[42] This clarification was in part a response to the common excuse made by financiers and owners that the crew of their vessels acted on their own accord without the knowledge of their masters, but it was also a political signal to other imperial powers on the part of the government, reassuring them that the Swedish Empire was indeed committed to the cause of abolition.

If transatlantic shipping of slaves was a relatively uncommon occurrence in the post-abolition Leeward Islands, intercolonial slave trade was a pervasive and entrenched practice in the microregion. British, Danish, Dutch, and Swedish colonies were deeply implicated in such activities, and they seem to have taken place within well-established trans-imperial networks. While the degree to which colonial officials were involved in the trade seems to have differed from island to island, magistrates of all empires played some role in facilitating these practices, either by turning a blind eye to the presence of slave markets within their jurisdictions, as on St. Thomas, or by selling or otherwise providing the necessary paperwork to transport slaves between colonies. As late as 1831 slaves were frequently smuggled between islands and resold, often through the use of registries and certificates that were either forged or obtained from corrupt magistrates.[43]

As opposed to the direct shipping of slaves across the Atlantic, which was a clear violation of abolition and tended to take place faraway from official scrutiny, the intercolonial slave trade within the Leewards often happened just below the radar of or with the direct collusion of colonial officials. While moving slaves between different islands with the aim of selling them was ostensibly illegal, moving them from one estate to another belonging to the same family was within the letter of the law, as long as an official approval was granted. The Danish West Indies saw many requests for such approvals in the years after abolition, and a closer

[42] Royal Proclamation on the Prohibition against the African Slave Trade, January 12, 1825, in RKA, LC 2424/22.
[43] "Customs, Tortola: Papers relating to plantations, 1816–1853," TNA, CUST 34/814, ff. G and H.

reading of these moments of official involvement in the movement of slaves illustrates the many ways in which slaves were bought and sold within the intercolonial plantation networks. It also highlights the role played by slaves in objecting to their owners' transgressions against imperial law.

One example of this dynamic can be seen in the 1825 case of the enslaved woman Madlane, whose owner, the widow Sarah Daguilard, requested to move her from St. Croix to St. Thomas.[44] Daguilard had originally brought Madlane with her to the Danish island from Curaçao during the period of British occupation, eventually opening up a dry goods store in Christiansted.[45] The widow seems to have been a somewhat notorious personage in the town, having been under investigation previously for the maltreatment of her slaves and their children. According to Madlane, the intention of Daguilard in 1825 was not to move her from one estate to another within the Danish islands, but rather to send her to St. Thomas and from there sell her to a foreign buyer on St. Barthélemy, separating her from her children and family in the process. Another of Daguilard's slaves being moved, Catalina, similarly reported to officials that her ultimate destination was not St. Thomas, but "a place much further away."[46] This type of transshipment seems to have been a fairly common practice in the period, as St. Thomas was the center for a well-known, if underground, intercolonial slave market. In the 1810s and 1820s most of the requests for transporting slaves in the Danish islands were focused on movement between St. Croix and St. Thomas, but a growing number also requested transport to nearby Puerto Rico, likely as a consequence of the increasing demand for slaves in the Spanish colony during the sugar boom.[47]

That the illegal slave trade to Puerto Rico was widely recognized in the region is illustrated by a different case concerning the movement of free and enslaved individuals between the Danish and Spanish colonies. Frederikke Amalia, a free woman of color born on St. Thomas, had allegedly been kidnapped and sold into slavery in Puerto Rico in the late 1820s. While the Danish Governor, Peter von Scholten, made several inquiries to the Spanish colonial authorities regarding Amalia's

---

[44] "Requests to send slaves and servants between islands," in the Caribbean Collection: Virgin Island Documents, the Florence Williams Library, Christiansted, St. Croix.

[45] St. Croix Census, Christiansted, 1841, in the Caribbean Collection: Virgin Island Documents, the Florence Williams Library, Christiansted, St. Croix.

[46] "Requests to send slaves and servants between islands."

[47] Ibid. For Puerto Rico's changing plantation economy in this period, see, for example, Francisco A. Scarano, *Sugar and Slavery in Puerto Rico: The Plantation Economy of Ponce, 1800–1850* (Madison: University of Wisconsin Press, 1984).

circumstances, these seem to have been met with little information, and in 1837 von Scholten wrote:

I fear that it will be challenging to confirm the claims through the Spanish Tribunals, and I assume that the most important hindrance lies in the relevant authority's disinclination to investigate too closely the Documents of Title held by the slave owners in general, as these Documents in most cases would be highly inadequate, seeing as so many of the slaves there have been acquired through the illegal and forbidden, but very much active, African slave trade.[48]

The ultimate fate of Amalia is unknown. She might well have been kept in slavery in Puerto Rico, as her family on St. Thomas claimed, or she might have been transported from there to Cuba or another colony as part of the intercolonial slave trade, but she was undoubtedly not the only individual born into freedom in the Caribbean who nonetheless ended up enslaved in a different territory.

The third type of post-abolition slave trade was that involving prize slaves. Enslaved Africans seized by officials, either while on board slaving vessels or after having been illegally purchased, were to be "forfeited to the Crown."[49] As described in the previous chapter, this forfeiture typically meant that they were to serve a fourteen-year period of apprenticeship before being granted their freedom. The boundary between legal apprenticeships and the illegal resale of confiscated slaves was often blurred, particularly so at the Vice Court of Admiralty on Tortola. While the colonial government employed some confiscated slaves, many other Africans were auctioned off by prize courts under the guise of the laws of apprenticeship. This practice in turn created a somewhat paradoxical situation in which enforcement of the abolition itself fed an emerging market for captured prize slaves. While the period of servitude for these apprentices was finite and their potential children were not born into the same legal bonds as those of slaves, the daily life of an apprentice was hardly all that different from that of a slave. Indeed, many of them were auctioned off to work on plantations alongside slaves, and it is unclear how common the act of denying apprentices their eventual freedom was – a practice made all the easier due to the lax way in which courts such as the one on Tortola handled the records of prize slaves.[50]

According to the former Tortola prize agent Anthony Mackenrot, Admiral Alexander Cochrane of the Royal Navy had taken more than 200 Africans who had been condemned at the Tortola court and, rather

---

[48] Letter from Governor von Scholten to Frederick VI, May 4, 1837, RA, WILA 2.7.3.
[49] Report from Governor William Nicolay, May 1832, TNA, CO 239/29, f. 38.
[50] An incomplete example of such paperwork is preserved as "List of Prize Negroes condemned at Tortola," in TNA, CO 239/5, miscellaneous.

than free them or place them into legal apprenticeships, used them as slave labor on his own Trinidad plantation.[51] Captain Cochrane's actions were, according to Mackenrot, not a one-time happening but rather an example of a common practice of reselling captured prize slaves at the court – a practice in which many of the court's agents and the islands magistrates were involved, including the admiral's brother Andrew Cochrane-Johnstone, himself a prize agent on the island.[52] Later investigations indicated that this trade in African apprentices was not limited to the British Leewards, but that Africans confiscated at the Tortola court were also sold to the colonies of other empires, including Puerto Rico.[53] While Mackenrot can hardly be considered an impartial source, the gist of his accusations nonetheless seems to resonate with other accounts of Tortola in the post-abolition period.[54] Indeed, the entire region was suspected of disregarding the letter and the spirit of abolition by political elites in London, resulting in the creation of an investigative commission in the 1820s.

The British Commission of Enquiry into the State of Captured Negroes in the West Indies provides an illuminating glimpse into the practices of the illegal slave trade in the region. Set up in 1821 and operating throughout the 1820s, the aim of this commission was to look into the conditions and treatment of so-called liberated Africans, that is, slaves who had been confiscated by collectors of customs in accordance with the abolition of the trade. The commission was initially led by Thomas Moody, a major from a prominent Caribbean planter family, and John Dougan, a landowner and former prize agent on Tortola, until the latter's resignation in 1822 following a number of disputes with his colleague.[55] In short, the two men found themselves divided over the extent of planters' rights, as Moody was decidedly more on the side of the slave owners than was Dougan. According to a report to parliament, Dougan's conclusion from the investigations was that "free labour in the West Indies is preferable to compulsory labour; that of Major Moody on

---

[51] Anthony Mackenrot, *Secret Memoirs of the Honourable Andrew Cochrane Johnstone: Of the Honourable Vice-Admiral Sir Alex. Forrester Cochrane, K. B., and of Sir Thomas John Cochrane, a Captain in the Royal Navy, with an Account of the Circumstances Which Led to the Discovery of the Conspiracy of Lord Cochrane and Others to Defraud the Stock Exchange* (London: C. Chapple), 9–11. See also TNA, CO 239/10, f. 126.

[52] See Benton, "This Melancholy Labyrinth," 106–7.

[53] Letter from Governor Maxwell to Earl Bathurst, April 7, 1824, TNA, CO 239/10, f. 118.

[54] Indeed, many of these practices seem to have persisted throughout the 1810s, as indicated by the Commission of Enquiry, discussed below.

[55] See the account of the commissioner's dispute in Thomas Babington Macaulay, "Social and Industrial Capacities of the Negroes," in *Critical, Historical and Miscellaneous Essays*, vol. 6 (New York: Sheldon and Company, 1860), 361–404.

the contrary is, that without some species of coercion African labour would be worthless."[56]

The work of the commission is interesting here not so much for its assessments or final recommendations as for the many observational notes taken by the commissioners during their fieldwork in the region. In one of the dispatches from Commissioner Moody, dated August 17, 1823, the seizure and subsequent fate of the vessel *La Mouche* is described in some detail. The vessel, condemned on August 16, 1819, allegedly sailed out of St. Thomas with a number of slaves on board, quite possibly picked up as cargo to be sold. Mr. Robert Mason, the apparent master of the ship and a known resident of St. Thomas, was sailing under a letter of marque signed by José Artigas. Moody describes Mason as

a notorious privateersman in these seas, chiefly residing at St. Thomas. When vessels with slaves on board were captured, the vessels were brought to such retired small islands as Jos Van Dykes, and the sound at Spanish Town [on Virgin Gorda], to which the merchants from the Danish island of St. Thomas resorted and bought the slaves which were afterwards sold in foreign islands. This system was practiced quite openly, as there was neither military nor naval Force in the government of the Virgin Islands to prevent them.[57]

The following description of the challenges of stopping the Virgin Islands slave trade, by Moody, is worth quoting at length:

The slave trade with Africa is still carried on from the Danish island of St. Thomas, and the negroes sold in like manner. One schooner called the *Anna Barnes*, a swift sailing vessel has made fourteen voyages and is still employed in the Trade. Nothing but the guard of a British Man of War can prevent these vessels frequenting the small Keys which form this government. In Jos Van Dykes for example which once contained two Sugar Estates there is now no magistrate residing on the island, or persons possessing property beyond a very limited extent as its cultivation is now reduced to about 100 acres of land, and a little more than that quantity is cultivated in provisions, whilst its population of about 34 whites, 76 free black or coloured, and near 400 slaves, in a most insubordinate state, is employed chiefly in catching fish, cutting fire wood, which they take for sale to the Danish island of St. Thomas, on which they depend for supplies, and are more connected with the Danish subjects of that island, than they are with the inhabitants of Tortola. It will therefore be seen how unable the Officers of His Majesty's Custom House in the Island of Tortola would be to seize any foreign vessel at anchor off the British Island of Jos van Dykes, where there is neither a magistrate, a militia force, or an armed Battery.[58]

[56] *Parliamentary Abstracts Containing the Substance of All Important Papers Laid before the Two Houses of Parliament during the Session of 1825* (London: Longman, 1826), 239.
[57] Tortola Schedules from the Commissioners of Inquiry, in TNA, CO 318/82, G 6.
[58] Ibid.

As indicated by this description, the borders between the Danish and British Virgin Islands were not just porous but near impossible to control for either of the two imperial powers. Besides the practical obstacles to controlling the borders, there was little incentive for most local magistrates to attempt to rein in the intercolonial trade not least because many of them were themselves deeply involved in it. Only when confronted with the practices by imperial agents arriving from the outside were real efforts made to control them, and these efforts almost always came up short.

Anegada, the northernmost of the British Virgin Islands, posed its own set of challenges to the legal order of the colonies, primarily because of the treacherous natural environment that earned the island its name.[59] The extensive coral reefs off the coast of Anegada were a well-known threat to local sailors, and many a vessel had been wrecked there over the years, including a significant number involved in the illegal slave trade. The latter wrecks are documented in great detail in Moody's reports and appeared on multiple contemporary maps of the region (see Figure 6.1 for one such example).[60] One of the more interesting wrecks was that of the *Donna Paula*, a Portuguese ship that hit upon the Anegada shoals in September of 1819.[61] Besides rescuing the captain and crew of the vessel, which included fourteen slaves and two free people of color, the British rescued a total of 226 Africans from the wreck, of whom 126 were listed as men, 57 as women, and 43 as girls.[62] The Africans were from Portuguese Angola and were ostensibly being transported to the region to be sold as slaves in the Spanish Caribbean, although this proved hard to verify because of the limited information available to colonial authorities. Initially, the Portuguese captain was questioned and the Africans on board held temporarily, although never brought to court. What happened next is hard to piece together accurately. In a subsequent report to Governor Maxwell, George R. Porter, the president of the Council of the Virgin Islands, remarked: "It appeared to me at the time that these negroes ought not to have been permitted to be exported from a British colony as *slaves*."[63] This notion was confirmed by the King's Counsel on the island, but despite such legal determinations, it was,

---

[59] The Spanish name "Anegada" roughly translates as "drowned land" or "drowned island."

[60] A chart of the island of Anegada c. 1823, is contained in TNA, CO 318/82.

[61] TNA, CO 239/10, f. 95.

[62] "Register for the schooner Wellington, inwards to the port of Tortola from Anegada," in ibid.

[63] George R. Porter to Governor Maxwell, December 13, 1823, in ibid. Emphasis in original.

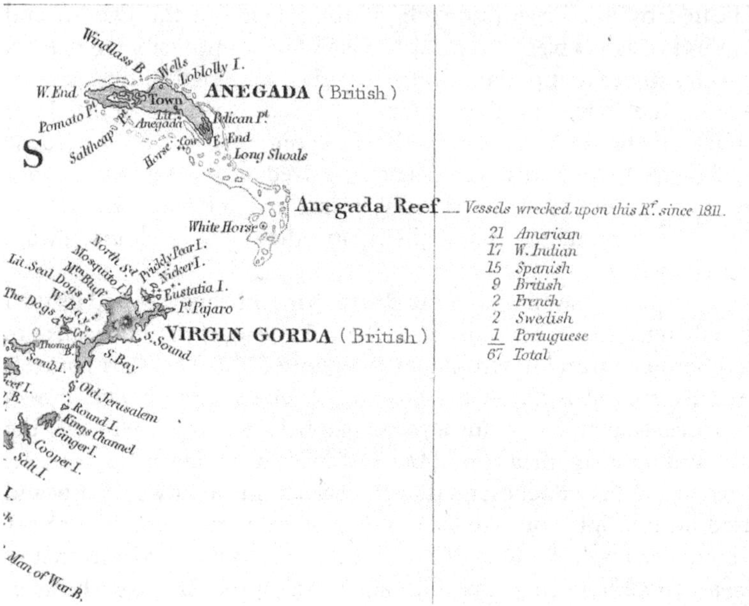

Figure 6.1 Detail showing the Anegada wrecks, 1842. From a map of the Leeward Islands in John Arrowsmith, *The London Atlas of Universal Geography*.
Source: The David Rumsey Map Collection

according to Porter, "a well known fact that they were carried to Porto Rico, where there is every reason to believe they were sold, and used as slaves." The act of carrying the Africans to Puerto Rico did not, seemingly, happen with the blessing of the Vice Admiralty Court on the island, or indeed with the knowledge of the president, but rather through the involvement of the influential Tortolan planter George Patnelli.[64] Porter was quick to emphasize that had he or any other official magistrate on the island known of the transportation of the confiscated Africans to the Spanish colony, they would of course have objected, but unfortunately this was not the case. How exactly several hundred slaves were carried out of the port unknown to any colonial authorities is hard to guess at, let alone believe, but the course of events surrounding the *Donna Paula* are indicative of the broader practices of the illegal slave trade in the Leewards. Local officials were slow to report cases but eager to wash their hands when imperial authorities got wind of them, and the actual

[64] Ibid.

perpetrators were rarely brought to justice by a local judicial system manned by individuals who, in many cases, profited handsomely from the trade themselves.

Conclusion

The abolition of the slave trade was an event with deep ramifications for the microregion of the Leeward Islands. Despite the fact that the trade in slaves continued to a significant degree after 1807, the practices through which this trade was conducted and the legal and political institutions surrounding it in the 1810s and 1820s looked different from those of a few decades earlier. Such subtle shifts are hard to trace when viewing events from European capitals or even from the large slave markets of Cuba or the Americas, but they become illuminated when employing a microregional, bottom-up perspective.

The changes in the slave trade brought about by the British abolitionist regime had at least three consequences for the political landscape of the Leeward Islands. First, it further separated imperial and colonial interests from one another. While there were outspoken abolitionists in the Caribbean championing an end to the trade, and proslavery lobbyists continued to argue the opposite in London and Copenhagen, the Caribbean islands were far less interested in ceasing the importation of enslaved labor than were most of the imperial metropoles of Europe.

Second, the illegal trade between colonies following 1807 served to further tie the merchants and planters of different islands together in increasingly integrated intercolonial and, very often, trans-imperial networks. While many of the networks through which the trade in slaves continued to flow had existed prior to abolition, the new dynamics and risks associated with abolition meant that the links between members were in some sense stronger than before. Although smuggling had always been prevalent throughout the region, the illicit transportation of human beings under the radar of imperial authorities was a source of somewhat novel logistical challenges. These activities also opened up different markets to traders and altered both supply and demand, as large-scale transatlantic shipping of slaves gradually gave way to shorter intercolonial circuits and new centers of transshipment.

Third, inter-imperial relations within the microregion witnessed a decided shift in the relative balance of power, with British naval superiority after 1812 being channeled through the attempted enforcement of the abolition regime. While a certain hierarchical relationship between imperial powers was in this way made explicit, the actual enforcement of the slave trade abolition was much less successful, since the presence of the Royal Navy did little to deter local slave traders. Small crafts and sailors with intimate knowledge of the local geography dominated the intercolonial trade, and colonial magistrates found new ways to partake in and profit from the outlawing of the trade. While outright corruption and the selling of false paperwork was one way imperial middlemen could make a profit, the selling of confiscated prize slaves and the speculating in African apprentices was another.

In this and other ways, many of the individuals responsible for enforcing the abolition of the trade were thus complicit in its continuation, especially in the first unruly decade after 1807, when the imperial apparatus at large was more occupied by the pressing issues of inter-imperial warfare than with policing the trade in humans. The complicity of officials alone does not explain the longevity of the illegal trade after its official cessation, however. The fact that Africans were still being bought and sold in the Leeward Islands well into the nineteenth century underscores the resilience of the practices on the ground associated with slavery as well as the limited capacity of European empires to control a maritime landscape that was almost made for clandestine commerce. Reining in the rampant smuggling had proven nearly impossible in the previous century, and the task was hardly more feasible when the cargo being smuggled consisted of human beings.

Conclusion

As revolutions swept across the Atlantic Ocean and the republics of the continental Americas forged a new postcolonial order for the western hemisphere, most of the Caribbean Sea remained a zone of enduring colonialism, commercial opportunism, and oppressive racial hierarchies. The Leeward Islands were defined not by imperial interests and activity as much as by cross-colonial practices and the interests of trans-imperial networks, integrated at a microregional level. The strongest drivers of this regional integration at the turn of the century were contraband trade, slavery, and local security concerns associated with these practices. The prevalence of trans-imperial networks and the high priority given to social and economic stability by colonial elites goes some way toward explaining the remarkable continuities in practices during these decades of otherwise revolutionary upheaval and sustained inter-imperial warfare – a period that reshaped much of Europe and the Americas, but, with a few notable exceptions, left Caribbean colonial institutions comparatively stable.[1]

For the individuals living in or traversing the Leeward Islands, the connectedness of life between the different colonies was an obvious truth. So much of the lived experience in the colonial Caribbean went beyond the confines of the small island colonies of the region, regardless of whether the person in question was an Afro-Caribbean slave toiling on a plantation or a wealthy white merchant in one of the region's bustling entrepôts. Slaves and sailors, magistrates and merchants alike, all lived in a world of border-crossings and intercultural connectivity, and all were embedded in one or more social networks, connecting them with spaces that were removed from their daily existence, whether these were in a

---

[1] The obvious exception was of course the Haitian Revolution. See Laurent Dubois, *Avengers of the New World: The Story of the Haitian Revolution* (Cambridge, MA: Harvard University Press, 2005); David Geggus, "Saint-Domingue on the Eve of the Haitian Revolution," in *The World of the Haitian Revolution*, ed. David Geggus and Norman Fiering (Bloomington: Indiana University Press, 2009), 3–20; Geggus, "The Caribbean in the Age of Revolution," 83–100; Ferrer, *Freedom's Mirror*, 329–46.

neighboring colony or in a far-flung continent. The existence of a trans-imperial public sphere, through the widespread circulation of newspapers and pamphlets, and the polyglot nature of the islands and their inhabitants meant that there was a constant ongoing conversation between the subjects of different empires. Intercolonial political struggles and rivalries between groups or individuals could be waged not just on the waves but also in the pages of the *St. Kitts Advertiser* or the *St. Thomae Tidende*.

News and rumors did not require printed media to spread, however, as word of mouth proved a most efficient method of disseminating both information and paranoia. The Leeward Islands were a world on the move with some degree of mobility as a constant in many people's lives, even if this mobility was not always wanted. From the forced transportation of African captives and European convicts to the newfound freedom of movement enjoyed by entrepreneurial traders and free people of color, traversing national and imperial borders was a constant element in the daily practices of Leeward Islanders, even as this mobility came with its own share of risks and opportunities. All of this movement fostered a region dense in networks and rich with crossings from one society to another, not all of which were confined to the microregion alone. Rather, the Leeward Islands were an increasingly globalized space, with strong ties to the greater Atlantic region as well as to the larger world of European global empires.

The Leewards were a border region, to be sure – a maritime borderland shaped by the presence of multiple empires – but this Caribbean microregion does not fit neatly into the categories usually employed in the historiography of borderlands. Part of the misalignment stems from the fact that borderlands scholarship has tended to focus on interpolity relations on land involving one or two European imperial powers and their interactions with indigenous polities, primarily in the continental Americas.[2] This focus has led to a research program that leaves out crucial components influencing most border regions across the globe that had relatively little role in the North American historical experience.[3] Such

---

[2] See, for example, Karl Jacoby, *Shadows at Dawn: An Apache Massacre and the Violence of History* (New York: Penguin, 2008); Richard White, *The Middle Ground: Indians, Empires, and Republics in the Great Lakes Region, 1650–1815* (2nd edition) (New York: Cambridge University Press, 2010); Michael Witgen, *An Infinity of Nations: How the Native New World Shaped Early North America* (Philadelphia: University of Pennsylvania Press, 2012). For an early overview of the borderlands historiography, see Jeremy Adelman and Stephen Aron, "From Borderlands to Borders: Empires, Nation-States, and the Peoples in between in North American History," *American Historical Review* 104:3 (1999): 814–40.

[3] This historiographical focus on North America is one possible reason why the conceptual framework of borderlands studies has been relatively slow in penetrating the historiographies of other world regions, with the possible exception of Europe, despite the prevalence of such frontier zones across the globe. See, for example, Emmanuel

overlooked dynamics include the centrality of land–sea connections and the role of port towns as nodes connecting maritime and land-based networks; the fragmented nature of imperial territorial control, often leading to colonial enclaves existing side by side in relative stability for decades; and the complicated dynamics between multiple coexisting imperial polities of unequal regional and global power.[4] The framework of the inter-imperial microregion presented here is in part an attempt to forge a new perspective through which to study such colonial frontier zones, drawing on the insights of borderlands studies but incorporating a more expansive and global horizon in the process. More than just maritime borderlands, inter-imperial microregions were zones of integration, cross-polity entanglement, and novel institutions.

The continuities of practices on the ground in the Leeward Islands should not blind us to the transformations that did take place during this crucial period of history, especially in the tumultuous early decades of the nineteenth century. In the case of the colonial Caribbean, these changes included a tightening of intra-imperial control, a partial shift from de facto to de jure free trade, the gradual and contested dissolution of the institution of slavery, and the transformation of inter-imperial relations brought about by geopolitical and revolutionary events. This concluding chapter begins with some thoughts on two historical changes that seem especially pertinent to the study at hand: the relationship between imperial authority and colonial autonomy, and the rise of British power in the nineteenth-century Atlantic world. The chapter then returns to the microregional framework of analysis presented in Chapter 1 and its specific dynamics in the context of the colonial Leeward Islands, followed by a discussion of the relevance of the concept for global imperial and maritime history more broadly, as well as for the study of nineteenth-century globalization.

Imperial Authority and Colonial Autonomy

One of the defining conflicts in the Leeward Islands at the turn of the century was the clash between imperial and local interests. Contestation of political and jurisdictional authority was a frequent phenomenon

Brunet-Jailly, "The State of Borders and Borderlands Studies 2009: A Historical View and a View from the Journal of Borderlands Studies," *Eurasia Border Review* 1:1 (2010): 1–15.

[4] On the first point, see Adam Arenson, Barbara Berglund, and Jay Gitlin, eds., *Frontier Cities: Encounters at the Crossroads of Empire* (Philadelphia: University of Pennsylvania Press, 2013). On the second point, see Benton, *A Search for Sovereignty*, 37–38. On the third point, see Andrew Phillips and J. C. Sharman, *International Order in Diversity: War, Trade and Rule in the Indian Ocean* (Cambridge: Cambridge University Press, 2015), chapter 5.

across colonial territories, but the Caribbean experienced this pattern in particular ways tied to the practices of trade, security, and slavery that prevailed in the region.[5] The struggles over authority highlighted the inherent limits of local autonomy within an imperial system, as well as the difficulties faced by imperial administrators in exercising metropolitan control over distant territories that did not always display strong ties of loyalty to their nominal European governments.

Commerce was a central activity in the microregion and one of the main causes of conflicts between local and imperial authorities. In the eighteenth century, the rampant smuggling in the region was either a deliberate strategy or a cause for concern on the part of European policy makers, depending on the empire in question. As free ports became increasingly common at the turn of the century, this new regime of partial free trade was in part a way to mitigate the practices of illegal trade. Its implementation was also frequently due to the lobbying efforts of colonial interests, who saw the benefits of gaining economic privileges and, through those, the potential to topple their regional competitor ports. When the granting of free port status was only partially successful at controlling the rampant smuggling, this was due in part to the continued collaboration between local intermediaries and regionally anchored trans-imperial networks of informal trade. As with corruption everywhere, colonial officials who enjoyed relatively low pay and had easy access to increased wealth through seemingly low-risk engagement with smugglers often succumbed to the temptation of contraband trade.

One type of illicit trade particular to the early nineteenth century was the illegal slave trade. Abolition itself was partly motivated by a British imperial goal of limiting the local autonomy of its colonies, but its implementation in the Leeward Islands highlighted the limits of imperial control.[6] The first decade of abolition especially saw many of the local agents who were tasked with its implementation using their position in creative ways to profit handsomely from the continued trade, using the very institutions of abolition as convenient channels through which to disseminate confiscated Africans, as exemplified by the prize court on Tortola. Beyond official involvement, informal regional markets continued to drive the trade in slaves well into the 1820s, and locals looking to buy or sell slaves would likely have intimate knowledge of markets such as those on Jost Van Dyke or St. Thomas.[7]

---

[5] For the broader tensions between local and imperial authorities, see Bayly, *Imperial Meridian*, 193–96; Benton and Ford, "Magistrates in Empire," 173–98.

[6] For the argument that the impetus behind abolition was related to intra-imperial concerns over legal reform, see Benton, "Abolition and Imperial Law," 364–69.

[7] See the description of these markets in Chapter 6.

The institution of slavery was the source of numerous conflicts over political as well as legal authority. Slavery was first and foremost contested by enslaved individuals themselves. Africans and Afro-Caribbeans challenged the institution in myriad ways, from filing legal petitions in imperial metropoles to throwing off their chains in more direct ways, through marronage or outright revolt. But jurisdictional and political conflicts related to the system of slavery also took place within colonial networks that actively excluded the victims of this system. The widespread fear of slave uprisings was one obvious point of contention, as the lack of local capacity to safeguard the colonial social order against such revolts in many places led individual colonies to rely on their neighbors, rather than on their respective empires, for day-to-day security guarantees. This was particularly true for smaller colonies, such as the main islands explored in the previous chapters, a fact that strained not just the relationship between these colonies and their European capitals, but also the local hierarchy between individual British colonies. If St. Christopher could not provide assistance to the British Virgin Islands in times of perceived need, they would have to go elsewhere for help, as happened in 1828 when Danish, rather than British, forces heeded the call for assistance from Tortola. This mutual reliance on security was a primary feature of the inter-imperial microregion and a prime driver of regional integration, but it was also the cause of some intra-imperial anxiety and conflicts between local and central authorities.

Beyond issues of security, slavery was also a frequent cause for tensions in the area of legal practice. Exactly who held the right to mete out punishment to slaves, to define the minimum standards of their daily treatment, and to uproot them and transport them from one territory to another were questions hotly contested at both local and imperial levels. While the introduction of the Amelioration Acts at the end of the eighteenth century was arguably an early attempt at diffusing some of this tension, these acts did little to reassure abolitionist-leaning policy makers in Britain and even less to affect the daily practices of slaveholding in the Leeward Islands. The shocking crimes and trials of Edward Huggins and Arthur Hodge further cemented the need for rethinking the notion of the planters' prerogative, but reform was a slow-moving process, especially in colonial territories where the magistracy had little interest in overhauling the system and potentially destabilizing the local social order. While there was undoubtedly a paternalistic humanitarian impulse behind some of the push for reforms of the slave laws in the Caribbean, sometimes springing from particular religious outlooks, this impulse had little to do with anything resembling the concept of the rights of man, and even less with a present-day human rights discourse. Rather, one of the main drivers behind slave law reform was the perceived need from European metropoles to regulate in the autonomy of local colonial interests, enshrine the centrality of law, and place slaves as well as slaveholders within a legal system that was imperially sanctioned and ultimately under imperial control.

The conflict between imperial authority and colonial autonomy did not take place at the institutional level alone. A large part of the contest was at the level of individual magistrates and intermediaries – the very people who were in some sense put in place to mediate between local and central interests. The way in which this responsibility was handled very often came down to issues of personal connections and career trajectories, or in other words the conflicting allegiances of individuals to imperial and colonial interests. Thus, those magistrates, governors, and imperial agents with strong personal ties to the Caribbean tended to favor local interests over those of the centralized imperial authorities, whereas those men who served in the region in a temporary fashion, often as part of a longer career within the civil service or the military of the British, Danish, or Swedish empires, generally exhibited a more pronounced loyalty to European concerns. As the example of Johan Norderling, the Swedish governor of St. Barthélemy in the 1820s, shows, such distinctions were not set in stone but were likely to shift over the course of a lifetime, especially if governors and magistrates bought land or settled down in the Caribbean, creating deeper personal connections in the process.

A related division could often be found between those imperial agents who were part of the civil service and those who belonged to the military arm of the empire. While the lines between these groups were also blurry, with several individuals crossing over from one branch to the other, the general tendency was toward a higher degree of loyalty to central author-ities among military and naval officers, who were usually serving in the Caribbean in a temporary fashion before being relocated to another region. This situation meant that they were often less likely to own property in the colonial territories and that their personal ties were of a less substantial nature, leading to a position somewhat disconnected from regionally anchored interest networks.

Inter-imperial Configurations and the Rise of Britain

The rise of British power in the nineteenth-century Caribbean is an interesting example of historical contingency, especially when viewed from within the microregion of the Leeward Islands. An examination of the British Empire's rise to hegemony in the Leewards illuminates key aspects of how this development unfolded on the ground and of the inter-imperial environment in which it took place.

Britain had arguably been on an upward trajectory for many years prior to the turn of the nineteenth century, despite the loss of the thirteen North American colonies, but the trend intensified beginning in the 1790s.[8] As the French Empire was hit first by a national revolution in France and then by a colonial revolution in Saint-Domingue, most of the Atlantic was cast into two decades of revolutionary war, resulting in France's loss of considerable portions of its Atlantic empire. This major setback for one of the strongest European empires naturally increased the relative dominance of Britain, and with Spain rapidly losing control over colonial territory in the Americas, the trend toward British regional hegemony seemed manifest.[9]

Growing naval power was central to the overall strength of the British Empire, as the might of the navy made projections of British influence across the seas possible.[10] Naval power was central to British victory in the Revolutionary and Napoleonic Wars, but the reach of the British navy also became a critical factor during peacetime in the early nineteenth century. The new uses of the navy were in large part due to the abolition of the slave trade and the resulting British-led treaty regime, which made it possible for British ships to stop and search numerous foreign vessels in the Caribbean and off the African coast, leading to a growing presence of naval patrols cruising these waters. The combination of diplomatic treaty-making and the display of maritime superiority made the abolition of the slave trade a particularly stark moment in the exercise of British power in shaping inter-imperial hierarchy, alongside the internal dimension of taming colonial magistrates described above. The visibility of British warships cruising Caribbean waters was particularly important for the regional projection of imperial dominance, especially given the

---

[8] On the relationship between the Caribbean and the North American territories in British imperial strategy, see Andrew Jackson O'Shaughnessy, *An Empire Divided: The American Revolution and the British Caribbean* (Philadelphia: University of Pennsylvania Press, 2000), 185–211.

[9] While Britain was poised to dominate much of the Caribbean, a claim to the role of hegemon in the Americas was significantly more dubious. In this context, the Monroe Doctrine, with the support of both Britain and the United States, was a way to ensure a certain type of postcolonial order in the Western Hemisphere following the defeat of Spain, with Britain as the only significant European imperial power remaining. See Osterhammel, *The Transformation of the World*, 475–80; Jeppe Mulich, "Empire and Violence: Continuity in the Age of Revolution," *Political Power and Social Theory* 32 (2017): 181–204.

[10] See, for example, Roger Morriss, *The Foundations of British Maritime Ascendancy: Resources, Logistics and the State, 1755–1815* (Cambridge: Cambridge University Press, 2011).

limited success these ships had in carrying out their ostensible task, namely, ending the slave trade.

Two colonial institutions were key in the configuration of power between colonies in the period of British ascendance – prize courts and free ports. The more powerful the British Empire itself was in the region, the more important these geographically bounded institutions became for the individual colonies that could lay claim to them. The presence of prize courts and free ports spurred on intercolonial integration within the microregion by increasing foreign traffic to British colonial territories and opening up new opportunities for legal and illegal commerce. By granting increased privileges of trade and maritime jurisdiction to individual ports within the British colonial system, the placement of these institutions reshaped the geographical dimensions of local trans-imperial networks. Their presence placed particular colonies at the center of regional networks, thus enhancing the relative influence of certain ports within the British Empire itself and in their relations to other regional powers. Thus the existence of a court of vice admiralty on Tortola was important not just vis-à-vis the relative power of Tortola to other British colonies, including St. Christopher, but also to the relationship between Tortola and the neighboring Danish islands, as the prize court's presence created new opportunities for legitimate trade, legal legerdemain, and even maritime predation.[11]

The smaller islands of neutral imperial powers in the region played an important role in the course of British regional ascendance. Danish, Dutch, and Swedish colonies were deeply entangled in the intercolonial relations of the region, and they frequently functioned as a buffer zone between the larger Caribbean empires, namely, the French and the British. When peace treaties were negotiated and political borders redrawn, giving the territorial rights of contested spaces to neutral third parties was often a useful way to defuse inter-imperial rivalries over particular ports and islands. This logic was one of the reasons why Sweden gained St. Barthélemy in the 1780s and, however briefly, was granted Guadeloupe in the aftermath of the Napoleonic Wars. At times, small colonial powers in the microregion looked more like political proxies for their larger neighbors than independent actors. Thus St. Barthélemy seemed little more than an extension of the French Empire in the 1790s, providing a convenient port for French sailors and privateers, complete with a temporary prize court and readily available manpower to replace fallen crew members. The same was true for the Danish

---

[11] See the case of arranged seizures and acquittals between St. Thomas and Tortola described in Chapter 4 for an example of this dynamic.

West Indies and their relationship to Britain at various points over the half-century. When the European capitals of these neutral powers were not willing to give up on their de facto neutrality in the face of political pressure, the British proved willing to invade and hold the colonies in question, with little to no local resistance.

The relationships between the neutral islands and the British colonies were more complicated than that, however. The control extended over these seemingly convenient proxies by the British Empire was partial at best, and if Britain's own colonies proved unruly at times, this went double for neutral islands such as St. Thomas and St. Eustatius. At the intercolonial level, these neutral free ports were perfectly positioned to directly or indirectly subvert the restrictions placed on British subjects on neighboring islands, either through participation in legal free trade or via the trans-imperial networks of illicit commerce, in which the neutral islands were key nodes. Such relations between British and neutral colonies at the local level went both ways, with islands such as Tortola doing their part in securing the trade and prosperity of St. Thomas merchants through legal legerdemain at the prize court or elsewhere, while at the same time engaging in a healthy intercolonial rivalry with their neighbors over land and capital. In this way, the presence of Danish, Dutch, and Swedish colonial territories in the Leeward Islands served a purpose for British administrators at the metropolitan level as well as for colonial intermediaries and subjects at the local level, despite the fact that such neutral territories could also be recurring nuisances to all of them. Their presence made political and commercial maneuvering possible for multiple actors – maneuvering that would otherwise not have been feasible. Thus, the intricate relationship between British and neutral islands in the Leewards sustained British regional hegemony at the level of inter-imperial politics at the same time as it helped subvert British imperial authority at the level of trans-imperial networks.

Revisiting the Microregional Framework

The inter-imperial microregion has been a useful perspective through which to view the history of the Leeward Islands. It seems worth considering in some detail the ways in which the case at hand differs from the contours of the analytical ideal-type, in order to refine the model as well as to tease out certain aspects of the historical dynamics of the Leewards themselves. The ideal-typical microregion is defined primarily by the existence of multiple imperial polities within a particular area, with a high degree of interaction across and between the borders of these polities. This interaction leads to the creation of relatively robust trans-imperial networks and, in the extreme, to a greater degree of integration between different imperial peripheries than between imperial peripheries and their respective metropoles, at least in certain spheres.[12]

Arguably, the primary divergence from the ideal-type lies in the way in which Caribbean imperial actors attempted to enforce, and at times succeeded in enforcing, imperial boundaries over the course of the early nineteenth century. The half-century examined here saw an emerging tendency for imperial centers to rein in the autonomy and privileges of their colonial territories, enforce the centrality of imperial authority, and solidify territorial borders between empires. Such efforts were sporadic at best and were often borne out in ambiguous ways, in fits and starts depending on the specific political and economic circumstances of the moment: freedom of trade was granted or restricted depending on the currents of war and the imperial balance of power; jurisdictional autonomy depended on the lobbying efforts and influence of both planters and abolitionists; the power of magistrates was seen as, at various times, a bulwark against local unrest or a threat to centralized imperial authority. The strength of the inter-imperial microregion was thus at once a key component of European imperialism in the Atlantic world and a phenomenon that imperial powers struggled with and, at times, attempted to regulate. These attempts at enforcing central authority also highlight more complicated connections of power and allegiances, as networks between groups of actors who otherwise had relatively little common ground formed over critical issues, such as the abolition of the slave trade, the limits of the planters' prerogative, and the advocacy of free trade. These and other topics became key points of contention, both between metropoles and colonies and within colonial territories themselves.

Another divergence from the ideal-type can be found in the particular dynamics of the trans-imperial networks existing among free African and Afro-Caribbean subjects in the Leeward Islands. While many of these subjects were integrated to some degree into the commercial networks of the microregion, others were separated from the existing structures by the pervasive force of colonial racial hierarchies. Strong, direct ties between white elites and prominent people of color, such as the one between Governor von Scholten and the free people of color of Charlotte Amalie, were rare and rather slow to emerge in colonial societies where the very notions of rights and privileges were restricted to white subjects, and where black people were generally assumed by authorities to be

---

[12] See Chapter 1 for the full definition and discussion of the ideal-type.

slaves unless proven otherwise.[13] This partial separation between white and black free people meant that parallel networks existed within the region, in effect adding another layer to the three separate levels of the inter-imperial microregion – one that tied together free black communities across colonial and imperial borders without always connecting these communities directly to the existing structures of colonial society, dominated as they were by the privileges of white subjects.[14]

Such divergences are not arguments against the usefulness of the ideal-type, but rather examples of the specificity of the historical case of the Leeward Islands. The dynamics of a racially contingent slave society, such as the one in the colonial Caribbean, were not likely to be found in all places with inter-imperial frontier zones, but they were nonetheless deeply embedded into the sociopolitical configuration of the Leeward Islands. The same is true for the attempts at exerting increased imperial control over the colonial territories on these islands. Such efforts might well be reflective of a broader trend across European overseas empires in the early nineteenth century but need not be an integral part of the ideal-type. These divergences from the theoretical model, then, should be taken not as arguments against an ideal-typical approach but as concrete examples of the model's ability to single out and highlight individual distinctiveness while keeping in mind wider historical parallels.

By disaggregating the state into its component parts, and in particular into the institutions and practices that it encompasses, we can reveal that the nineteenth-century world was not exclusively one of state units. Rather, the specific practices that are usually prescribed to the state were in many places handled by quite different institutions and networks, including those I have here located within the ideal-type of the inter-imperial microregion. The intercolonial networks of the Leeward Islands took on the role of security guarantors in the face of internal uprisings; they shaped and constituted informal markets that were often more important for local commerce than those formalized by imperial sanctions; and they even created legal practices that spread across different colonial legal regimes of the region, in recognizable if not always uniform ways. If this insight – that regionally anchored networks crossing national and colonial boundaries took on certain practices otherwise ascribed solely to the realm of the state – is taken seriously, it follows that

---

[13] See Chapter 5 for a discussion of these points.

[14] For other examples of such parallel and partially overlapping networks in the Caribbean, see Adderley, *"New Negroes from Africa,"* 92–152; Bolster, *Black Jacks*, 158–89; Jenny Shaw, *Everyday Life in the Early English Caribbean: Irish, Africans, and the Construction of Difference* (Athens: University of Georgia Press, 2013), 71–100.

traditional narratives of the development of global politics dominated by either the continuities of empires or the proliferation of nation-states must give way to the recognition of a broader variety of political configurations with varying stability and degrees of formalization that defy the modeling of traditional political units.[15]

Inter-Imperial Microregions across Global History

In order to illustrate the utility of the analytical framework presented in this book, it is useful to briefly consider some other examples of inter-imperial microregions. Each of these cases would be an obvious subject for an in-depth microregional study, either on its own or as part of a broader comparative analysis.

The West African region known by contemporaries as the Gold Coast is an area in the Atlantic world that approximates the ideal-typical model. From the late seventeenth century to the early nineteenth century, this relatively narrow stretch of land, today a part of the country of Ghana, saw the interaction of multiple small European communities with a number of local polities and the resulting formation of commercial, political, and cultural networks – structures that lasted until the eventual regional hegemony of the British Empire in the 1850s.[16] In the seventeenth century, British, Danish, Dutch, and Swedish agents built a range of new fortifications along the coast. These agents sought alliances with various Fante polities to set up forts far enough from their rivals' trading posts so that they could trade unhindered and also maintain access to the sea.[17] Regardless of their relative positions of strength, European companies on the coast were wholly dependent on good relations with

---

[15] For more on the development of such political units at a global scale, see Jeppe Mulich, "Transformation at the Margins: Imperial Expansion and Systemic Change in World Politics," *Review of International Studies* 44:4 (2018): 694–716.

[16] European outposts included at various times those of Brandenburg, Britain, Denmark, the Dutch Republic, Portugal, and Sweden. African polities included the different Akan states of the Akim, the Akwapim, and the Ashanti Empire. See George Nørregård, *Danish Settlements in West Africa, 1658–1850* (Boston: Boston University Press, 1966); Harvey M. Feinberg, *Africans and Europeans in West Africa: Elminans and Dutchmen on the Gold Coast during the Eighteenth Century* (Philadelphia: American Philosophical Society, 1989); Ivor Wilks, *Forests of Gold: Essays on the Akan and the Kingdom of Asante* (revised edition) (Athens: Ohio University Press, 1995); Daniel P. Hopkins, "The Danish Ban on the Atlantic Slave Trade and Denmark's African Colonial Ambitions," *Itinerario* 25:4 (2001): 154–84; Rebecca Shumway, *The Fante and the Transatlantic Slave Trade* (Rochester, NY: University of Rochester Press, 2011); Randy J. Sparks, *Where the Negroes Are Masters: An African Port in the Era of the Slave Trade* (Cambridge, MA: Harvard University Press, 2014).

[17] This was not a static set of players. Several chartered companies were forced out by rivals within a few decades, as was the case with both the Swedish Africa Company in 1663 and

African leaders in order to facilitate the slave trade, secure profits, and guarantee the safety of their agents. These conditions created multiple layers of formal and informal networks, both between different European groups and between Africans and Europeans. Some forts and entrepôts became so linked to local polities that the rise and fall of the political position of one directly affected the relative power of the other.[18] In the early nineteenth century, the rising Asante Empire, hitherto primarily an inland polity, forced the Europeans on the coast to acknowledge its political power in the region. Through a series of local wars, including with the Fante in 1806 and the Akim–Akwapim Alliance in 1814–16, the Asante established their political authority and eventually forced British agents from the African Company of Merchants to sign a treaty partially recognizing Asante claims to much of the coastal territory and its African inhabitants.[19]

Moving beyond the Atlantic, Mauritius and the Seychelles are an Indian Ocean example of a microregion that witnessed a complex web of interactions between both European and indigenous polities, particularly in connection with the widespread slave trade and later British attempts at suppressing it.[20] Hostility to the British colonial authorities was widespread among the predominantly Francophone planters and traders, not least when it came to the issue of the slave trade abolition after 1807.[21] The stream of human contraband subsided only when the sanctioned importation of indentured labor from Africa and Asia became more profitable than illegal slave importation in the 1830s.[22]

---

the Brandenburger Africa Company in 1717. See Ray A. Kea, *Settlements, Trade, and Polities in the Seventeenth-Century Gold Coast* (Baltimore: Johns Hopkins University Press, 1982); Lauren Benton and Jeppe Mulich, "The Space between Empires: Coastal and Insular Microregions in the Early Nineteenth-Century World," in *The Uses of Space in Early Modern History*, ed. Paul Stock (New York: Palgrave Macmillan, 2015), 155–57.

[18] Feinberg, *Africans and Europeans in West Africa*, 155–58. See also Ludewig Ferdinand Rømer, *A Reliable Account of the Coast of Guinea (1760)*, trans. Selena Axelrod Winsnes (Oxford: Oxford University Press, 2000).

[19] "The 'Bowdich' Treaty with Ashanti, 7 September 1817," in *Great Britain and Ghana: Documents of Ghana History, 1807–1957*, ed. George E. Metcalfe (London: University of Ghana, 1964), 46–47; Thomas E. Bowdich, *Mission from Cape Coast Castle to Ashantee* (London: J. Murray, 1819).

[20] See Moses D. E. Nwulia, *The History of Slavery in Mauritius and the Seychelles, 1810–1875* (Madison, NJ: Fairleigh Dickinson University Press, 1981); Deryck Scarr, *Seychelles since 1770: History of a Slave and Post-Slavery Society* (Trenton, NJ: Africa World Press, 1999).

[21] Marina Carter and Hubert Gerbeau, "Covert Slaves and Coveted Coolies in the Early Nineteenth Century Mascareignes," *Slavery and Abolition* 9:3 (1988): 194–208; Richard B. Allen, "Licentious and Unbridled Proceedings: The Illegal Slave Trade to Mauritius and the Seychelles during the Early Nineteenth Century," *The Journal of African History* 42:1 (2001): 91–116.

[22] Carter and Gerbeau, "Covert Slaves," 203–5.

The nineteenth-century Pacific offers numerous cases that are worth exploring, from the relatively loose networks of traders and missionaries in Melanesia and Micronesia to the more firmly established settlements and trading posts along the Strait of Malacca, connecting the Indian and Pacific Oceans.[23] The Straits Settlements, and in particular Singapore, were arguably dominated by the presence of British colonial administrators, but their inhabitants operated within a much broader world of inter-imperial and Eurasian connections.[24] This rapidly growing port, which, despite a much earlier history as maritime hub, was little more than a hamlet when acquired by Stamford Raffles for the British East India Company in 1819, grew to a bustling and thoroughly polyglot city in the 1830s.[25] English sailor George Windsor Earl, who arrived in Singapore in February of 1833, described a port in which "ships from all parts of the world are constantly arriving," where "the flags of Great Britain, Holland, France, and America, may often be seen intermingled with the streamers of the Chinese junks, and the fanciful colours of the native *perahus*" and where "Chinese, Malays, Bugis, Javanese, Balinese, natives of Bengal and Madras, Parsees, Arabs, and Caffrees, are to be found."[26] While some of this trade activity was carried out by European merchants and imperial agents, non-European regional traders were also heavily involved. A multitude of sailors had used the Straits of Malacca to

---

[23] On the island nations of the Pacific and their interactions with Europeans and each other, see David A. Chappell, *Double Ghosts: Oceanic Voyagers on Euroamerican Ships* (New York: M. E. Sharpe, 1997); Paul D'Arcy, *The People of the Sea: Environment, Identity and History in Oceania* (Honolulu: University of Hawai'i Press, 2006); Nicholas Thomas, *Islanders: The Pacific in the Age of Empires* (New Haven: Yale University Press, 2010); Matt K. Matsuda, *Pacific Worlds: A History of Seas, Peoples, and Cultures* (Cambridge: Cambridge University Press, 2012). Another key example of an interpolity microregion was the so-called Sulu zone, encompassing the islands and maritime networks of the Sulu and Celebes Seas, described in great detail in James Francis Warren, *The Sulu Zone 1768–1898: The Dynamics of External Trade, Slavery, and Ethnicity in the Transformation of a Southeast Asian Maritime State* (2nd edition) (Singapore: NUS Press, 2007).

[24] See Paul Battersby, *To the Islands: White Australians and the Malay Archipelago since 1788* (Lanham, MD: Lexington Books, 2007); C. M. Turnbull, *A History of Modern Singapore* (revised edition) (Singapore: NUS Press, 2009), 1–127; Mark Ravinder Frost and Yu-Mei Balasingamchow, *Singapore: A Biography* (Hong Kong: Hong Kong University Press and National Museum of Singapore, 2009); Stephen Dobbs, "The Singapore River/Port in a Global Context," in *Singapore in Global History*, ed. Derek Heng and Syed Muhd Krairudin Aljunied (Amsterdam: Amsterdam University Press, 2011), 51–66.

[25] For a treatment of the early beginnings of Singapore and Temasik in the fourteenth century, see Derek Heng, "Situating Temasik within the Larger Regional Context: Maritime Asia and Malay State Formation in the Pre-modern Era," in *Singapore in Global History*, ed. Derek Heng and Syed Muhd Krairudin Aljunied (Amsterdam: Amsterdam University Press, 2011), 27–50.

[26] Quoted in Frost and Balasingamchow, *Singapore: A Biography*, 84.

travel from South Asia to the Chinese coast for centuries before colonial contact, and "the silk road of the sea" provided a preexisting network structure into which European, Chinese, and Southeast Asian entrepreneurial traders could insert themselves.[27]

Similar descriptions can be found of the city of Shanghai, which, following the creation of the United Municipal Council in 1854, became an inter-imperial microregion in its own right, albeit a uniquely institutionalized one with representatives from most of the Western empires as well as the Qing Empire dividing the city between them, creating a space of complex and overlapping sovereignty in the process.[28] Before Shanghai grew to prominence, a different coastal region of the Middle Kingdom had foreign imperial powers scrambling for influence – the South China Coast. Much of the Sino-European trade of the eighteenth and nineteenth centuries took place in an inter-imperial zone, spanning the triangular space from Macau in the southeast to Canton in the north and down to Hong Kong in the southwest. This area included both the sanctioned trading posts in Canton and Macau and the smuggling centers on Lingding Island and in Whampoa (Huangpu).[29] While the Portuguese and British Empires had a more stable hold on the coast due to their colonial ports, there was a plethora of other commercial and political actors, ranging from individual European or Eurasian entrepreneurs to organized trading companies, such as the Danish, Dutch, and Swedish East India Companies.[30] All these actors operated in complex

---

[27] John N. Miksic, *Singapore and the Silk Road of the Sea, 1300–1800* (Singapore: NUS Press, 2013). See also Carl A. Trocki, "Opium as a Commodity in the Chinese Nanyang Trade," in *Chinese Circulations: Capital, Commodity, and Networks in Southeast Asia*, ed. Eric Tagliacozzo and Wen-Chin Chang (Durham, NC: Duke University Press, 2011), 84–104; Takeshi Hamashita, "The *Lidai Baoan* and the Ryukyu Maritime Tributary Trade Network with China and Southeast Asia, the Fourteenth to Seventeenth Centuries," in ibid., 107–29.

[28] See, in particular, J. H. Hann, "Origin and Development of the Political System in the Shanghai International Settlement," *Journal of the Hong Kong Branch of the Royal Asiatic Society* 22 (1982): 207–29; Marie-Claire Bergère, *Histoire de Shanghai* (Paris: Librairie Arthème Fayard, 2002); Meng Yue, *Shanghai and the Edges of Empires* (Minneapolis: University of Minnesota Press, 2006).

[29] Jonathan Goldstein, "A Clash of Civilizations in the Pearl River Delta: Stephen Girard's Trade with China, 1787–1824," in *Americans and Macau: Trade, Smuggling, and Diplomacy on the South China Coast*, ed. Paul A. Van Dyke (Hong Kong: Hong Kong University Press, 2012), 17–32; Van Dyke, "Smuggling Networks of the Pearl River Delta before 1842: Implications for Macau and the American China Trade," in ibid., 49–72; Rogério Puga, *The British Presence in Macau, 1635–1793* (Hong Kong: Hong Kong University Press, 2013).

[30] On the history of empire in Macau, see R. D. Cremer, "From Portugal to Japan: Macau's Place in the History of World Trade," in *Macau: City of Commerce and Culture*, ed. Cremer (Hong Kong: UEA Press, 1987), 23–37; Zidong Hao, *Macau: History and Society* (Hong Kong: Hong Kong University Press, 2011). On the early

172   Conclusion

and layered commercial networks, laid claims to a variety of legal or
jurisdictional privileges, and, despite fierce rivalries, often cooperated
in the face of the common threat of Chinese sanctions or expulsion.[31]

The examples just described represent a number of variations on the
ideal-typical microregion. For one, the majority of them represent
interpolity zones with a mix of both imperial and indigenous actors.
While some of these indigenous actors were nominally placed under
the political control of imperial intermediaries, others maintained their
independence for much of the period in question, as was the case for the
Akan states of Western Africa up until the middle of the nineteenth
century. This variation introduces a new dynamic in the networked
relationships within the microregions, as some actors are operating under
formal ties to external authorities, while others have at least nominal
political independence.

Another variation is the degree of formal institutionalization of the
inter-imperial interactions. Such institutionalization is particularly
striking in the case of Shanghai, which saw a jurisdictional system
and a local administrative apparatus specifically designed to function
within an interpolity zone. A lack of institutionalization does not itself
account for all of the principal–agent problems of other microregions,
however, as there was a considerable disconnect between the formal
institutions in Shanghai, sanctioned by the metropolitan authorities
involved, and the actual practices by magistrates and private actors
on the ground.[32]

A third and final variation of importance to several of these cases is that
of regional hegemony. Some of the inter-imperial regions considered
came into existence under conditions of hegemony, while others had
those conditions introduced over the course of their history as a consequence of geopolitical or economic shifts. In the case of Singapore and
the Straits Settlements, this was arguably the case from the beginning,

---

period of Hong Kong history, see, in particular, Elizabeth Sinn, "A History of Regional
Associations in Pre-war Hong Kong," in *Between East and West: Aspects of Social and
Political Developments in Hong Kong*, ed. Sinn (Hong Kong: Centre of Asian Studies,
1990); John M. Carroll, *Edge of Empires: Elites and British Colonials in Hong Kong*
(Cambridge, MA: Harvard University Press, 2005); Christopher Munn, *Anglo-China:
Chinese People and British Rule in Hong Kong, 1841–1880* (Hong Kong: Hong Kong
University Press, 2009).
[31] On legal and jurisdictional tensions between the Chinese and the European empires, see
Ulrike Hillemann-Delaney, *Asian Empire and British Knowledge: China and the Networks
of British Imperial Expansion* (Cambridge: Cambridge University Press, 2009), 45–66.
[32] See some of the examples presented in Pär Kristoffer Cassel, *Grounds of Judgment:
Extraterritoriality and Imperial Power in Nineteenth-Century China and Japan* (Oxford:
Oxford University Press, 2012), 39–84.

with the British Empire dominating the region but allowing other imperial actors to operate within it, creating inter- and trans-imperial networks in the process. In the Leeward Islands the shift toward British hegemony was a gradual one, in part due to the declining power of the French Empire in the Caribbean and the growing presence of the Royal Navy along the major Atlantic trade routes, particularly following the decision to enforce the slave trade abolition at the end of the Napoleonic Wars. In many ways the enforcement of the abolition was the first of several manifestations of growing British inter-imperial hegemony during the global nineteenth century.

Regional Globalization

Microregions functioned as cogs in the grand wheel of global connectivity, as tightly integrated transnational networks within looser and more expansive transoceanic networks. This relationship between the levels of regional globalization and the larger, commonly understood, level of worldwide globalization underlines the geographic and spatial dimensions of the process of globalization.[33] The case of the Leeward Islands also illustrates the relationship between colonial empires and the push toward global connectivity taking place in the nineteenth century, in part due to the increased interdependence between regional markets. This growing interdependence did not just take the form of bilateral economic relations between colonial territories and European metropoles, but also manifested as direct links between different colonial regions across the globe.

Globalization as a *longue durée* process took place not simply on a worldwide scale, but rather through the intensification of transnational, or more accurately trans-imperial, microregional networks. These networks were linked to wider oceanic and even global networks that displayed lesser degrees of integration and cohesion, creating a system of networks-within-networks where strong regional integration spilled over into growing global or near-global connectivity. In this sense, early globalizing processes might be thought of as emanating from increasingly integrated regional spaces, manifesting as layered networks of trans-polity connections and activity – from tightly knit microregions at the local level to transoceanic migratory and commercial flows on the global

---

[33] In this way maritime microregions are similar to the "portals of globalization" conceptualized by Matthias Middell and Katja Naumann in "Global History and the Spatial Turn: From the Impact of Area Studies to the Study of Critical Junctures of Globalization," *Journal of Global History* 5:1 (2010): 162–63.

level. The activities of the Leeward Islands in the early nineteenth century were one example of such a pattern. The microregion was an integrated local space but also illustrated the role of wider transoceanic and global processes that expanded over the first decades of the century and ultimately contributed to the decline of the Caribbean within the global economy.

The globalizing characteristics of the microregion were most clearly visible in the area of intercolonial commerce, as the Leeward Islands were very much an integrated zone of trans-imperial economic activity. But while the islands had been at the center of a regional and even an Atlantic system of growing globalization in trade and production at the turn of the century, this centrality was replaced by decline and a decidedly peripheral economic role in the latter half of the century. The global markets for sugar and cotton shifted dramatically over the course of the nineteenth century, with entire supply chains moving away from the Caribbean as new spaces for production opened up or became significantly more competitive, particularly in South and Southeast Asia and in the continental Americas. While the trans-imperial economic integration within the Leewards did not itself fade away, this regional system was increasingly disconnected from the wider globalizing circuits of trans-regional trade and production, and the microregion would never again achieve the global economic importance that it experienced during its financial zenith at the turn of the century.

Another example of the linkage between microregional and global networks can be found in the development of slavery and the slave trade. Slavery and colonial labor were institutions deeply affected by the growing connectivity across regions. At the regional level, slavery was one of the primary drivers of intercolonial integration, but the market for slave labor was never contained within the Leeward Islands alone. The circuits of trade and forced migration within which the trade in slaves took place reached across the Atlantic, linking the African coast with the continental Americas and the Greater Caribbean region. Furthermore, the substantial slave markets within the Leewards, centered on ports of transshipment such as those of the Danish West Indies, catered not only to neighboring colonies but also to larger islands of empires with higher demands for slaves, including Puerto Rico, Hispaniola, and Jamaica. During the decades of illegal slave trade following the British abolition, new opportunities opened up for individuals with expertise in the practices of smuggling human beings, and as markets dried up in one region of the world, growing demands in other regions made some of these slave traders relocate from the Caribbean to more vibrant markets, including those of Brazil and the western Indian Ocean region.[34] Following the abolition of slavery, the demographic composition of the Caribbean, and particularly the British Caribbean, was significantly affected by the importation of South and East Asian indentured laborers, as the plantation economies of the region shifted from one type of unfree labor to another.[35] These migratory flows connected two world regions in ways that went beyond economic linkages, creating cultural and social ties between the otherwise relatively disparate geographical spheres of the British Empire and the wider global economy.

Since globalization as a conceptual framework for understanding the present shows no sign of disappearing from the social sciences anytime soon, it would perhaps behoove historians to devote more effort to tackling the issue of historicizing globalization, rather than dismiss the notion outright.[36] Such work has already been done when it comes to anchoring globalization in a temporal sense, with several historians and sociologists tracing the origins and precedents of global connectivity by locating the history of globalization within the longer histories of cross-cultural contact, long-distance trading, colonial expansion, or European imperialism.[37] What I have attempted here is somewhat different. Rather than solely focusing on the timing of globalization, I believe more needs to be done to anchor the concept in specific geographies and practices. The very notion of globalization might seem an inherent abstraction – a concept that works only when employed through a macro view of human experience. But if globalization is to make sense in an applicable analytical sense, it needs to be connected to the lived experience of historical and contemporary subjects. By locating globalizing currents within specific geographical spaces, we can see that the process of forging global

[34] There is, for example, some evidence to suggest that Cabot, Bailey, & Co., the company engaged in both privateering and the illegal slave trade, relocated to the Indian Ocean after their near-lethal brush with authorities in the Leeward Islands. See Chapter 4.

[35] Kale, *Fragments of Empire*, 12–37; Walton Look Lai, *Indentured Labor, Caribbean Sugar: Chinese and Indian Migrants to the British West Indies, 1838–1918* (Baltimore: Johns Hopkins University Press, 1993), 19–85.

[36] Osterhammel and Petersson, *Globalization*, 1–11; Charles Bright and Michael Geyer, "World History in a Global Age," *American Historical Review* 100:4 (1995): 1034–60. For an opposing view, see Cooper, "What Is the Concept of Globalization Good For?," 189–213.

[37] See, for example, Andre Gunder Frank, *ReOrient: Global Economy in the Asian Age* (Berkeley: University of California Press, 1998); Giovanni Arrighi, *The Long Twentieth Century: Money, Power and the Origins of Our Times* (revised edition) (New York: Verso, 2010); Magee and Thompson, *Empire and Globalisation*, 22–44; Ballantyne and Burton, "Empire and the Reach of the Global," 285–434. See also Kevin O'Rourke and Jeffrey G. Williamson, "When Did Globalisation Begin?," *European Review of Economic History* 6:1 (2002): 23–50; Flynn and Giraldez, "Path Dependence, Time Lags and the Birth of Globalisation."

connections did not take place through top-down macro developments alone, but also through the bottom-up activities of people making a living in spaces that became increasingly integrated into widening networks of connectivity and interdependence. And by focusing on the patterns of this integration in everyday practices, rather than in purely structural changes, we might be able to free the concept of globalization from the shackles of abstraction, imbuing it with a renewed dose of analytical purchase.

Bibliography

Archives and Collections

Rigsarkivet, Copenhagen, Denmark [RA]
Audited Accounts [AA]
Chamber of Customs [COC]
Chamber of Revenue [COR]
Department of Foreign Affairs [DFA]
West Indian Local Archives [WILA]

The Royal Library, Copenhagen, Denmark
Caribbean and American Newspaper Collection

Riksarkivet, Stockholm, Sweden [RKA]
The Collection of Sten Simonsson [CSS]
The Lamborn Collection [LC]
The St. Barthélemy Collection, 1784-1878 [SBS]
Trade and Shipping Collection – The West India Company [TSC]

The National Library of Sweden, Stockholm, Sweden

Archives nationales d'outre-mer, Aix-en-Province, France [ANOM]
Secrétariat d'État à la Marine

The National Archives, Kew, UK [TNA]
Domestic Records of the Public Record Office [PRO]
Records of the Admiralty and related bodies [ADM]
Records of the Boards of Customs and Excise [CUST]
Records of the Colonial Office and related bodies [CO]
Records created or inherited by HM Treasury [T]
Records of the High Court of Admiralty and colonial Vice-Admiralty courts [HCA]
Records of the Privy Council [PC]
Records of the War Office and related bodies [WO]

Gladstone's Library, Hawarden, UK

The Florence Williams Library, Christiansted, St. Croix
The Caribbean Collection: Virgin Islands Documents

The American Antiquarian Society, Worcester, MA [AAS]
Caribbean Newspaper Collection

The New-York Historical Society, New York, NY
Patricia D. Klingenberg Library

The David Rumsey Historical Map Collection, Stanford, CA

Printed Primary Sources

The Annual Register, or a View of History, Politics, and Literature of the Year 1828. London: T. S. Hansard, 1829.

Arrowsmith, John. *The London Atlas of Universal Geography, Exhibiting the Physical & Political Divisions of the Various Countries of the World.* London: John Arrowsmith, 1842.

Belisario, A. M. *A Report of the Trial of Arthur Hodge, Esquire (late one of the Members of His Majesty's Council for the Virgin Islands), at the Island of Tortola, on the 25th of April 1811, and Adjourned to the 29th of the Same Month; for the Murder of His Negro Man Slave Named Prosper.* Middletown, CT: Tertius Dunning, 1812.

Bellin, Jacques Nicolas. *Le petit atlas maritime recueil de cartes et plans des quatre parties du monde en cinq volumes,* vol. 1. Paris: J. Arrivet, 1764.

Bergius, O. E. *Om Westindien.* Stockholm: A. Gadeliues, 1819.

Bowdich, Thomas E. *Mission from Cape Coast Castle to Ashantee.* London: J. Murray, 1819.

Bowles, Thomas Gibson. *The Declaration of Paris of 1856.* London: Sampson Low, Marston and Co., 1900.

British and Foreign State Papers, vol. 1. London: HMSO, 1841.

British and Foreign State Papers, vol. 12. London: HMSO, 1846.

Buxton, Charles, ed. *Memoirs of Sir Thomas Fowell Buxton, Baronet* (3rd edition). London: John Murray, 1849.

Calendar of State Papers Colonial, America and West Indies, vol. 41. London: HMSO, 1953.

Caron, Aimery P. and Arnold R. Highfield, eds. *The French Intervention in the St. John Slave Revolt of 1733–34.* Christiansted: Bureau of Libraries, Museums and Archeological Services, 1981.

Carstens, J. L. *St Thomas in Early Danish Time: A General Description of all the Danish, American or West Indian Islands,* edited and translated by Arnold R. Highfield. St. Croix: Virgin Islands Humanities Council, 1997.

Dahlman, Sven. *Beskrifning om St Barthelemy, Svensk Ö uti Westindien.* Stockholm: A. J. Nordström, 1786.

Goes, Axel. *Några Minnen från St. Barthelemy.* Stockholm: P. A. Norstedt & Söner, 1878.

Gurney, Joseph John. *A Winter in the West Indies, Described in Familiar Letters to Henry Clay, of Kentucky.* London: John Murray, 1840.

Jonnès, Alexandre Moreau de. *Recherches statistiques sur l'esclavage colonial sur les moyens de le supprimer.* Paris: Imprimerie de Bourgogne et Martinet, 1842.

Kongl. Maj:ts Nådige Kungörelse, Som förklarar Ön St. Barthelemy i Westindien för en Fri Hamn eller Porto Franco. Drottningholm, 1785.

Mackenrot, Anthony. *Secret Memoirs of the Honourable Andrew Cochrane Johnstone: Of the Honourable Vice-Admiral Sir Alex. Forrester Cochrane, K. B., and of Sir*

Thomas John Cochrane, a Captain in the Royal Navy, with an Account of the Circumstances Which Led to the Discovery of the Conspiracy of Lord Cochrane and Others to Defraud the Stock Exchange. London: C. Chapple, 1814.

Malzac, John. *Piracy: Details of the Case of the Brig Carraboo of Liverpool, Together with an Account of the Capture of the Pirate-Vessel, the Schooner Las Damas Argentinas.* St. Christopher: J. A. Howe, 1828.

Metcalfe, George E., ed. *Great Britain and Ghana: Documents of Ghana History, 1807–1957.* London: University of Ghana, 1964.

Nissen, Johan Peter. *Reminiscences of a 46 Years' Residence in the Island of St. Thomas, in the West Indies.* Nazareth, PA: Senseman and Co., 1838.

Pannet, Pierre J. *Report on the Execrable Conspiracy Carried out by the Amina Negroes on the Danish Island of St. Jan in America, 1733,* edited and translated by Aimery P. Caron and Arnold R. Highfield. St. Croix: Antilles Press, 1984.

Papers Relative to the Slave Trade Presented to Parliament in 1819, vol. 1. London: R. G. Clarke, 1820.

Parliamentary Abstracts Containing the Substance of All Important Papers Laid before the Two Houses of Parliament during the Session of 1825. London: Longman, 1826.

Report of Cases Argued and Adjudged in the Supreme Court of the United States, January Term 1832. Philadelphia: D. B. Canfield & Co., 1853.

Rømer, Ludewig Ferdinand. *A Reliable Account of the Coast of Guinea (1760),* edited and translated by Selena Axelrod Winsnes. Oxford: Oxford University Press, 2000.

Schmidt, Johan Christian. *Various Remarks Collected on and about the Island of St. Croix in America,* edited and translated by Svend E. Holsoe. St. Croix: Virgin Islands Humanities Council, 1998.

St. John Backtime: Eyewitness Accounts from 1718 to 1956, edited by Ruth Hull Low and Rafael Valls. St. John: Eden Hill Press, 1985.

Stephen, James. *England Enslaved by Her Own Slave Colonies: An Address to the Electors and People of the United Kingdom.* London: R. Taylor, 1826.

Sucking, George. *An Historical Account of the Virgin Islands in the West Indies.* London: Benjamin White, 1780.

United Kingdom. *Hansard Parliamentary Debates,* 1st ser., vol. 7 (1806).

Hansard Parliamentary Debates, 1st ser., vol. 32 (1816).

Westergaard, Waldemar, trans. "Account of the Negro Rebellion on St. Croix, Danish West Indies, 1759." *The Journal of Negro History* 11:1 (1926): 50–61.

Secondary Sources

Abu-Lughod, Janet. *Before European Hegemony: The World System A.D. 1250–1350.* Oxford: Oxford University Press, 1989.

Adams, Julia. *The Familial State: Ruling Families and Merchant Capitalism in Early Modern Europe.* Ithaca, NY: Cornell University Press, 2007.

Adderley, Rosanne Marion. *"New Negroes from Africa": Slave Trade Abolition and Free African Settlement in the Nineteenth-Century Caribbean.* Bloomington: Indiana University Press, 2006.

Adelman, Jeremy. *Sovereignty and Revolution in the Iberian Atlantic.* Princeton: Princeton University Press, 2009.

Adelman, Jeremy, and Stephen Aron. "From Borderlands to Borders: Empires, Nation-States, and the Peoples in between in North American History." *The American Historical Review* 104:3 (1999): 814–40.

Adler, Emanuel, and Vincent Pouliot, eds. *International Practices*. New York: Cambridge University Press, 2011.

Agamben, Giorgio. *State of Exception*. Chicago: University of Chicago Press, 2005.

Allain, Jean. "The Nineteenth Century Law of the Sea and the British Abolition of the Slave Trade." *British Yearbook of International Law* 78 (2008): 342–88.

Allen, John, Doreen Massey, and Allan Cochrane. *Rethinking the Region*. London: Routledge, 1998.

Allen, Richard B. "Licentious and Unbridled Proceedings: The Illegal Slave Trade to Mauritius and the Seychelles during the Early Nineteenth Century." *The Journal of African History* 42:1 (2001): 91–116.

"Suppressing a Nefarious Traffic: Britain and the Abolition of Slave Trading in India and the Western Indian Ocean, 1770–1830." *The William and Mary Quarterly* 66:4 (2009): 873–94.

Andreen, Per G. *Politik och Finansväsen från 1815 års Riksdag till 1830 års Realisationsbeslut*. Stockholm: Almqvist & Wiksell, 1958.

Andrew, John, *The Hanging of Arthur Hodge: A Caribbean Anti-slavery Milestone*. Bloomington: Xlibris, 2000.

Anghie, Antony. *Imperialism, Sovereignty, and the Making of International Law*. Cambridge: Cambridge University Press, 2007.

Applegate, Celia. "A Europe of Regions: Reflections on the Historiography of Sub-National Places in Modern Times." *The American Historical Review* 104:4 (1999): 1157–82.

Arenson, Adam, Barbara Berglund, and Jay Gitlin, eds. *Frontier Cities: Encounters at the Crossroads of Empire*. Philadelphia: University of Pennsylvania Press, 2013.

Arlyck, Kevin. "Plaintiffs v. Privateers: Litigation and Foreign Affairs in the Federal Courts, 1816–1825." *Law & History Review* 30:1 (2012): 245–78.

Armitage, David. "The Atlantic Ocean." In *Oceanic Histories*, edited by David Armitage, Alison Bashford, and Sujit Sivasundaram. Cambridge: Cambridge University Press, 2018.

Armitage, David, and Michael J. Braddick, eds. *The British Atlantic World, 1500–1800* (2nd edition). New York: Palgrave Macmillan, 2009.

Armitage, David, Alison Bashford, and Sujit Sivasundaram, eds. *Oceanic Histories*. Cambridge: Cambridge University Press, 2018.

Armytage, Frances. *The Free Port System in the British West Indies: A Study in Commercial Policy, 1766–1822*. London: Longmans, Green & Co., 1953.

Arrighi, Giovanni. *The Long Twentieth Century: Money, Power and the Origins of Our Times* (revised edition). New York: Verso, 2010.

Bailyn, Bernard. *Atlantic History: Concept and Contours*. Cambridge, MA: Harvard University Press, 2005.

Baker, Philip, and Peter Mülhäuser. "Creole Linguistics from Its Beginnings, through Schuchardt to the Present Day." In *Creolization: History, Ethnography, Theory*, edited by Charles Stewart, 84–107. Walnut Creek, CA: Left Coast Press, 2007.

Balasingamchow, Yu-Mei, and Mark Ravinder Frost. *Singapore: A Biography.* Hong Kong: Hong Kong University Press and National Museum of Singapore, 2009.

Ballantyne, Tony, and Antoinette Burton. "Empire and the Reach of the Global." In *A World Connecting, 1870–1945,* edited by Emily S. Rosenberg, 285–434. Cambridge, MA: Belknap Press, 2012.

Banks, Kenneth J. *Chasing Empire across the Sea: Communication and the State in the French Atlantic, 1713–1763.* Montreal: McGill University Press, 2006.

Bannister, Jerry. *The Rule of Admirals: Law, Custom, and Naval Government in Newfoundland, 1699–1832.* Toronto: University of Toronto Press, 2003.

Barka, Norman F. "Citizens of St. Eustatius, 1781: A Historical and Archeological Study." In *The Lesser Antilles in the Age of European Expansion,* edited by Robert L. Paquette and Stanley L. Engerman, 223–38. Gainesville: University Press of Florida, 1996.

Bassi, Ernesto. *An Aqueous Territory: Sailor Geographies and New Grenada's Transimperial Greater Caribbean World.* Durham, NC: Duke University Press, 2016.

Battersby, Paul. *To the Islands: White Australians and the Malay Archipelago since 1788.* Lanham, MD: Lexington Books, 2007.

Bayly, C. A. *The Birth of the Modern World, 1780–1914.* Oxford: Wiley-Blackwell, 2004.

"The First Age of Global Imperialism, c. 1760–1830." *The Journal of Imperial and Commonwealth History* 26:2 (1998): 28–47.

Imperial Meridian: The British Empire and the World, 1780–1830. London: Longman, 1989.

Beckert, Sven. *Empire of Cotton: A Global History.* New York: Alfred A. Knopf, 2014.

Benhabib, Seyla. "Rationality and Social Action: Critical Reflections on Max Weber's Methodological Writings." *Philosophical Forum* 12:4 (1981): 356–75.

Benjamins, Herman, and Johannes Snelleman, eds. *Encyclopedie van Nederlandsch West-Indië.* Leiden: Martinus Nijhoff, 1917.

Benton, Lauren. "Abolition and Imperial Law, 1790–1820." *The Journal of Imperial and Commonwealth History* 39:3 (2011): 355–74.

Law and Colonial Cultures: Legal Regimes in World History, 1400–1900. New York: Cambridge University Press, 2002.

A Search for Sovereignty: Law and Geography in European Empires, 1400–1900. New York: Cambridge University Press, 2010.

"This Melancholy Labyrinth: The Trial of Arthur Hodge and the Boundaries of Imperial Law." *Alabama Law Review* 64:1 (2012): 91–122.

"Toward a New Legal History of Piracy: Maritime Legalities and the Myth of Universal Jurisdiction." *International Journal of Maritime History* 23:1 (2011): 225–40.

"Una Soberanía Extraña: La Provincia Oriental en el Mundo Atlántico." *20/10: El Mundo Atlántico y la Modernidad Iberoameircana, 1750–1850* 1 (2012).

Benton, Lauren, and Jeppe Mulich. "The Space between Empires: Coastal and Insular Microregions in the Early Nineteenth-Century World." In *The Uses of Space in Early Modern History*, edited by Paul Stock, 151–71. New York: Palgrave Macmillan, 2015.

Benton, Lauren, and Richard J. Ross. "Empires and Legal Pluralism: Jurisdiction, Sovereignty, and Political Imagination in the Early Modern World." In *Legal Pluralism and Empires, 1500–1850*, edited by Benton and Ross, 1–20. New York: New York University Press, 2013.

Bergère, Marie-Claire. *Histoire de Shanghai*. Paris: Librairie Arthème Fayard, 2002.

Bilder, Mary Sarah. *The Transatlantic Constitution: Colonial Legal Culture and the Empire*. Cambridge, MA: Harvard University Press, 2004.

Blackburn, Robin. *The American Crucible: Slavery, Emancipation and Human Rights*. New York: Verso, 2013.

Blaufarb, Rafe. "The Western Question: The Geopolitics of Latin American Independence." *The American Historical Review* 112 (2007): 742–63.

Block, Kristen. *Ordinary Lives in the Early Caribbean: Religion, Colonial Competition, and Politics of Profit*. Athens: University of Georgia Press, 2012.

Blume, Helmut. *The Caribbean Islands*. London: Longman, 1974.

Bolster, W. Jeffrey. *Black Jacks: African American Seamen in the Age of Sails*. Cambridge, MA: Harvard University Press, 1997.

The Mortal Sea: Fishing in the Atlantic in the Age of Sail. Cambridge, MA: Harvard University Press, 2012

Bourdieu, Pierre. *Outline of a Theory of Practice*. New York: Cambridge University Press, 1977.

Boyce, Gordon. *Information, Mediation, and Institutional Development: The Rise of Large-Scale Enterprise in British Shipping, 1870–1919*. Manchester: Manchester University Press, 1995.

Bright, Charles, and Michael Geyer. "World History in a Global Age." *American Historical Review* 100:4 (1995): 1034–60.

Bro-Jørgensen, J. O. *Vore Gamle Tropekolonier, bind 1: Dansk Vestindien indtil 1755*. Copenhagen: Fremad, 1966.

Brook, Timothy. *Vermeer's Hat: The Seventeenth Century and the Dawn of the Global World*. London: Bloomsbury, 2007.

Brown, Christopher L. *Moral Capital: Foundations of British Abolitionism*. Chapel Hill: University of North Carolina Press, 2006.

"The Politics of Slavery." In *The British Atlantic World, 1500–1800* (2nd edition), edited by David Armitage and Michael J. Braddick, 214–32. New York: Palgrave Macmillan, 2009.

Brunet-Jailly, Emmanuel. "The State of Borders and Borderlands Studies 2009: A Historical View and a View from the Journal of Borderlands Studies." *Eurasia Border Review* 1:1 (2013): 1–15.

Bulmer-Thomas, Victor. *The Economic History of the Caribbean since the Napoleonic Wars*. Cambridge: Cambridge University Press, 2012.

Burbank, Jane. *Russian Peasants Go to Court: Legal Culture in the Countryside, 1905–1917*. Bloomington: Indiana University Press, 2004.

Burbank, Jane, and Frederick Cooper. *Empires in World History: Power and the Politics of Difference*. Princeton: Princeton University Press, 2010.

Burns, Alan. *History of the British West Indies* (revised edition). New York: Barnes and Noble, 1965.

Burton, Antoinette, ed. *Archive Stories: Facts, Fictions, and the Writing of History.* Durham, NC: Duke University Press, 2005.

Buzan, Barry, and George Lawson. *The Global Transformation: History, Modernity and the Making of International Relations.* Cambridge: Cambridge University Press, 2015.

Buzan, Barry, and Richard Little. *International Systems in World History: Remaking the Study of International Relations.* Oxford: Oxford University Press, 2000.

Calafat, Guillaume. *Une mer jalousée: Contribution à l'histoire de la souveraineté.* Paris: Éditions du Seuil, 2019.

Camp, Stephanie. *Closer to Freedom: Enslaved Women and Everyday Resistance in the Plantation South.* Chapel Hill: University of North Carolina Press, 2004.

Cañizares-Esguerre, Jorge, Matt Childs, and James Sidbury, eds. *The Black Urban Atlantic in the Age of the Slave Trade.* Philadelphia: University of Pennsylvania Press, 2013.

Carroll, John M. *Edge of Empires: Elites and British Colonials in Hong Kong.* Cambridge, MA: Harvard University Press, 2005.

Carter, Marina, and Hubert Gerbeau. "Covert Slaves and Coveted Coolies in the Early Nineteenth Century Mascareignes." *Slavery and Abolition* 9:3 (1988): 194–208.

Cassel, Pär Kristoffer. *Grounds of Judgment: Extraterritoriality and Imperial Power in Nineteenth-Century China and Japan.* Oxford: Oxford University Press, 2012.

Chappell, David A. *Double Ghosts: Oceanic Voyagers on Euroamerican Ships.* New York: M. E. Sharpe, 1997.

Chatterjee, Partha. *The Black Hole of Empire: History of a Global Practice of Power.* Princeton: Princeton University Press, 2012.

Chaudhuri, Nupur, Sherry J. Katz, and Mary Elizabeth Perry, eds. *Contesting Archives: Finding Women in the Sources.* Champaign: University of Illinois Press, 2010.

Cheney, Paul. *Revolutionary Commerce: Globalization and the French Monarchy.* Cambridge, MA: Harvard University Press, 2010.

Childs, Gregory L. "Scenes of Sedition: Publics, Politics, and Freedom in Late Eighteenth-Century Bahia, Brazil." PhD dissertation, New York University, 2012.

Chinea, Jorge L. "A Quest for Freedom: The Immigration of Maritime Maroons into Puerto Rico, 1656–1800." *The Journal of Caribbean History* 31:1–2 (1997): 51–87.

Clulow, Adam. *The Company and the Shogun: The Dutch Encounter with Tokugawa Japan.* New York: Columbia University Press, 2014.

Coclanis, Peter A. "Atlantic World or Atlantic/World?" *The William and Mary Quarterly* 63:4 (2006): 725–42.

Colás, Alejandro, and Bryan Mabee. "The Flow and Ebb of Privatised Seaborne Violence in Global Politics: Lessons from the Atlantic World, 1689–1815." In *Mercenaries, Pirates, Bandits and Empires: Private Violence in Historical Context,* edited by Colás and Mabee, 93–116. New York: Columbia University Press, 2010.

Coleman, D. C., ed. *Revisions in Mercantilism.* London: Methuen, 1969.

Colledge, J. J., and Ben Warlow. *Ships of the Royal Navy: A Complete Record of All Fighting Ships of the Royal Navy from the 15th Century to the Present*. Havertown: Casemate, 2010.

Connelly, Matthew. *A Diplomatic Revolution: Algeria's Fight for Independence and the Origins of the Post–Cold War Era*. Oxford: Oxford University Press, 2002.

Conrad, Sebastian, and Prasenjit Duara. *Viewing Regionalisms from East Asia*. Washington, DC: American Historical Association, 2013.

Cooley, Alexander. *Logics of Hierarchy: The Organization of Empires, States, and Military Occupations*. Ithaca, NY: Cornell University Press, 2012.

Cooper, Frederick. "Empire Multiplied: A Review Essay." *Comparative Studies in Society and History* 46:2 (2004): 247–72.

"What Is the Concept of Globalization Good For? An African Historian's Perspective." *African Affairs* 100:399 (2001): 189–213.

Corradi, Gessica, Silvia Gherardi, and Luca Verzelloni. "Through the Practice Lens: Where Is the Bandwagon of Practice-Based Studies Heading?" *Management Learning* 41:3 (2010): 265–83.

Cottret, Bernard. "La révolution atlantique, une question mal posée?" In *Cosmopolitismes, patriotismes, Europe et Amériques, 1773–1802*, edited by Mark Bélissa and Bernard Cottret, 183–98. Rennes: Perséides, 2005.

Craton, Michael John. "The Caribbean Vice Admiralty Courts, 1763–1815; Indispensable Agents of an Imperial System." PhD dissertation, McMaster University, 1968.

Empire, Enslavement and Freedom in the Caribbean. Kingston: Ian Randle Publishers, 1997.

Testing the Chains: Resistance to Slavery in the British West Indies. Ithaca, NY: Cornell University Press, 1982.

Cremer, R. D. "From Portugal to Japan: Macau's Place in the History of World Trade." In *Macau: City of Commerce and Culture*, edited by R. D. Cremer, 23–37. Hong Kong: UEA Press, 1987.

Crump, Helen Josephine. *Colonial Admiralty Jurisdiction in the Seventeenth Century*. London: Longmans, 1931.

Curtin, Philip D. *The Rise and Fall of the Plantation Complex: Essays in Atlantic History* (2nd edition). Cambridge: Cambridge University Press, 1998.

Daget, Serge. "France, Suppression of the Illegal Trade, and England, 1817–1850." In *The Abolition of the Atlantic Slave Trade: Origins and Effects in Europe, Africa, and the Americas*, edited by David Eltis and James Walvin, 193–217. Madison: University of Wisconsin Press, 1981.

D'Arcy, Paul. *The People of the Sea: Environment, Identity and History in Oceania*. Honolulu: University of Hawai'i Press, 2007.

Darwin, John. *After Tamerlane: The Rise and Fall of Global Empires, 1400–2000*. New York: Penguin, 2007.

Davis, David Brion. *The Problem of Slavery in the Age of Emancipation*. New York: Alfred A. Knopf, 2014.

Dawdy, Shannon Lee. *Building the Devil's Empire: French Colonial New Orleans*. Chicago: University of Chicago Press, 2008.

Diouf, Sylviane A. *Slavery's Exiles: The Story of the American Maroons*. New York: New York University Press, 2014.

Dobbs, Stephen. "The Singapore River/Port in a Global Context." In *Singapore in Global History*, edited by Derek Heng and Syed Muhd Krairudin Aljunied, 51–66. Amsterdam: Amsterdam University Press, 2011.

Dookhan, Isaac. *A History of the British Virgin Islands, 1672–1970*. Epping: Caribbean Universities Press, 1975.

A History of the Virgin Islands of the United States. Kingston: Canoe Press, 1994.

Doyle, Michael W. *Empires*. Ithaca, NY: Cornell University Press, 1986.

Drayton, Richard. *Nature's Government: Science, Imperial Government, and the "Improvement" of the World*. New Haven: Yale University Press, 2000.

Drescher, Seymour. *Abolition: A History of Slavery and Antislavery*. New York: Alfred A. Knopf, 2009.

"Emperors of the World: British Abolitionism and Imperialism." In *Abolitionism and Imperialism in Britain, Africa, and the Atlantic*, edited by Derek R. Peterson, 129–49. Athens: Ohio University Press, 2010.

"History's Engines: British Mobilization in the Age of Revolution." *The William and Mary Quarterly* 66:4 (2009): 737–56.

Du Bois, W. E. B. *The Suppression of the African Slave-Trade to the United States of America, 1638–1870*. New York: Longmans, Green & Co., 1896.

Dubois, Laurent. *Avengers of the New World: The Story of the Haitian Revolution*. Cambridge, MA: Harvard University Press, 2005.

"Citizen Soldiers: Emancipation and Military Service in the Revolutionary French Caribbean." In *Arming Slaves: From Classical Times to the Modern Age*, edited by Christopher L. Brown and Philip D. Morgan, 233–54. New Haven: Yale University Press, 2006.

A Colony of Citizens: Revolution and Slave Emancipation in the French Caribbean, 1787–1804. Chapel Hill: University of North Carolina Press, 2004.

Duffy, Michael. "The French Revolution and British Attitudes to the West Indian Colonies." In *A Turbulent Time: The French Revolution and the Greater Caribbean*, edited by David Barry Gaspar and David Patrick Geggus, 78–101. Bloomington: Indiana University Press, 1997.

Dunn, Richard S. *Sugar and Slaves: The Rise of the Planter Class in the English West Indies, 1624–1713*. Chapel Hill: University of North Carolina Press, 1972.

Eich, Stefan, and Adam Tooze. "The Allure of Dark Times: Max Weber, Politics, and the Crisis of Historicism." *History and Theory* 56:2 (2017): 197–215.

Eisenstadt, S. N. *The Political Systems of Empire*. New York: Free Press, 1963.

Ekman, Ernst. "St. Barthélemy and the French Revolution." *Caribbean Studies* 3:4 (1964): 17–29.

"Sweden, the Slave Trade and Slavery, 1784–1847." *Revue française d'histoire d'outre-mer* 69 (1975): 221–31.

"A Swedish Career in the Tropics: Johan Norderling (1760–1828)." *The Swedish Pioneer Historical Quarterly* 15:1 (1964): 33–44.

Elliott, John H. *Empires of the Atlantic World: Britain and Spain in America 1492–1830*. New Haven: Yale University Press, 2007.

Eltis, David. *Economic Growth and the Ending of the Transatlantic Slave Trade*. Oxford: Oxford University Press, 1987.

The Rise of African Slavery in the Americas. Cambridge: Cambridge University Press, 2000.

"The U.S. Transatlantic Slave Trade, 1644–1867: An Assessment." *Civil War History* 54:4 (2008): 347–78.

"Was Abolition of the US and British Slave Trade Significant in the Broader Atlantic Context?" *The William and Mary Quarterly* 66:4 (2009): 717–36.

Emirbayer, Mustafa. "Manifesto for a Relational Sociology." *American Journal of Sociology* 103:2 (1997): 281–317.

Emirbayer, Mustafa, and Jeffrey Goodwin. "Network Analysis, Culture, and the Problem of Agency." *American Journal of Sociology* 99:6 (1994): 1141–54.

Emmer, Pieter C. "Abolition of the Abolished: The Illegal Dutch Slave Trade and the Mixed Courts." In *The Abolition of the Atlantic Slave Trade: Origins and Effects in Europe, Africa, and the Americas*, edited by David Eltis and James Walvin, 177–92. Madison: University of Wisconsin Press, 1981.

Fatah-Black, Karwan. "A Swiss Village in the Dutch Tropics: The Limitations of Empire-Centred Approaches to the Early Modern Atlantic World." *BMGN – Low Countries Historical Review* 128:1 (2013): 31–52.

Feinberg, Harvey M. *Africans and Europeans in West Africa: Elminans and Dutchmen on the Gold Coast during the Eighteenth Century*. Philadelphia: American Philosophical Society, 1989.

Feldbæk, Ole. *Slaget på Reden*. Copenhagen: Politikens Forlag, 1985.

Ferguson, Niall. *Empire: The Rise and Demise of the British World Order and the Lessons for Global Power*. London: Allen Lane, 2002.

Ferrer, Ada. *Freedom's Mirror: Cuba and Haiti in the Age of Revolution*. New York: Cambridge University Press, 2014.

"Haiti, Free Soil, and Antislavery in the Revolutionary Atlantic." *The American Historical Review* 117:1 (2012): 40–66.

Flynn, Dennis O., and Arturo Giraldez. "Path Dependence, Time Lags and the Birth of Globalisation: A Critique of O'Rourke and Williamson." *European Review of Economic History* 8:1 (2004): 81–108.

Ford, Lisa. *Settler Sovereignty: Jurisdiction and Indigenous Peoples in America and Australia, 1788–1836*. Cambridge, MA: Harvard University Press, 2010.

Foucault, Michel. *L'archéologie du savoir*. Paris: Éditions Gallimard, 1969.

Histoire de la sexualité II: L'usage des plaisirs. Paris: Éditions Gallimard, 1984.

Frank, Andre Gunder. *ReOrient: Global Economy in the Asian Age*. Berkeley: University of California Press, 1998.

Franzén, Gösta. *Svenskstad i Västindien: Gustavia på Saint Barthélemy i Språk- och Kulturhistorisk Belysning*. Stockholm: Almqvist & Wiksell, 1974.

Fuente, Alejandro de la. *Havana and the Atlantic in the Sixteenth Century*. Chapel Hill: University of North Carolina Press, 2011.

Fuentes, Marisa J. *Dispossessed Lives: Enslaved Women, Violence, and the Archive*. Philadelphia: University of Pennsylvania Press, 2016.

Gaffield, Julia. *Haitian Connections in the Atlantic World: Recognition after Revolution*. Chapel Hill: University of North Carolina Press, 2015.

Galloway, J. H. *The Sugar Cane Industry: An Historical Geography from Its Origins to 1914*. New York: Cambridge University Press, 1989.

Games, Alison. "Atlantic History: Definitions, Challenges, Opportunities." *The American Historical Review* 111:3 (2006): 741–57.

Webs of Empire: English Cosmopolitans in an Age of Expansion, 1560–1660. Oxford: Oxford University Press, 2009.

Garde, H. F. "Anna Heegaard og Peter von Scholten." *Personalhistorisk Tidsskrift* 78 (1958): 25–37.

Geels, Frank W. "Technological Transitions as Evolutionary Reconfiguration Processes: A Multi-level Perspective and Case-Study." *Research Policy* 31:8 (2002): 1257–74.

Geggus, David Patrick. "The Caribbean in the Age of Revolution." In *The Age of Revolutions in Global Context, c. 1760–1840,* edited by David Armitage and Sanjay Subrahmanyam, 83–100. New York: Palgrave Macmillan, 2010.

"Saint-Domingue on the Eve of the Haitian Revolution." In *The World of the Haitian Revolution,* edited by David Patrick Geggus and Norman Fiering, 3–20. Bloomington: Indiana University Press, 2009.

Geill, Torben. "Den Gule Feber i Dansk Vestindien." *Dansk Vestindisk Selskab* 16 (1981).

Ghachem, Malick W. *The Old Regime and the Haitian Revolution.* Cambridge: Cambridge University Press, 2012.

Ginzburg, Carlo. "Microhistory: Two or Three Things That I Know about It." *Critical Inquiry* 20:1 (1993): 10–35.

Go, Julian. "For a Postcolonial Sociology." *Theory and Society* 42:1 (2013): 25–55.

Patterns of Empire: The British and American Empires, 1688 to Present. Cambridge: Cambridge University Press, 2011.

Gøbel, Erik. "The Danish Edict of 16th March 1792 to Abolish the Slave Trade." In *Orbis in Orbem: Liber Amicorum John Everaert,* edited by Jan Parmentier and Sander Spanoghe, 259–64. Ghent: Academia Press, 2001.

Goebel, Michael. *Overlapping Geographies of Belonging: Migrations, Regions, and Nations in the Western South Atlantic.* Washington, DC: American Historical Association, 2013.

Gould, Eliga H. "Zones of Law, Zones of Violence: The Legal Geography of the British Atlantic, circa 1772." *The William and Mary Quarterly* 60:3 (2003): 471–510.

Goveia, Elsa V. *Slave Society in the British Leeward Islands at the End of the Eighteenth Century.* New Haven: Yale University Press, 1965.

The West Indian Slave Laws of the Eighteenth Century. Mona: Caribbean Universities Press, 1970.

Green-Pedersen, Svend Erik. "The History of the Danish Negro Slave Trade, 1733–1807." *Revue française d'histoire d'outre-mer* 69 (1975): 196–220.

"The Scope and Structure of the Danish Negro Slave Trade." *Scandinavian Economic History Review* 19:2 (1971): 149–97.

"Slave Demography in the Danish West Indies and the Abolition of the Danish Slave Trade." In *The Abolition of the Atlantic Slave Trade: Origins and Effects in Europe, Africa, and the Americas,* edited by David Eltis and James Walvin, 231–58. Madison: University of Wisconsin Press, 1981.

Greene, Jack P., and Philip D. Morgan, eds. *Atlantic History: A Critical Appraisal.* Oxford: Oxford University Press, 2009.

Grendi, Edoardo. "Micro-analisi e storia sociale." *Quaderni storici* 35(1977): 506–20.

Hall, Neville A. T. "Maritime Maroons: 'Grand Marronage' from the Danish West Indies." *The William and Mary Quarterly* 42:4 (1985): 476–98.
   Slave Society in the Danish West Indies: St. Thomas, St. John, and St. Croix. Mona: University of the West Indies Press, 1992.
Hancock, David. *Oceans of Wine: Madeira and the Emergence of American Trade and Taste.* New Haven: Yale University Press, 2009.
Hann, J. H. "Origin and Development of the Political System in the Shanghai International Settlement." *Journal of the Hong Kong Branch of the Royal Asiatic Society* 22 (1982): 207–29.
Hao, Zhidong. *Macau: History and Society.* Hong Kong: Hong Kong University Press, 2011.
Hardt, Michael, and Antonio Negri. *Empire.* Cambridge, MA: Harvard University Press, 2000.
Harrigan, Norwell, and Pearl Varlack. *The Virgin Islands Story.* Mona: Caribbean Universities Press, 1975.
Hartog, J. *St Marten, Saba, St. Eustatius* (5th edition). Aruba: De Wit Stores, 1978.
Harvey, David. *The Limits to Capital.* Chicago: University of Chicago Press, 1982.
   Spaces of Capital: Towards a Critical Geography. New York: Routledge, 2001.
Head, David. "A Different Kind of Maritime Predation: South American Privateering from Baltimore, 1816–1820." *International Journal of Naval History* 7:2 (2008): 1–38.
Helfman, Tara. "The Court of Vice Admiralty at Sierra Leone and the Abolition of the West African Slave Trade." *Yale Law Review* 115 (2006): 1122–56.
Heng, Derek. "Situating Temasik within the Larger Regional Context: Maritime Asia and Malay State Formation in the Pre-modern Era." In *Singapore in Global History*, edited by Derek Heng and Syed Muhd Krairudin Aljunied, 27–50. Amsterdam: Amsterdam University Press, 2011.
Highfield, Arnold R., and George F. Tyson, eds. *The Danish West Indian Slave Trade: Virgin Islands Perspectives.* St. Croix: Virgin Islands Humanities Council, 1994.
Hildebrand, Ingegerd. *Den Svenska Kolonin S:t Barthélemy och Västindiska Kompaniet fram til 1796.* Lund: P. Lindstedt, 1951.
Hillemann-Delaney, Ulrike. *Asian Empire and British Knowledge: China and the Networks of British Imperial Expansion.* Cambridge: Cambridge University Press, 2009.
Hirst, Paul, and Grahame Thompson. *Globalization in Question: The International Economy and the Possibilities of Governance.* Cambridge: Polity Press, 1996.
Hobsbawm, Eric. *The Age of Revolution: Europe 1789–1848.* London: Abacus, 1862.
Hofman, Corinne L., and William F. Keegan. *The Caribbean before Columbus.* Oxford: Oxford University Press, 2017.
Högström, E. O. E. "S. Barthelemy under Svenska Välde." PhD dissertation, University of Uppsala, 1888.
Holt, Thomas C. *The Problem of Freedom: Race, Labor, and Politics in Jamaica and Britain, 1832–1938* (Baltimore: Johns Hopkins University Press, 1992.
Hont, Istvan. *Jealousy of Trade: International Competition and the Nation-State in Historical Perspective.* Cambridge, MA: Belknap Press, 2005.

Hoonhout, Bram. "Smuggling for Survival: Self-Organized, Cross-Imperial Colony Building in Essequibo and Demerara, 1746–1793." In *Beyond Empires: Global Self-Organizing, Cross-Imperial Networks, 1500–1800*, edited by Cátia Antunes and Amélia Polónia, 212–35. Leiden: Brill, 2016.

Hopkins, Daniel H. "The Danish Ban on the Atlantic Slave Trade and Denmark's African Colonial Ambitions." *Itinerario* 25:4 (2001): 154–84.

Horden, Peregrine, and Nicholas Purcell, "The Mediterranean and 'the New Thalassology.'" *The American Historical Review* 111:3 (2006): 722–40.

Hulsebosch, Daniel J. *Constituting Empire: New York and the Transformation of Constitutionalism in the Atlantic World, 1664–1830*. Chapel Hill: University of North Carolina Press, 2005.

Hussain, Nasser. *The Jurisprudence of Emergency: Colonialism and the Rule of Law*. Ann Arbor: University of Michigan Press, 2003.

Huzzey, Richard. *Freedom Burning: Anti-slavery and Empire in Victorian Britain*. Ithaca, NY: Cornell University Press, 2012.

Jackson, Patrick T. *The Conduct of Inquiry in International Relations: Philosophy of Science and Its Implications for the Study of World Politics*. New York: Routledge, 2011.

Jackson, Patrick T., and Daniel H. Nexon. "Relations before States: Substance, Process, and the Study of World Politics." *European Journal of International Relations* 5:3 (1999): 291–332.

Jacoby, Karl. *Shadows at Dawn: An Apache Massacre and the Violence of History*. New York: Penguin, 2008.

Jameson, John Franklin. "St. Eustatius in the American Revolution." *The American Historical Review* 8:4 (1903): 683–708.

Jarvis, Michael. *In the Eye of All Trade: Bermuda, Bermudians, and the Maritime Atlantic World, 1680–1783*. Chapel Hill: University of North Carolina Press, 2010.

Johansen, Hans Christian. "The Reality behind the Demographic Arguments to Abolish the Danish Slave Trade." In *The Abolition of the Atlantic Slave Trade: Origins and Effects in Europe, Africa, and the Americas*, edited by David Eltis and James Walvin, 221–30. Madison: University of Wisconsin Press, 1981.

Kale, Madhavi. *Fragments of Empire: Capital, Slavery, and Indian Indentured Labor in the British Empire*. Philadelphia: University of Pennsylvania Press, 2011.

Karras, Alan L. *Smuggling: Contraband and Corruption in World History*. Lanham, MD: Rowman & Littlefield, 2010.

"Transgressive Exchange: Circumventing Eighteenth-Century Atlantic Commercial Restrictions, or The Discount of Monte Christi." In *Seascapes: Maritime Histories, Littoral Cultures, and Transoceanic Exchanges*, edited by Jerry H. Bentley, Renate Bridenthal, and Kären Wigen, 121–34. Honolulu: University of Hawai'i Press, 2007.

Katic, Ulla. "The Transportation of Mules from South America to the West Indies in the 1860s." *Historia Medicinae Veterinariae* 23 (1998): 3–25.

Keck, Margaret E., and Kathryn Sikkink. *Activists beyond Borders: Advocacy Networks in International Politics*. Ithaca, NY: Cornell University Press, 1998.

Keene, Edward. *Beyond the Anarchical Society: Grotius, Colonialism and Order in World Politics*. Cambridge: Cambridge University Press, 2002.

"A Case Study of the Construction of International Hierarchy: British Treaty-Making against the Slave Trade in the Early Nineteenth Century." *International Organization* 61:2 (2007): 311–39.

Kinsbruner, Jay. *Independence in Spanish America: Civil Wars, Revolutions, and Underdevelopment* (2nd edition). Albuquerque: University of New Mexico Press, 2000.

Klooster, Wim. *Illicit Riches: Dutch Trade in the Caribbean, 1648–1795.* Leiden: KTLV Press, 1998.

"Inter-imperial Smuggling in the Americas, 1600–1800." In *Soundings in Atlantic History: Latent Structures and Intellectual Currents, 1500–1830*, edited by Bernard Bailyn and Patricia L. Denault, 141–80. Cambridge, MA: Harvard University Press, 2009.

Revolutions of the Atlantic World: A Comparative History. New York: New York University Press, 2009.

Knox, John P. *An Historical Account of St. Thomas.* New York: Charles Scribner, 1852.

Kocka, Jürgen. "Comparison and Beyond." *History and Theory* 42:1 (2003): 39–44.

Koot, Christian J. *Empire at the Periphery: British Colonists, Anglo-Dutch Trade, and the Development of the British Atlantic, 1621–1713.* New York: New York University Press, 2011.

Lai, Walton Look. *Indentured Labor, Caribbean Sugar: Chinese and Indian Migrants to the British West Indies, 1838–1918.* Baltimore: Johns Hopkins University Press, 1993.

Lake, David A. *Hierarchy in International Relations.* Ithaca, NY: Cornell University Press, 2009.

Landers, Jane G. *Atlantic Creoles in the Age of Revolutions.* Cambridge, MA: Harvard University Press, 2010.

Lang, Michael. "Globalization and Its History." *Journal of Modern History* 78:4 (2006): 899–931.

Larsen, Kay. *Dansk Vestindien, 1666–1917.* Copenhagen: C. A. Reitzels Forlag, 1928.

Lavoie, Yolande. "Histoire sociale et démographique d'une communauté isolée: Saint-Barthélemy (Antilles françaises)." *Revue d'histoire de l'Amérique française* 42:3 (1989): 411–27.

Lavoie, Yolande, Carolyn Fick, and Francine-M. Mayer. "A Particular Study of Slavery in the Caribbean Island of Saint Barthelemy: 1648–1846." *Caribbean Studies* 28:2 (1995): 369–403.

Law, Robin. "Abolitionism and Imperialism: International Law and the British Suppression of the Atlantic Slave Trade." In *Abolitionism and Imperialism in Britain, Africa, and the Atlantic*, edited by Derek R. Peterson, 150–74. Athens: Ohio University Press, 2010.

Lawaetz, Hermann C. J. *Peter v. Scholten: Vestindiske Tidsbilleder fra den sidste Generalguvernørs Dage.* Copenhagen: Gyldendal, 1940.

Levi, Giovanni. "On Microhistory." In *New Perspectives on Historical Writing*, edited by Peter Burke, 93–113. Philadelphia: Pennsylvania State University Press, 1992.

Lewis, Martin, and Kären Wigen. *The Myth of Continents: A Critique of Metageography*. Berkeley: University of California Press, 1997.

Lewisohn, Florence. *St. Croix under Seven Flags*. Hollywood, FL: Dukane Press, 1970.

Tales of Tortola and the British Virgin Islands. Tortola: n.p., 1966.

Lieberman, Victor. *Strange Parallels, Southeast Asia in Global Context, c. 800–1830, vol. 2: Mainland Mirrors: Europe, Japan, China, South Asia, and the Islands*. Cambridge: Cambridge University Press, 2009.

Lightfoot, Natasha. *Troubling Freedom: Antigua and the Aftermath of British Emancipation*. Durham, NC: Duke University Press, 2015.

Liss, Peggy, and Franklin Wright, eds. *Atlantic Port Cities: Economy, Culture, and Society in the Atlantic World, 1650–1850*. Knoxville: University of Tennessee Press, 1991.

Lloyd, Christopher. *The Navy and the Slave Trade: The Suppression of the African Slave Trade in the Nineteenth Century*. London: Frank Cass and Company, 1968.

Luthin, Reinhard H. "St. Bartholomew: Sweden's Colonial and Diplomatic Adventure in the Caribbean." *The Hispanic American Historical Review* 14:3 (1934): 307–24.

Macaulay, Thomas Babington. *Critical, Historical and Miscellaneous Essays*, vol. 6. New York: Sheldon and Company, 1860.

MacMillan, Ken. *The Atlantic Imperial Constitution: Center and Periphery in the English Atlantic World*. New York: Palgrave Macmillan, 2011.

Sovereignty and Possession in the English New World. Cambridge: Cambridge University Press, 2009.

Madariaga, Isabel de. *Britain, Russia and the Armed Neutrality of 1780*. New Haven: Yale University Press, 1962.

Magee, Gary B., and Andrew Thompson. *Empire and Globalisation: Networks of People, Goods and Capital in the British World, 1850–1914*. Cambridge: Cambridge University Press, 2010.

Magnusson, Lars. *Mercantilism: The Shaping of an Economic Language*. London: Routledge, 1994.

Maier, Charles S. *Among Empires: American Ascendance and Its Predecessors*. Cambridge, MA: Harvard University Press, 2006.

Mamigonian, Beatriz. "In the Name of Freedom: Slave Trade Abolition, the Law, and the Brazilian Branch of the African Emigration Scheme." *Slavery and Abolition* 30:1 (2009): 41–66.

Mann, Michael. *The Sources of Social Power, vol. 1: A History of Power from the Beginning to A.D. 1760*. Cambridge: Cambridge University Press, 1986.

Marini, Ludovico. "On the Method of Studying Thalassology." *The Geographical Journal* 25:2 (1905): 191–97.

Martinez, Jenny. "Antislavery Courts and the Dawn of International Human Rights Law." *Yale Law Review* 117 (2008): 550–64.

Mason, Matthew. "Keeping up Appearances: The International Politics of Slave Trade Abolition in the Nineteenth-Century Atlantic World." *The William and Mary Quarterly* 66:4 (2009): 809–32.

Matsuda, Matt K. *Pacific Worlds: A History of Seas, Peoples, and Cultures*. Cambridge: Cambridge University Press, 2012.

McCarthy, Matthew. "'A Delicate Question of a Political Nature': The Corso Insurgente and British Commercial Policy during the Spanish-American Wars of Independence, 1810–1824." *International Journal of Maritime History* 23:1 (2011): 277–92.

    Privateering, Piracy, and British Policy in Spanish America, 1810–1830. Woodbridge: Boydell & Brewer, 2013.

McConnel, Michael N. *A Country Between: The Upper Ohio Valley and Its Peoples, 1724–1774.* Lincoln: University of Nebraska Press, 1992.

McDonald, Paul K. *Networks of Domination: The Social Foundation of Peripheral Conquest in International Politics.* Oxford: Oxford University Press, 2014.

McNeill, J. R. *Mosquito Empires: Ecology and War in the Greater Caribbean, 1620–1914.* Cambridge: Cambridge University Press, 2010.

Merritt, Jane T. *At the Crossroads: Indians and Empires on a Mid-Atlantic Frontier, 1700–1763.* Chapel Hill: University of North Carolina Press, 2003.

Middell, Matthias, and Katja Naumann. "Global History and the Spatial Turn: From the Impact of Area Studies to the Study of Critical Junctures of Globalization." *Journal of Global History* 5:1 (2010): 149–70.

Miller, Peter N., ed. *The Sea: Historiography and Thalassography.* Ann Arbor: University of Michigan Press, 2013.

Minshull, Roger. *Regional Geography.* London: Hutchinson University Library, 1967.

Mintz, Sidney W. *Sweetness and Power: The Place of Sugar in Modern History.* New York: Penguin, 1985.

Morgan, Philip D. "Ending the Slave Trade: A Caribbean and Atlantic Context." In *Abolitionism and Imperialism in Britain, Africa, and the Atlantic*, edited by Derek R. Peterson, 101–28. Athens: Ohio University Press, 2010.

Morieux, Renaud. *The Channel: England, France and the Construction of a Maritime Border in the Eighteenth Century.* Cambridge: Cambridge University Press, 2016.

    "Diplomacy from below and Belonging: Fishermen and Cross-Channel Relations in the Eighteenth Century." *Past and Present* 202:1 (2009): 83–125.

    "Indigenous Comparisons." In *History after Hobsbawm: Writing the Past for the Twenty-first Century*, edited by John Arnold, Matthew Hilton, and Jan Rüger, 50–75. Oxford: Oxford University Press, 2017.

Morriss, Roger. *The Foundations of British Maritime Ascendance: Resources, Logistics and the State, 1755–1815.* Cambridge: Cambridge University Press, 2011.

Motyl, Alexander J. *Imperial Ends: The Decay, Collapse, and Revival of Empires.* New York: Columbia University Press, 2001.

    Revolutions, Nations, Empires. New York: Columbia University Press, 1999.

Moyn, Samuel. *The Last Utopia: Human Rights in History.* Cambridge, MA: Belknap Press, 2010.

Mukherjee, Rila, ed. *Networks in the First Global Age, 1400–1800.* New Delhi: Indian Council of Historical Research, 2011.

Muldoon, James. *Popes, Lawyers, and Infidels: The Church and the Non-Christian World, 1250–1550.* Philadelphia: University of Pennsylvania Press, 1979.

Mulich, Jeppe. "Empire and Violence: Continuity in the Age of Revolution." *Political Power and Social Theory* 32 (2017): 181–204.

"Transformation at the Margins: Imperial Expansion and Systemic Change in World Politics." *Review of International Studies* 44(4) (2018): 694–716.

Munn, Christopher. *Anglo-China: Chinese People and British Rule in Hong Kong, 1841–1880*. Hong Kong: Hong Kong University Press, 2009.

Murray, David. *Odious Commerce: Britain, Spain, and the Abolition of the Cuban Slave Trade*. Cambridge: Cambridge University Press, 1980.

Neuman, Iver B. *At Home with the Diplomats: Inside a European Foreign Ministry*. Ithaca, NY: Cornell University Press, 2012.

"Returning Practice to the Linguistic Turn: The Case of Diplomacy." *Millennium* 31:3 (2002): 627–51.

Newman, Simon P. "Rethinking Runaways in the British Atlantic World: Britain, the Caribbean, West Africa, and North America." *Slavery and Abolition* 38:1 (2017): 49–75.

Nexon, Daniel H. *The Struggle for Power in Early Modern Europe: Religious Conflict, Dynastic Empires, and International Change*. Princeton: Princeton University Press, 2009.

Nexon, Daniel H., and Thomas Wright. "What's at Stake in the American Empire Debate." *American Political Science Review* 101:2 (2007): 253–71.

Nørregård, George. *Danish Settlements in West Africa, 1658–1850*. Boston: Boston University Press, 1966.

Nwulia, Moses D. E. *The History of Slavery in Mauritius and the Seychelles, 1810–1875*. Madison, NJ: Fairleigh Dickinson University Press, 1981.

Obadele-Starks, Ernest. *Smugglers and Freebooters: The Foreign Slave Trade in the United States after 1808*. Fayetteville: University of Arkansas Press, 2007.

Olsen, Poul Erik. "Danske Lov på de vestindiske øer." In *Danske og norske lov i 300 år*, edited by Ditlev Tamm, 289–321. Copenhagen: Djøf Forlag, 1983.

O'Rourke, Kevin, and Jeffrey G. Williamson. "When Did Globalisation Begin?" *European Review of Economic History* 6:1 (2002): 23–50.

O'Shaugnessy, Andrew Jackson. *An Empire Divided: The American Revolution and the British Caribbean*. Philadelphia: University of Pennsylvania Press, 2000.

Osiander, Andreas. "Sovereignty, International Relations, and the Westphalian Myth." *International Organization* 55:2 (2001): 251–87.

Osterhammel, Jürgen. *The Transformation of the World: A Global History of the Nineteenth Century*. Princeton: Princeton University Press, 2014.

Osterhammel, Jürgen, and Niels Petersson. *Globalization: A Short History*. Princeton: Princeton University Press, 2009.

Pagden, Anthony. *The Burdens of Empires, 1539 to Present*. Cambridge: Cambridge University Press, 2015.

Palmer, Michael A. *Stoddert's War: Naval Operations during the Quasi-War with France, 1798–1801*. Columbia: University of South Carolina Press, 1987.

Palmer, R. R. *The Age of Democratic Revolution*, vols. 1 and 2. Princeton: Princeton University Press, 1959 and 1964.

Pålsson, Ale. "Smugglers before the Swedish Throne: Political Activity of Free People of Color in Early Nineteenth-Century St. Barthélemy." *Atlantic Studies* 14:3 (2017): 318–35.

Pares, Richard. *Colonial Blockade and Neutral Rights, 1739–1763*. Oxford: Oxford University Press, 1938.

Paton, Diana. *No Bond but the Law: Punishment, Race, and Gender in Jamaican State Formation, 1780–1870*. Durham, NC: Duke University Press, 2004.

Pedersen, Christian Damm. "The Question of Rights in a Colour-Conscious Empire: The Danish West Indies and the Global Age of Revolutions (1800–1850)." In *Ports of Globalisation, Places of Creolisation: Nordic Possessions in the Atlantic World during the Era of the Slave Trade*, edited by Holger Weiss, 154–90. Leiden: Brill, 2015.

Peltonen, Matti. "Clues, Margins, and Monads: The Micro-Macro Link in Historical Research." *History and Theory* 40:3 (2001): 347–59.

Pérez Morales, Edgardo. *No Limits to Their Sway: Cartagena's Privateers and the Masterless Caribbean in the Age of Revolutions*. Nashville, TN: Vanderbilt University Press, 2018.

Pérotin-Dumon, Anne. "Cabotage, Contraband, and Corsairs: The Port Cities of Guadeloupe and Their Inhabitants, 1650–1800." In *Atlantic Port Cities: Economy, Culture, and Society in the Atlantic World, 1650–1850*, edited by Franklin W. Knight and Peggy K. Liss, 58–86. Knoxville: University of Tennessee Press, 1991.

 La ville aux îsles, la ville dans l'île: Basse-Terre et Pointe-à-Pitre, Guadeloupe, 1650–1820. Paris: Editions Karthala, 2000.

Perrone, Sean T. "John Stoughton and the Divina Pastora Prize Case, 1816–1819." *Journal of the Early Republic* 28:2 (2008): 215–41.

Phillips, Andrew. *War, Religion and Empire*. Cambridge: Cambridge University Press, 2011.

Phillips, Andrew, and J. C. Sharman. *International Order in Diversity: War, Trade and Rule in the Indian Ocean*. Cambridge: Cambridge University Press, 2015.

Pincus, Steven. "Rethinking Mercantilism: Political Economy, the British Empire, and the Atlantic World in the Seventeenth and Eighteenth Centuries." *The William and Mary Quarterly* 69:1 (2012): 3–34.

Poggi, E. Muriel. "The German Sugar Beet Industry." *Economic Geography* 6:1 (1930): 81–93.

Pomeranz, Kenneth. *The Great Divergence: China, Europe, and the Making of the Modern World Economy*. Princeton: Princeton University Press, 2000.

Pope, Dudley. *The Great Gamble: Nelson at Copenhagen*. London: Weidenfeld & Nicolson, 1972.

Postma, Johannes. "A Reassessment of the Dutch Atlantic Slave Trade." In *Riches from Atlantic Commerce: Dutch Transatlantic Trade and Shipping, 1585–1817*, edited by Johannes Postma and Victor Enthoven, 115–38. Leiden: Brill, 2003.

Prado, Fabricio. *Edge of Empire: Atlantic Networks and Revolution in Bourbon Río de la Plata*. Berkeley: University of California Press, 2015.

Pressly, Paul M. *On the Rim of the Atlantic: Colonial Georgia and the British Atlantic World*. Athens: University of Georgia Press, 2013.

Price, Richard, ed. *Maroon Societies: Rebel Slave Communities in the Americas* (3rd edition). Baltimore: Johns Hopkins University Press, 1996.

Prior, David. "After the Revolution: An Alternative Future for Atlantic History." *History Compass* 12:3 (2014): 300–9.

Pulsipher, Jenny Hale. *Subjects unto the Same King: Indians, English and the Contest of Authority in Colonial New England*. Philadelphia: University of Pennsylvania Press, 2005.

Restall, Matthew. "Crossing to Safety? Frontier Flight in Eighteenth Century Belize and Yucatan." *Hispanic American Historical Review* 94:3 (2014): 381–419.

Revel, Jacques. "L'histoire au ras du sol." In *Le pouvoir au village: Histoire d'un exorciste dans le Piémont du XVIIe Siècle*, by Giovanni Levi, translated by Monique Aymard, i–xxxiii. Paris: Gallimard, 1989.

Richards, Jake C. "Anti-slave-trade Law, 'Liberated Africans' and the State in the South Atlantic World, c. 1839–1852." *Past and Present* 241:1 (2018): 179–219.

Richardson, Bonham C. *The Caribbean in the Wider World, 1492–1992: A Regional Geography*. Cambridge: Cambridge University Press, 1992.

Ringmar, Erik. "The Search for Dialogue as a Hindrance to Understanding: Practices as Inter-paradigmatic Research Program." *International Theory* 6:1 (2014): 1–27.

Røge, Pernille. "Why the Danes Got There First: A Trans-imperial Study of the Abolition of the Danish Slave Trade in 1792." *Slavery and Abolition* 35:4 (2014): 576–92.

Roitman, Jessica V. "Land of Hope and Dreams: Slavery and Abolition in the Dutch Leeward Islands, 1825–1865." *Slavery and Abolition* 37:2 (2016): 375–98.

Rolph, George M. *Something about Sugar: Its History, Growth, Manufacture and Distribution*. San Francisco: John J. Newbegin, 1917.

Rouse, Irving. *The Tainos: Rise and Decline of the People Who Greeted Columbus*. New Haven: Yale University Press.

Rubin, Alfred P. *The Law of Piracy*. Newport, RI: Naval War College Press, 1988.

Rugemer, Edward Bartlett. *The Problem of Emancipation: The Caribbean Roots of the American Civil War*. Baton Rouge: Louisiana State University Press, 2009.

Rupert, Linda M. *Creolization and Contraband: Curaçao in the Early Modern Atlantic World*. Athens: University of Georgia Press, 2012.

"Marronage, Manumission, and Maritime Trade in the Early Modern Caribbean." *Abolition and Slavery* 30:3 (2009): 361–82.

Scanlan, Padraic X. "The Colonial Rebirth of British Anti-slavery: The Liberated African Villages of Sierra Leone, 1815–1824." *The American Historical Review* 121:4 (2016): 1085–113.

Freedom's Debtors: British Antislavery in Sierra Leone in the Age of Revolution. New Haven: Yale University Press, 2017.

Scarano, Francisco A. *Sugar and Slavery in Puerto Rico: The Plantation Economy of Ponce, 1800–1850*. Madison: University of Wisconsin Press, 1984.

Scarr, Deryck. *The Seychelles since 1770: History of a Slave and Post-slavery Society*. Trenton, NJ: Africa World Press, 1999.

Schatzi, Theodore R., Karin K. Cetina, and Eike von Savigny, eds. *The Practice Turn in Contemporary Theory*. New York: Routledge, 2001.

Schnakenbourg, Eric. "Sweden and the Atlantic: The Dynamism of Sweden's Colonial Projects in the Eighteenth Century." In *Scandinavian Colonialism and the Rise of Modernity: Small Time Agents in a Global Arena*, edited by Magdalena Naum and Jonas Nordin, 229–42. New York: Springer, 2013.

Scott, Julius C. *The Common Wind: Currents of Afro-American Communication in the Age of the Haitian Revolution*. London: Verso, 2018.

"Crisscrossing Empires: Ships, Sailors, and Resistance in the Lesser Antilles in the Eighteenth Century." In *The Lesser Antilles in the Age of European Expansion*, edited by Robert L. Paquette and Stanley L. Engerman, 128–43. Gainesville: University Press of Florida, 1996.

Seed, Patricia. *Ceremonies of Possession in Europe's Conquest of the New World, 1492–1640*. New York: Cambridge University Press, 1995.

Shaw, Jenny. *Everyday Life in the Early English Caribbean: Irish, Africans, and the Construction of Difference*. Athens: University of Georgia Press, 2013.

Sheehan, James J. "The Problem of Sovereignty in European History." *The American Historical Review* 111:1 (2006): 1–15.

Shovlin, John. "Rethinking Enlightened Reform in the French Context." In *Enlightened Reform in Southern Europe and Its Atlantic Colonies, c. 1750–1830*, edited by Gabriel Paquette, 47–62. Baltimore: Johns Hopkins University Press, 2009.

Shumway, Rebecca. *The Fante and the Transatlantic Slave Trade*. Rochester, NY: University of Rochester Press, 2011.

Simonsen, Gunvor. "Magic, Obeah and Law in the Danish West Indies, 1750s–1840s." In *Ports of Globalisation, Places of Creolisation: Nordic Possessions in the Atlantic World during the Era of the Slave Trade*, edited by Holger Weiss, 245–79. Leiden: Brill, 2016.

"Skin Colour as a Tool of Regulation and Power in the Danish West Indies in the Eighteenth Century." *Journal of Caribbean History* 37:2 (2003): 256–76.

Singleton, Theresa. "Islands of Slavery: Archeology and Caribbean Landscapes of Intensification." In *What Is a Slave Society? The Practice of Slavery in Global Perspective*, edited by Noel Lenski and Catherine Cameron, 290–309. Cambridge: Cambridge University Press, 2018.

Sinn, Elizabeth. "A History of Regional Associations in Pre-war Hong Kong." In *Between East and West: Aspects of Social and Political Developments in Hong Kong*, edited by Elizabeth Sinn, 159–86. Hong Kong: Centre of Asian Studies, 1990.

Sloan, Edward W. "The First (and Very Secret) International Steamship Cartel, 1850–1856." In *Global Markets: The Internationalization of the Sea Transport Industries since 1850*, edited by Clara Eugenia Núñez, 41–48. Seville: Universidad de Sevilla, 1998.

Smith, Adam. *An Inquiry into the Nature and Causes of the Wealth of Nations*, edited by Edwin Cannan. London: Methuen & Co., 1904.

Sommers, Margaret R. "'We're No Angels': Realism, Rational Choice, and Relationality in Social Science." *American Journal of Sociology* 104:3 (1998): 79–98.

Sparks, Randy J. *Where the Negroes Are Masters: An African Port in the Era of the Slave Trade*. Cambridge, MA: Harvard University Press, 2014.

Stern, Philip J. "'Bundles of Hyphens': Corporations as Legal Communities in the Early Modern British Empire." In *Legal Pluralism and Empires,*

1500–1850, edited by Lauren Benton and Richard J. Ross, 21–48. New York: New York University Press, 2013.

The Company-State: Corporate Sovereignty and the Early Modern Foundations of the British Empire in India. Oxford: Oxford University Press, 2011.

Stern, Phillip J., and Carl Wennerlind, eds. *Mercantilism Reimagined: Political Economy in Early Modern Britain and Its Empire.* Oxford: Oxford University Press, 2014.

Subrahmanyam, Sanjay. "Connected Histories: Notes towards a Reconfiguration of Early Modern Eurasia." *Modern Asian Studies* 31:3 (1997): 735–62.

Swahn, Jan-Öjvind, and Ola Jennertsen. *Saint-Barthélemy: Sveriges sista koloni.* Höganäs: AB Wiken, 1984.

Tagliacozzo, Eric. *Secret Trades, Porous Borders: Smuggling and States along a Southeast Asian Frontier, 1865–1915.* New Haven: Yale University Press, 2005.

Tagliacozzo, Eric, and Wen-chin Chang. *Chinese Circulations: Capital, Commodities, and Networks in Southeast Asia.* Durham, NC: Duke University Press, 2011.

Tarrade, Jean. *Le commerce colonial de la France à la fin de l'Ancien Régime: L'evolution du régime de "l'Exclusif" de 1763 à 1789*, vols. 1 and 2. Paris: Presses Universitaires de France, 1972.

Teschke, Benno. *The Myth of 1648: Class, Geopolitics, and the Making of Modern International Relations.* New York: Verso, 2003.

Thomas, Nicholas. *Islanders: The Pacific in the Age of Empires.* New Haven: Yale University Press, 2010.

Thomasson, Fredrik. "'Contre la Loi mais en considérant les Circonstances dangereuses du moment.' Le tribunal suédois de l'île de Saint-Berthélemy pendant la periode révolutionnaire." In *Les colonies, la révolution française, la loi*, edited by Frédéric Régent, Jean-François Niort, and Pierre Serna, 231–49. Rennes: Presses Universitaires de Rennes, 2014.

"Thirty-Two Lashes at Quatre Piquets: Slave Laws and Justice in the Swedish Colony of St. Barthélemy ca. 1800." In *Ports of Globalisation, Places of Creolisation: Nordic Possessions in the Atlantic World during the Era of the Slave Trade*, edited by Holger Weiss, 280–306. Leiden: Brill, 2016.

Thompson, Alvin O. *Flight to Freedom: African Runaways and Maroons in the Americas.* Mona: University of the West Indies Press, 2006.

Thomson, Janice E. *Mercenaries, Pirates, and Sovereigns: State-Building and Extra-territorial Violence in Early Modern Europe.* Princeton: Princeton University Press, 1994.

Thornton, A. P. *West India Policy under the Restoration.* Oxford: Clarendon Press, 1956.

Tilly, Charles. *Stories, Identities, and Political Change.* Lanham, MD: Rowman & Littlefield, 2002.

"To Explain Political Processes." *American Journal of Sociology* 100:6 (1995): 1594–610.

Trivellato, Francesca. *The Familiarity of Strangers: The Sephardic Diaspora, Livorno, and Cross-Cultural Trade in the Early Modern Period.* New Haven: Yale University Press, 2009.

"Is There a Future for Italian Microhistory in the Age of Global History?" *California Italian Studies* 2(1) (2011): 1–23.

Trouillot, Michel-Rolph. *Silencing the Past: Power and the Production of History.* Boston: Beacon Press, 1995.

Turnbull, C. M. *A History of Modern Singapore* (revised edition). Singapore: Singapore University Press, 2009.

Turnbull, Patricia G. *Can These Stones Talk? St. Philip's Church Ruins at the Liberated African Settlement in Kingstown, Tortola.* Tortola: Rainwater Institute, 2012.

Vibæk, Jens. *Vore Gamle Tropekolonier, bind 2: Dansk Vestindien, 1755–1848.* Copenhagen: Fremad, 1966.

Vink, Markus P. M. "Indian Ocean Studies and the 'New Thalassology.'" *Journal of Global History* 2:1 (2007): 41–62.

Wallerstein, Immanuel. *The Modern World-System I: Capitalist Agriculture and the Origins of the European World-Economy in the Sixteenth Century.* New York: Academic Press, 1947.

Ward, Kerry. *Networks of Empire: Forced Migration in the Dutch East India Company.* Cambridge: Cambridge University Press, 2009.

Warren, James Francis. *The Sulu Zone 1768–1898: The Dynamics of External Trade, Slavery, and Ethnicity in the Transformation of a Southeast Asian Maritime State* (2nd edition). Singapore: NUS Press, 2007.

Weber, Max. "Objectivity in the Social Sciences." In *The Methodology of the Social Sciences,* edited by Edward Shils and Henry Finch, 50–112. New York: Free Press, 1949.

Werner, Michael, and Bénédicte Zimmerman. "Beyond Comparison: *Histoire Croisée* and the Challenge of Reflexivity." *History and Theory* 45:1 (2006): 30–50.

Westergaard, Waldemar. *The Danish West Indies under Company Rule, 1671–1754.* New York: Macmillan, 1917.

White, Richard. *The Middle Ground: Indians, Empires, and Republics in the Great Lakes Region, 1650–1815* (2nd edition). New York: Cambridge University Press, 2010.

Wigen, Kären. *The Making of a Japanese Periphery, 1750–1920.* Berkeley: University of California Press, 1995.

A Malleable Map: Geographies of Restoration in Central Japan, 1600–1912. Berkeley: University of California Press, 2010.

Wilks, Ivor. *Forests of Gold: Essays on the Akan and the Kingdom of Asante* (revised edition). Athens: Ohio University Press, 1995.

Williams, Greg H. *The French Assault on American Shipping, 1793–1813.* Jefferson, NC: McFarland, 2009.

Wilson, Samuel M. "The Cultural Mosaic of the Indigenous Caribbean." *Proceedings of the British Academy* 81 (1992): 37–66.

Wilson, Victor. *Commerce in Disguise: War and Trade in the Caribbean Free Port of Gustavia, 1793–1815.* Turku: Åbo Akademi University Press, 2016.

Witgen, Michael. *An Infinity of Nations: How the Native New World Shaped Early North America.* Philadelphia: University of Pennsylvania Press, 2012.

Wright, Donald R. *The World and a Very Small Place in Africa: A History of Globalization in Niumi, the Gambia* (3rd edition). New York: M. E. Sharpe, 2010.

Young, Elliott. "Regions." In *The Palgrave Dictionary of Transnational History*, edited by Akira Iriye and Pierre-Yves Saunier, 882–87. New York: Palgrave Macmillan, 2009.

Yue, Meng. *Shanghai and the Edges of Empires.* Minneapolis: University of Minnesota Press, 2006.

Zacek, Natalie A. *Settler Society in the English Leeward Islands, 1670–1776.* Cambridge: Cambridge University Press, 2010.

Zarakol, Ayşe, ed. *Hierarchies in World Politics.* Cambridge: Cambridge University Press, 2017.

Index

9 781108 747479